Studies in Comparative Legal History

Current Issues in Korean Law

Edited by
Laurent Mayali
and
John Yoo

The Robbins Collection   2014

The Robbins Collection
Berkeley Law
University of California at Berkeley
Berkeley, California 94720
(510) 642-5094 (510) 642-8325
http://www.law.berkeley.edu/robbins

This book is printed on acid-free paper.

ISBN 1-882239-22-9
978-1-882239-22-1

Library of Congress Cataloging-in-Publication Data

Current issues in Korean law / Edited by Laurent Mayali and John Yoo.
    p. cm.
Includes bibliographical references.
    ISBN 978-1-882239-22-1
    1. Law—Korea (South) 2. Constitutional law—Korea (South) I. Mayali, Laurent, editor of compilation. II. Yoo, John, editor of compilation.
    KPA120.C87 2014
    349.5195—dc23   2014010979

Contents

Introduction

Laurent Mayali[1]

This volume is the first in a series of comparative studies that focuses on Korea's legal system and its political institutions under the sponsorship of the Korea Law Center at UC Berkeley Law School. During the first decades following Korea's retrieval of its national sovereignty, legal reforms were limited in scope by a formalist approach that struggled to reconcile ancient legal traditions with the relics of the recent colonial past. Curiously the broadly accepted opinion that Korea was henceforth the master of its own legal heritage did not entail a substantial change in the legal paradigms that validated the authority of law. The conservative dependence on legal transplants and the idealized conception of ancient customs still enjoyed the favors of jurists who understandably sought to uphold legal predictability and stability. The drafting of the Civil Code heralded Korea's befitting pride in its law but its promulgation did not dispel the legacy of the colonial era.[2] The homogeneity of the legal profession united lawyers, judges and scholars in the same pursuit of the jurisprudential status quo that relied heavily on foreign models.

By the end of the 1980's, the structural conservatism of the legal order could no longer meet the expectations of a society that had definitely come to terms with its most recent past. People's renewed confidence in a better

---

1. Lloyd M. Robbins Professor of Law; Co-Director, Korea Law Center, Berkeley Law.

2. Marie Seong-Hak Kim, *Law and Custom in Korea. Comparative Legal History* (Cambridge: 2012). The author rightly observes that "The myth of customary law looms large in Korean legal history," at 267 and 272–273.

1

future was prompted by spectacular economic success that also expanded Korea's role on the international scene. This transformation both required and justified significant adjustments in the established conception of people's rights. It also forced reconsideration of the legal order's long-accepted dependence on political institutions, and asserted its intellectual autonomy from previous jurisprudential models.

As a result, Korea has experienced an astonishing pace of legal reforms within an interval of two generations, since the late 1980's. The collapse of the authoritarian regime started an irreversible process of democratization that has not yet completed its full course. But Korean society's firm embrace of democratic values reinforces the current trend in favor of the full acceptance of the standards of the Rule of Law.[3] In this perspective, the perceived tension between democratization and the implementation of the Rule of Law outlines the shortcomings of legal reforms that reflect society's attempt in reinventing its past and its ambivalent attitude toward deeply entrenched cultural beliefs.[4] For instance, the idealization of Confucian values constitutes undoubtedly one of the most salient aspects of this process of historical reconstruction. But the precise assessment of its social benefit leaves us with mixed results. On one hand, it certainly constitutes a solid reference for the acceptance of ethical norms that define Korean society. On the other hand, it also justifies a social conservatism that is at times out of touch with the social reality and with people's personal experience.[5] The solution of this conflict requires basic legal adjustments in the absence of any effective political remedy and the courts represent the preferred venue in light of their ability to address at once pressing social concerns within a broad constitutional framework.

At any rate, the historical changes of the past thirty years permanently transformed Korea's political institutions while fostering widespread

---

3. Haim Chaihark, "Uneasy about the Rule of Law. Reconciling Constitutionalism and "Participatory Democracy," in *The Rule of Law in South Korea*, ed. Jongryn Mo and David W. Brady (Palo Alto: 2009), 23–59,

4. Chulwoo Lee, "The rule of law and forms of power: theorizing the social foundations of the rule of law in South Korea and East Asia," in *Law and Society in Korea*, ed. Hyunah Yang (Northampton, Mass.: 2013), at 20–44

5. Hyunah Yang, "Colonialism and Patriarchy: Where the Korean Family-Head (hoju) System had been Located," in *Law and Society in Korea*, at 45–63.

economic expansion and ushering a new cycle of social changes. Many challenges remain ahead.[6] The Asian economic crisis and more recent tragedies have exposed undercurrent dysfunctions that threaten a system where legal reforms outpace social habits and deep-rooted political practices. The formidable test for upholding the authority of the legal institutions resides in their capacity to strike a delicate balance between the beliefs and the strong sense of national identity that are the product of a multi-secular tradition and the goals of a modernized civil society that is also part of the development of the globalized market economy and transnational culture.[7]

The success of the democratization process reflects the concrete accomplishments of the mature political process that is gradually forsaking the remnants of an outdated culture of power. But this success will ultimately rest upon a stable yet innovative legal system and the willingness of judicial institutions to fully assume the powers granted by the constitution in addition to the increasing responsibilities that the Korean people associate with their function. In doing so, the courts remain closely engaged in the juridification of the political and economical systems while also being attentive to the protection of individual rights and the civil society's wide-ranging expectations.

The papers included in this volume cast new lights on these challenges and the institutions that define the substance and the structure of current legal reforms. Although it is not the purpose of this volume to provide a comprehensive report on the current state of Korean law, the selective range of the themes is not a simple happenstance. It is representative of the current political debate which echoes the Korean society's determination to resolve the paradoxes of its legal tradition and overcome the trials of its democratic aspirations.

Justice Kang-Kook Lee, underscores the essential role played by the Constitutional Court in strengthening the legal foundations of Korean de-

6. For a rather pessimist assessment of these prospects, see Robert Compton, *East Asian Democratization. Impact of Globalization, Culture and Economy* (Westport and London: 2000). Chapter 6: "South Korea: Imperfect Legitimation Leads to Democracy?," at 143–161

7. Francis Fukuyama, "Asian Values, Korean Values, and Democratic Consolidation," in *Institutional Reform and Democratic Consolidation in Korea*, ed. Larry Diamond and Doh Chull Shin (Palo Alto: 2000), 305–334.

mocracy. As the Court's past president, he provides a unique insight on its operating structure and legal reasoning. Justice Lee notes how, for instance, the unique procedure of norm-control appeal has become essential in defining Korea's proactive constitutional adjudication process. Various polls regularly attest to the prestige of the court in public opinion. Popular endorsement of its accomplishments is clearly due to its assertive and socially attuned interpretation of the Constitution. But popular approval reflects also the cultural dominance achieved by the concept of fundamental rights in a society which traditionally favored—and still favors—the group's interest over private individuals' concerns. What is remarkable is that after more than a quarter century of its existence, the court's decisions attract intense scrutiny as it faces institutional and political challenges that question its legitimacy. The criticisms leveled at the Court owe less to its activism than to the ambiguities of a democracy that has not yet reached its age of reason.

Justice Lee's assessment of the Court's influence on legal and social changes is further confirmed by Professor Jibong Lim's detailed analysis of the debate generated by the enforcement of the Marriage limitation act. The question of the constitutionality of the provision forbidding marriage between members of the same family name posed a fundamental challenge to the authority of tradition with the recognition a new "social appropriateness and reasonableness." It also forced reconsideration of the State's power to limit individual freedom. Professor Lim shows how an initially divided court which could not, in the absence of a quorum, impose a definitive decision, could nevertheless revisit the issue and decide its final legal outcome after the legislature's failure to repeal the challenged provision. Just like in many similar modern democracies, Korea's political institutions are crippled by the polarization of political life that has significantly altered the democratic balance between majority and minority. Under these circumstances, the subsequent interpretation of the court's pro- or anti-majoritarian stance requires, as professor Lim observes, a more nuanced judgment on the place of judicial activism in the democratization process.

Judicial governance is also the subject of professor Hong Sik Cho's more theoretical reflection on the judicial power and the role of courts in the development of democratic institutions. In this regard, Korea's model might not differ from the political patterns observed in other countries with a different legal tradition such as the United States. Professor Cho rightly observes that the complex concept of judicialization may describe a variety of circumstances involving judicial decision-making and governance. Its multi-form manifestation, as noted by Malcolm Feeley and Ed Rubin, has transformed the overarching normative model of the separation of power in contemporary democracies.[8] Most of the current debate, however, focuses on the most salient political features of this new form of governance while neglecting its major consequences for the definition of the modern State's power to create and implement administrative policies. This less visible aspect of judicial governance represents nevertheless a formidable challenge to the democratic canons of a political doctrine that still honors the beliefs of a two-century old tradition. Professor Cho's careful assessment of the contemporary trend toward more judicialization advocates an active role for the court as protector of the rights of the minority in a liberal democracy where majority rule remains within the limits drawn by the legal system in balancing the necessities of public order with the defense of private interest.

Professor Dai-Kwon Choi provides a sweeping review of the various fundamental rights protections in Korea in light of the country political history and social transformation since the country's independence in 1948. He stresses both the practical and the symbolic importance of the constitution as a bridge between a post-independence normative ideal and the political reality of the authoritarian regime. From the beginning of the new constitutional order, the gap separating this formal legal model from its social and political environment resulted from a double set of international and domestic circumstances. On one hand, the Korean War and its immediate aftermath imposed the militarization of the power structures. On the other hand, the adoption of a democratic system presented a significant cultural challenge for a society which had not been prepared to this change by the years of Japanese occupation and whose only sense of identity resided in the idealized history of the Choson dynasty and its Confucian legacy. Curiously enough, the ethical model of social behavior that was supposed to define the independent nation encouraged attitudes that increasingly

---

8.　Malcolm Feeley and Edward Rubin, *Judicial Policy Making and the Modern State: How the Courts Reformed America's Prisons*, (New York: 1998).

conflicted with people's expectations in an urban environment that no longer corresponded to the former rural society. The constitution was in many ways ahead of its time in a society that could not think of its future without a return to its past. Nowadays, as professor Choi suggests, the protection of fundamental rights necessarily coincides with the reinvention of a social moral that may complement people's full adherence to democratic values in the respect individual diversity.

A former member of the Korean Human Rights Commission, Professor Kuk Cho is well aware of the existing challenges in providing equal protection for all citizens. He draws our attention to article 92(5) of the military penal code and its discrimination against sexual minorities. The code's criminalization of sodomy raises a fundamental rights issue that challenges Korean society's commitment to legal equality and the protection of human dignity. In contrast with the laws implemented in Western democracies, the Korean military exception stands out as a clear instance of discrimination. The Supreme Court and the Constitutional Court on the motive that military discipline requires stricter rules in order to protect the cohesiveness of the fighting units nevertheless condoned it. This argument is familiar to legal scholars who followed the U.S. government's indecision leading to the adoption of the "Don't ask, don't tell" policy. This imperfect compromise was eventually abandoned in the U.S. It remains in effect in Korea but does not remove the threat of criminal punishment.

Fundamental rights protection and social legislation represent the most visible part of Korea's reform movement in the course of the democratization. They constitute however only one facet of the legal changes that, over the past thirty years, have sustained the country's emergence on the international scene as a financial and economic power. The Asian economic crisis in the late 90's was a brutal reminder of the fragility of an economic system based on outdated management practices and opaque financial rules. Any successful response to the financial crisis required a departure from the traditional way of doing business in close cooperation with the political powers that had been the hallmark of the early post war era. Professor Jaewan Park reminds us that sustainable economic expansion relies upon adequate legal institutions that not only facilitate its growth but also provide dependable structures of governance. By the turn of the twenty-first century, the legal response to the economic challenges opened up a new era of more regulations Time is thus of the essence in considering corporate re-organization in concurrence with the basic principles of transparency and efficiency. Taking into account the Seoul central district court's decisions, Professor Park proposes to adopt in Bankruptcy proceedings the Merger and Acquisition practices which, in his opinion, provide several incentives for a more efficient reorganization. He thus gives a detailed evaluation of the M&A features that could be implemented for the benefit of expediency in the decision-making process, the selection of potential buyers, and the restructuring of debt.

Technology and its byproducts are one of the most vaunted examples of Korea's current economic success. They illustrate its industry's capacity to influence an entire sector of the global market economy. Numerous studies have addressed the economic and social consequences of the technological revolution but they failed to fully assess the challenges it created for a legal system that mostly relies on written procedure and textual evidence. Professor Sang Won Lee reminds us that criminal procedure is not immune to these changes when he considers the conditions of admissibility of electronic evidence. Digitization has not only provided a new type of electronic support, it has also transformed our relationship to the text by altering the parameters defining its storage, its transmission and its treatment. The management of E-evidence requires thus a very different form of handling than the one traditionally used for typical textual support. What are then the criteria that should define the authenticity of electronic documents that may be reproduced many times? The answer is not simply theoretical but bears very practical consequences on the course of criminal trials at a time when electronic channels are the main avenue for communicating and sharing documents between diverse judicial institutions. In the absence of a uniform procedure, Professor Lee's recommendation to adopt a more flexible interpretation of the "original evidence rule" provides a sensible base for a much needed legislative clarification.

The conception and publication of this volume would not have been possible without the unflinching support of Berkeley Law's devoted Korean alumni and the institutions (Courts, the Ministry of Justice, law firms and Universities) that they so brilliantly represent. Dean Christopher Edley, Jr. and Acting Dean Gillian Lester of the UC Berkeley Law School were instrumental in providing indispensable institutional support. Their encouragements fueled the intellectual synergy that sustained the entire project. As co-editors of the volume, John Yoo and I owe a great debt to Max Withers, manager of the Robbins Collection's publications. His superb editorial experience and constant dedication contributed greatly to give this volume its final shape. For translating and preparing several articles, we were fortunate to benefit from the invaluable assistance of Youna Kim, Beatrice Na, Hae Ri You and Tongkun Kim.

The Past and Future of Constitutional Adjudication in Korea

Kang-Kook Lee[1]

The Constitution and Constitutional Adjudication

We learn from the history of mankind that it is only after the establishment of the constitution that the guarantees for the rights of citizens and the limits on government power of a liberal democracy can be built on a firm legal foundation. It was also the constitution that brought law and order and the social integration that respected and protected the socially disadvantaged. The ideals of constitutional democracy that checks and balances state powers and guarantees for individual liberty, equality, and justice, are a valuable asset of our humanity.

However, the supremacy of the constitutional guarantees for citizens' freedom and rights have often been infringed or restricted by state actions or governmental authority. For this reason, the luminaries of mankind created a constitutional adjudication system to effectively protect the constitution as an instrument for people to pursue happiness while enjoying human dignity and worth. This development has allowed the nominal, formal constitution to become a living norm in people's everyday lives, as well as a standard for controlling the exercise or abuse of state power. The constitution also led to the advancement of democracy and the rule of law by me-

---

1.   Former President, Constitutional Court of Korea.

diating and integrating ideological conflicts and confrontations. Moreover, the constitutional court came to serve as the focal point that assimilates and integrates state and society into one political entity. Accordingly, most of the advanced democratic welfare states today are equipped with systematic and stable constitutional adjudication systems, and in that sense, we may be able to define today's era as the era of constitutional adjudication.

With respect to the constitutional adjudication system that protects constitutional ideals and values of guaranteeing citizens' fundamental rights, I wish to briefly introduce the establishment of the Constitutional Court of Korea, its past decisions, its contribution to the development of Korean society, and the direction of the Court in the future.

FOOTSTEPS OF THE CONSTITUTIONAL COURT OF KOREA

In 1987, the people of Korea expressed their strong aspiration to demolish the long-standing authoritarian regime and build a democratic state embodying freedom, human rights, equality, and justice. This public demand produced the ninth Korean Constitution, which led to the establishment of a constitutional court designed to safeguard the long-neglected basic rights of citizens and to effectively control the abuse of state power.

Though the constitutional review system formally existed prior to its establishment in September, 1988, it was nominal and had held merely four statutes unconstitutional over 40 years of its existence. In those years, the notions of constitutional supremacy and fundamental rights of the people were merely formal, and constitutional control over state power remained passive and limited. As a result, many doubted that the new Constitutional Court would be able to properly fulfill its function.

Despite various forms of challenges presented before the Constitutional Court during its early period, the Court consistently stressed and reaffirmed the principles and values of the constitution as the supreme, fundamental law of the nation. At the same time, it renewed people's understanding of the *raison d'être* and the value of constitutional justice by emphasizing the state's duty to protect human dignity and worth and to guarantee citizens' fundamental rights. By earning the trust of the people who had long desired the rule of law and the guarantee of fundamental human rights, the Court was able to establish itself as an important institution of stature and influence.

From the early days of its inception, the Constitutional Court broadly read the legal requirements for a constitutional petition and expanded the scope of its jurisdiction to include statutes and government decrees in an effort to invigorate the function of constitutional adjudication. As a result, the number of cases filed increased every year from as few as 425 cases in 1989 to 1,720 cases by the year 2010. As of August 31, 2012, 22,826 cases had been filed and the Court handled approximately 21,272 cases, in which 457 cases found some government action to be unconstitutional, 146 cases held a law to be unconformable to the constitution, 63 cases ruled a law unconstitutional as applied, and 28 cases found a law conditionally constitutional. Moreover, there are now 417 cases where the Court has decided a constitutional complaint in favor of the plaintiff.

Corresponding to the efforts and commitment of the Constitutional Court, the constitution in Korea is no longer a mere ornament in the code of laws; it has become a living norm in our daily lives and a standard for controlling state powers. The Constitutional Court thereby came to be a trustworthy guardian of constitutional principles and values that form the norm for integration of social conflicts. In recent polls, the Constitutional Court has been chosen as the most trusted and influential government institution in Korea, reflecting Korean citizens' appreciation of the Court's efforts.

A New Form of Constitutional Appeal Prescribed by Article 68, Section 2 of the Constitutional Court Act

Article 68, Section 2 of the Constitutional Court Act prescribes a special form of constitutional complaint, also known as the "norm-control," which is one of the institutional factors that enabled early stabilization of the constitutional adjudication system in Korea and that facilitated public recognition of constitutional review as the last resort in protecting individuals' fundamental rights.

As mentioned earlier, Korea followed Germany and several European countries in adopting a constitutional court system that plays an important role in protecting the constitution and safeguarding people's basic rights in 1987, as a result of people's strong desire for an actualization of the rule of law and reinforcement of the guarantee of people's basic rights.

The participants of the 1987 constitutional amendments adopted the constitutional court system based on the Basic Law for the Federal Republic of Germany. However, they simply included a broad provision creating an appeal system by which people may directly seek legal remedies for the violation of their constitutional rights in the Constitutional Court, and delegated all the specifics and procedural steps to the legislature. Consequently, the legislators who were authorized to formulate the details and procedures of the constitutional complaint system heatedly debated whether to adopt a key element of the German model—judicial review of decisions of ordinary courts.

Each country has its own structure and method for the constitutional complaint. For instance, Austria, which established the world's first independent constitutional court in 1920, only allows constitutional complaints for administrative actions while Germany permits constitutional review of court decisions. Germany's approach is now accepted as a standard form of constitutional petition throughout the world. The German system requires complete exhaustion of all legal remedies against state actions available in ordinary courts first before the constitutional court can review whether the judgment of appellate courts and the Supreme Court regarding the lower courts' interpretation or application of laws violated the constitutional rights of citizens.

When Korea was considering the adoption of a constitutional court, the Korean courts were already exercising jurisdiction with the accumulated experience and excellent human and material resources of nearly 100 years. Thus, it was hard for courts to accept the idea that their decisions will be reviewed by a constitutional court, a fledgling institution. Moreover, unlike Germany where the constitutional court functions as the nation's highest court in the hierarchy of the court system under the constitution, Korea envisioned its constitutional court as a separate branch of state powers with independent jurisdiction. This emphasis on the separateness and independence of the constitutional court was also somewhat problematic as a matter of legal principles for the constitutional court to exercise jurisdiction for constitutional complaints.

In this context, the legislators devised a new avenue for filing a constitutional complaint by prescribing in Article 68(2) of the Constitutional Court Act that any party to an ordinary court proceeding has recourse to the Constitutional Court to receive a final decision on the constitutionality of the statutes that were rejected by the court of original jurisdiction. This is in addition to the general constitutional complaint system where people are entitled to file a complaint when their fundamental rights have been infringed by the government's exercise or non-exercise of its power.

In other words, under the typical German system, courts file a motion with the constitutional court only when they are certain about the unconstitutionality of statutes at issue in pending trials. Otherwise, they proceed with the trials according to the constitutional interpretation of laws and their rulings may eventually be subject to review by the appellate courts. Under this system, a party to a case must exhaust all legal recourse before requesting the constitutional court to review the constitutionality of the ordinary courts' interpretation and application of the disputed law. However, under the Korean system, a party can immediately file a constitutional complaint under Article 68(2) and need not wait for the judgment from an appellate court when a court dismisses the party's motion requesting constitutional review of a disputed statute in a pending trial. Put differently, the party can have the constitutionality of the statute reviewed even in lower court proceedings and promptly prevent or remedy the trial court's erroneous ruling on the constitutionality of a statute which may infringe the party's constitutional rights. Hence, a party to a case can obtain a legal remedy either through the binding effect of the Constitutional Court's decision if the ordinary court proceedings are yet to be finalized or through initiating a retrial if the proceedings are finalized.

The reason for introducing an alternative avenue of constitutional complaint was to enable people to directly request that the Constitutional Court review the constitutionality of disputed statutes in pending trials because ordinary courts were extremely passive in exercising their constitutional review powers. Accordingly, there were scarcely any filed motions for the constitutional review of laws. And this meant that litigants had little, if any, real opportunity to have the Constitutional Court review the constitutionality of disputed statutes. The operation of this complaint system for about 10 years reveals that the public largely resorts to this avenue;

requests for constitutional review under Article 68(2) accounted for about 40% of the total constitutional complaints and 11.8% of these complaints were held in favor of the plaintiffs. This is a much higher rate than the rate by which general constitutional complaint cases in both Korea and Germany find in favor of plaintiffs—2.9% and 2.4% respectively.

Korean scholars positively evaluate this form of constitutional complaint as an unprecedented system unique to Korea. Academics conclude that it has played a major role in effectively addressing the problems of the norm control system and providing expeditious assistance in guarding the people's basic rights, activating constitutional adjudication, and stabilizing the Constitutional Court.

Even practitioners and scholars of other countries assess Korea's constitutional complaint system to be an effective scheme in promoting constitutional justice and raising people's awareness for countries with newly formed constitutional courts. Moreover, they deem that such a system can adequately adjust the inevitable conflicts between a newly created constitutional court and ordinary courts.

The Impact of the Constitutional Court of Korea on Political and Social Development

One of the most critical accomplishments of the Constitutional Court of Korea over the past 24 years is the Court's performance of its duty of safeguarding constitutional principles and values by guaranteeing its citizens' freedom and basic rights and controlling the state's abuse of powers.

Moreover, the government agencies involved in the legislative process have recognized the importance of preliminary constitutional review. Statutes used as a tool to sustain the past authoritarian regime or to protect the interests of special groups have been declared void by the Constitutional Court. The public now also believes that the constitutional review of governmental action is a way to protect the freedom and fundamental rights of the people, as well as the constitution as the supreme law of the nation.

The Constitutional Court's landmark decisions have found unconstitutional: 1, a provision of the Social Protection Act that mandates protective custody for criminal offenses irrespective of punishment; 2, a provision of the Criminal Procedure Act that maintains the effect of an arrest warrant even when the defendant is later found not guilty if he or she was sentenced to a severe punishment; 3, a provision of the Correctional Administration Act that compels a prison guard to attend a meeting between a pretrial detainee and his/her defense counsel; and 4, a provision of the National Security Act that criminally punishes those who praise, incite or produce expressive materials for anti-government organizations.

Meanwhile, as the legal legacies of the past authoritarian regime to some extent disappeared, an increasing number of high-profile cases that could influence the course of social stability and the future of the nation were brought before the Constitutional Court. Issues of great national and social importance arising from the political, economic, and social sectors that failed to be resolved through satisfactory dialogue and compromise in the political process came to the Constitutional Court for judicial review. This distorted the decision-making process of a democratic political system, which also raised serious questions regarding the separation of powers and the limitation of constitutional review.

Major decisions during this time include: 1, holding the statute for the relocation of Korea's capital unconstitutional; 2, dismissing health requirements for imports of U.S. beef; 3, invalidating a provision of the Public Election Act which denied the voting rights of Korean people living overseas; and 4, ruling unconstitutional criminal penalties for conscientious objectors to military service and a statutory ban on night time outdoor rallies and assemblies. In handling these cases, the Court modified its pleading and procedures and developed more universal and compelling review standards that improved the predictability of its decisions and the people's trust in the Constitutional Court. Further, the Court strengthened the necessity and legitimacy of constitutional review throughout this time.

Recently, the Court strengthened its control over legislative procedures as well as substantive matters of law. In a suit brought by a congressman of the opposition party against the chairman of the National Assembly, a congressman claimed that the majority party railroaded a bill through the legislature. The Constitutional Court held that the chairman would have violated assembly members' right to vote on a bill if the voting proceeded under significant impairment in freedom and fairness. Hence, the Court emphasized the procedural legitimacy of laws over the autonomy of the National Assembly in its proceedings. This accelerated the realization of democracy within the National Assembly and the advancement of political democracy in Korea.

THE RELATIONSHIP BETWEEN THE CONSTITUTIONAL COURT AND THE OTHER COURTS

The constitution of Korea separates judicial functions between the ordinary courts and the Constitutional Court by distinguishing between the judicial power of the Supreme Court of Korea, the highest judicial tribunal, and other lower courts in chapter 5 and that of the Constitutional Court in Chapter 6.

Article 101(1) of the Constitution entrusts courts with expansive judicial power by declaring that the "judicial power shall be vested in courts composed of judges." This empowers the courts to exercise their judicial power to the full extent unless otherwise specified in the constitution. However, since Article 111 of the Constitution spells out the details of the Constitutional Court's exclusive jurisdiction, the ordinary courts are restricted in exercising their judicial power.

Article 107, section 1 of the Constitution embodies this limitation by stating that "the court shall request for constitutional review from the Constitutional Court when the constitutionality of a statute is at issue in a trial and adjudge the matter in accordance with the decision of the Constitutional Court." This provision prevents the ordinary courts from making their own decisions on whether a challenged statute violates the constitution. In principle, the ordinary courts are required to interpret and apply statutes in conformity with the constitution. Thus, when the constitutionality of a disputed statute is in question, the court should halt the proceeding, request review by the Constitutional Court, and follow the Court's decision. If the Constitutional Court holds that the challenged statute is unconstitutional, that statute becomes invalid under Article 47 of the Constitutional Court Act and all courts are bound by the decision. This means that they may not apply the statute to a case at issue. Put another way, though the ordinary courts may possess the power to review the constitutionality of statutes, they do not have the final say in invalidating or upholding statutes. This authority is exclusively granted to the Constitutional Court. At the same time, when a party files a motion with an ordinary court to request a constitutional review of a disputed statute but is rejected by the court through a denial or a dismissal of the motion, the party may file a constitutional complaint to the Constitutional Court. Even in this case, the ruling of the Constitutional Court binds all other courts.

Furthermore, one may file a constitutional complaint with the Constitutional Court when a particular statute directly infringes upon his or her constitutional rights because this amounts to the legislature's illegitimate exercise of power. Under Article 75(1) of the Constitutional Court Act, if the Constitutional Court rules in favor of the petitioner, the ruling will bind all state agencies including all other courts. The statute will lose its effect from the day of the decision and the other courts may not apply the statute to their pending cases. Ultimately, the adjudicatory power of the constitutionality of statutes is vested exclusively in the Constitutional Court.

FUTURE DIRECTION OF THE CONSTITUTIONAL COURT OF KOREA

The Supreme Court of the United States first adopted the concept of judicial review and the Federal Constitutional Court of Germany laid the groundwork of the system that we have adopted in Korea. Originally, the creation and operation of the Constitutional Court of Korea was modeled after that of Germany and Austria. These days however, the precedents and case law of the common law countries, including the United States, exert considerable influence.

Moving forward, this is a perfect time for the Constitutional Court of Korea to explore its own approach for constitutional adjudication. It should develop a standard and a method for constitutional review that fits within the framework of both global and local practices. While a constitution generally contains universal ideas and values, it also embodies the tradition, culture, and values unique to each country. The Constitutional Court is thus confronted with the new challenge of balancing the universal characteristics of constitutional values with the regional and national uniqueness of Korea through its function of constitutional adjudication. Although the Constitutional Court of Korea still needs to import and study the theories of other countries, such as Germany and the United States, it must go beyond merely following other countries. In the future, it should seek out a new approach that would suit Korean history and culture, as well as its ideology and future. In other words, while the Constitutional Court should broadly adopt the jurisprudence of countries with advanced institutions for constitutional adjudication, it should also be critical of, and selective in, embracing foreign jurisprudence. It should focus on establishing Korea's own, creative constitutional review system and standards that would best serve Korean values and culture.

To respond to this need, the Court took a systematic and holistic approach by establishing the Constitutional Research Institute as the Court's legal research hub. The institute collects, analyzes, and studies various precedents and jurisprudence of foreign institutions of constitutional adjudication, as well as conducts a comprehensive study and review of the Constitutional Court's mid-to-long-term research and policy projects. Korea's Constitutional Research Institute is recognized as the only institution in the world established as a separate national research institute dedicated to mid-and long-term constitutional studies and research. The Constitutional Court has received an increasing number of visitors and inquiries from other countries interested in the development of the institute.

THE IMPORTANCE OF INTERNATIONAL RELATIONS FOR CONSTITUTIONAL JUSTICE AND EFFORTS OF THE CONSTITUTIONAL COURT OF KOREA

The early stabilization and remarkable achievements of the Constitutional Court of Korea in a fairly short period of time were possible primarily due to the support of the Korean people who respected and put their faith in the Court's decisions. But it must be noted that in addition to the citizens' help, the unstinting support and cooperation from foreign states with advanced constitutional adjudication systems also played an indispensable role.

When the Constitutional Court of Korea was founded in 1988, Korea began the work of constitutional adjudication with limited knowledge and experience in modern constitutional jurisprudence. Through the support and cooperation of other institutions of constitutional adjudication, which had already blazed a trail, the Court was able to make up for its lack of experience. The accumulated practice and wisdom of countries with developed democracy and the rule of law provided a good example for the Korean Constitutional Court during its rudimentary stage. Further, the advice and aid from these seasoned countries played a major role in the successful establishment of the constitutional adjudication system in Korea.

Inspired by the support and cooperation of countries with advanced constitutional jurisprudence, the Constitutional Court of Korea strives to further strengthen the international solidarity in promoting the advancement of the rule of law, democracy, and human dignity by sharing and discussing with various countries the experiences and lessons it has acquired over time.

Beginning in 2003, the chief justices or justices of constitutional courts and equivalent institutions from Korea and other Asian countries convened for the "Conference of Asian Constitutional Court Judges" to share experiences and insights on constitutional adjudication and to promote democracy and the rule of law throughout Asia. At the third conference held in September 2005, members agreed to establish the "Association of Asian Constitutional Courts and Equivalent Institutions (AACC)." After four preparatory meetings, the Association was officially launched in July of 2010 and the President of the Korean Constitutional Court was selected as the Association's first chair.

Currently, the AACC members include constitutional courts and equivalent institutions of Indonesia, Korea, Malaysia, Mongolia, Philippines, Russia, Tajikistan, Thailand, Turkey, Pakistan, and Uzbekistan. In May 2012, its inaugural assembly was successfully held in Seoul with delegations from 30 countries. The Constitutional Court of Korea will continue to help realize universal values, including the advancement of democracy, the rule of law, and human rights protection in Asia, by collaborating with its neighboring countries.

Further, the Constitutional Court of Korea is exerting its best efforts to expand cooperation and exchange with not only its Asian neighboring countries but also nations in other parts of the world, in order to find ways to further advance the constitution and constitutional justice. For instance, in September 2008, the Constitutional Court held an international symposium on the "Separation of Powers and Constitutional Adjudication in the Twenty-First Century" to commemorate the Court's twentieth anniversary. A total of 39 chief officials of constitutional courts and equivalent institutions, as well as representatives of regional alliances, attended. In 2009, constitutional courts and equivalent institutions across the world launched "The World Conference on Constitutional Justice" and brought the representatives of over 100 countries together in one place to create a global platform for the exchange of ideas. This movement stemmed from an accurate recognition that advancing the protection of human dignity, as well as democracy and the rule of law across the world, must necessarily be grounded in the collective efforts of all countries, not just one.

At the second world conference held in Brazil in January 2011, members selected Korea to host the third conference scheduled for 2014. It is a great honor that the Constitutional Court of Korea can host a conference that assembles many key constitutional courts and equivalent institutions across the world for an open exchange of experiences and insights, as well as foster solidarity to further constitutional justice.

CONCLUSION

Historically, an unrestrained power eventually leads to an abuse of power. Over the last two decades, the Constitutional Court of Korea brought all state powers under its scrutiny and set the constitution as the normative framework for checking and balancing state powers. It also provided guidance to the state's exercise of power in a way that protects peoples' fundamental constitutional rights.

Yet, new challenges lie ahead of the court. For instance, the risk of states infringing civil rights through the abuse of power—one of the major reasons why countries originally adopted constitutional adjudication systems—is significantly lower today as a result of the development of democracy and the advancement of human rights. Accordingly, the people's perspective on fundamental rights is changing drastically as the subject of interest is shifting from liberty rights to economic, social and cultural rights. Various social interest groups, including non-governmental organizations, are now more influential than ever and the remarkable development of information technology and biotechnology also raises a range of new constitutional questions regarding the people's rights to human dignity and worth and the pursuit of happiness.

In addition, the "globalization of human rights" and cooperation and solidarity between various international human rights organizations pose yet another challenge on issues such as the supremacy, boundaries, and limitations of constitutional review between the state's national courts and the International Court of Justice.

Therefore, institutions with constitutional review power around the world, including the Constitutional Court of Korea, should continue their efforts in defining their role and limits in guarding peoples' basic rights and preserving the constitution. The institutions should endeavor to judiciously resolve constitutional challenges emerging from changing times and circumstances to firmly implant the constitution as a living standard of the people and a control norm for governmental power.

Judicial Intervention in Policy-Making by the Constitutional Court in Korea

Jibong Lim[1]

INTRODUCTION

The Constitutional Court was established in 1988 as one of the highest courts in Korea, separate from the general courts. Before then, there had been a Constitutional Committee in Korea that seemingly imitated the French Constitutional Council, but it was only an ineffective constitutional institution where not a single statute was declared unconstitutional. In contrast, the Korean Constitutional Court has been fairly active since its establishment, settling 21,403 out of 22,294 filed cases by the end of April 2012, and declaring 223 statutes and 226 governmental measures unconstitutional.[2] The Korean Constitutional Court has become a focus of public concern, contributing much to the protection of the people's rights, and nurturing genuine constitutionalism in Korean society.[3]

This study aims at exploring the role of the Korean Constitutional

---

1. Professor of Law, Sogang University Law School (Seoul, Korea). Academic Adviser, Korean Constitutional Court.

2. For the statistics, please refer to http://english.ccourt.go.kr/home/english/decisions/stat_pop01.jsp.

3. For the details on the role of the Constitutional Court and the Constitutional Committee in Korea, see Jibong Lim, "A Comparative Study of the Constitutional Adjudication Systems of the U.S., Germany and Korea," *Tulsa Journal of Comparative and International Law* 6 (1999), 124.

Court through judicial intervention in policy-making, comparing it with that of the U.S. Supreme Court. To that end, it will examine a Korean Constitutional Court decision[4] on the marriage limitation provision in the Korean Civil Code and explore why it should not be the Korean Congress but the Korean Constitutional Court that take the lead in abolishing the system prohibiting marriage between persons of same surname and family origin. It will also explore whether the courts in Korea and in the U.S. are either pro-majoritarian or anti-majoritarian institutions. Finally, it will examine the reasons behind the existence of the Constitutional Court or the Supreme Court in the two countries and explain when and why judicial intervention into policy-making is necessary.

SUMMARY OF THE KOREAN CONSTITUTIONAL COURT DECISION ON THE MARRIAGE LIMITATION PROVISION IN THE KOREAN CIVIL CODE[5]

Section 1 of the Korean Civil Code Article 809 provides, "[T]he kin of [the] same surname and family origin[6] cannot marry each other." This provision

---

4. Marriage Limitation case. Constitutional Court [Const. Ct.] 95Hun-Ga6-13 (consol.) [adjudication on the constitutionality of statutes, case from #6 to #13 combined], Jul. 16, 1995, (S. Kor.). Appeal for the judicial review of Sec. 1 of Korean Civil Code Art. 809.

5. For more details of the case, see Jibong Lim, "Korean Constitutional Court, a Leader of Social Change and Judicial Activism in Korea," *Korean Journal Of Public Law* 1 (2004) (Special Issue of *Public Law*, Vol. 32-5, Korean Public Law Association), at 2–4.

6. "Family origin" means the place where the progenitor of the family established the family for the first time. Thus, it is usually the name of a town or city. Within the same family name, there could be several family origins. Accordingly, family origin is a subcategory of family name. For example, in the surname "Lim," there are three different family origins: Pyungtaek, Najoo, and Yecheon. That means three progenitors whose surname was "Lim," who could have been brothers or relatives long ago, established and started the Lim family in three different places. Therefore, among Lims, there are three different kinds: Lim from Pyungtaek, Lim from Najoo, and Lim from Yecheon. Persons with the same surname but different family origin can marry each other. Thus, for example, although a man and a woman are Lims, if the man is Lim originated from Pyungtaek and the woman is Lim originated from Najoo, they can marry each other. Only the persons

has existed since the enactment of the Korean Civil Code on February 2, 1958.

Facts

Mr. Heung-Sun Park and Ms. Mi-Ja Park and six other couples objected to the disposition of the registrar who did not accept their marriage registrations because each couple shared the same surname with the same family origin. Subsequently, the couples initiated a lawsuit in the Seoul District Family Court. On May 17, 1995, the Family Court combined the seven cases and examined the constitutionality of Section 1 of Civil Code Article 809, which was the basis of the registrar's decisions.[7] The Korean Constitutional Court accepted review of the combined case on May 29, 1995.

Reasoning

Majority Opinion by Five Justices: Unconstitutional

Five Justices ruled Section 1 to be unconstitutional for the following reasons.

First, the majority opinion focused on the social history and basis of the marriage limitation system and asserted that the marriage limitation system was not indigenous to Korea but originated from China's clan system. Then, it acknowledged that the system's moral base, Confucianism, respected the values of loyalty and filial piety of the traditionally agricultural Korean society.

Second, the majority articulated the change in the social environment and system basis in modern Korean society. They discussed changes in the Korean people's concept of marriage, family and gender equality, economic structure, and the increased urbanization of Korean society. In addition, the majority emphasized that the large number of couples that were given legal relief through the "Special Temporary Act on Marriage" was strong evidence that the marriage prohibition had lost its appropriateness in modern Korean society.

---

with same family origin among same surname cannot marry each other under Sec. 1 of the Korean Civil Code Art. 809.

7. *Republic of Korea v. Heung-Sun Park and Mi-Ja Park et al.* Seoul Family Court [Seoul Family Ct.], 95Ho-Pa3029–3036 (consol.) [cases from #3029 to #3036 combined], 1995 (S. Kor.).

Third, the majority stressed the unconstitutionality of Section 1 of Korean Civil Code Article 809 ("Art. 809, Sec. 1 of the Civil Code"). According to the majority, Article 809 directly violated Article 10 of Korean Constitution (protecting human value and dignity and the right to pursue happiness) by intruding on the freedom to marry; this freedom includes the freedom to choose one's partner and the time of the marriage. Article 809 also violated Article 11 (ensuring equal protection) and Section 1 of Article 36 (protecting marriage and family life on the basis of individual dignity and equality of genders) because one's surname and family origin is purely patrilineal.

The majority opinion concluded that the Civil Code provision was unconstitutional because it did not mirror the current Korean social environment and it conflicted directly with the above constitutional provisions.

First Dissenting Opinion by Two Justices: Constitutional

The first dissenting opinion ruled the Civil Code provision constitutional for the following reasons.

First, it emphasized that the origin of the marriage limitation system lay in Korea—not China—and that the system had been firmly established as a tradition in current Korean society. The first dissenting opinion further regarded the Civil Code provision as the heir of Korean traditional culture that should be protected by Article 9 of the Korean Constitution.[8]

Second, it asserted that although there were some fundamental changes in the social environment and the Korean people's way of thinking, such changes did not necessarily lead to the conclusion that the society's general ideology had changed as well.

Second Dissenting Opinion by Two Justices: Nonconforming to the Constitution

The second dissenting opinion agreed with the majority opinion's conclusion that the Civil Code provision was against the Constitution, but it did not consider it to be unconstitutional. Rather, the second dissenting opinion declared it to be "nonconforming to the constitution," and stressed that

---

8.   Art. 9 of the Korean Constitution provides, "[T]he government should make efforts to succeed and develop the traditional culture and enhance the national culture."

the decision to invalidate and revise the Civil Code provision should be left to the Congress—not the Court.

Holding of the Constitutional Court: Variation Type

While seven Justices agreed that the concerned provision was against the Korean Constitution, only five of them, including the Chief Justice, viewed it to be unconstitutional and the remaining two Justices of the second dissenting opinion regarded to be nonconforming with the Constitution. Although the opinion of the five Justices was the majority opinion, it did not satisfy the quorum necessary to declare the provision unconstitutional.[9] Accordingly, the Court finally decided to make a decision that the Article was nonconforming to the Constitution:

First, Art. 809 Sec. 1 of the Korean Civil Code (enacted on February 2, 1958 as Act No. 471) is nonconforming to the Constitution.

Second, unless Congress revises the concerned provision by December 31, 1998, it will lose its force starting on January 1, 1999. The courts and local and national government would suspend the application of the provision until the Congress revises it.

THE COURTS: PRO-MAJORITARIAN OR ANTI-MAJORITARIAN INSTITUTION

Among the three branches of government under the separation of power doctrine, the Legislative and Executive branches are called the "majoritarian institutions," because their formation and existence require the majority of the people. The members of the Legislature and the head of the Executive are elected according to the will of the majority of the people. Due to this characteristic, the two majoritarian institutions pay more attention to the opinion of the majority because they need the votes to be elected. Hence, they tend to represent the majority's will more often than that of the minority.

9.   Sec. 1 of Korean Constitution Art. 113 provides,"[W]hen the Constitutional Court makes a decision on the unconstitutionality of a law, impeachment, dissolution of political party or an affirmative decision regarding the constitutional complaint, the concurrence of six Justices or more shall be required."

From this perspective, it is evident that the Judiciary, compared to the Legislature and the Executive, is not a majoritarian institution. Generally,[10] judges are not elected, but appointed. How then does the relationship between the Judiciary and the two majoritarian institutions play out under the separation of powers doctrine? On one hand, the Judiciary represented by the Supreme Court or the Constitutional Court performs judicial review and strengthens the two majoritarian institutions by justifying what they do. There, the Judiciary is pro-majoritarian institution. On the other hand, the Judiciary can weaken the two majoritarian institutions by invalidating what they do. Here, the Judiciary could be labeled as anti-majoritarian institution. Focusing on the example of the U.S. Supreme Court, let us examine the two features of the Courts.

The Court as a Pro-Majoritarian Institution

On some occasions, the courts—especially the Supreme Court or Constitutional Court—function as a pro-majoritarian institution. The court can appear as a pro-majoritarian institution in the following two ways.

First, the court helps the other governmental branches by judicial legitimization. The court validates the exercise of power of the other branches by finding it to be constitutionally permissible. According to Professor Jesse H. Choper, the court's judicial legitimization provides dignity to laws the majoritarian institution makes and constitutionally justifies the majoritarian institution's actions: "The public knowledge that an independent tribunal has approved political assumptions of authority adds dignity to the laws of the central government and inspires confidence that it is acting within its constitution-limited boundaries."[11] Professor Choper states that the cooperation of all three governmental branches is necessary for the psychological acceptance by the American people, a prerequisite to successful administration of government and national unity.

This can also appear in the form of so-called 'judicial self-restraint' as well. Here, the judges participate passively in the decision of sensitive

---

10.   In Korea, all the judges are appointed. In the United States, while some judges are elected on the state court level, most are appointed.

11.   Jesse H. Choper, *Judicial Review And The National Political Process: A Functional Reconsideration Of The Role Of The Supreme Court* (Chicago: 1980), 229–30.

cases. They are reluctant to make a clear-cut decision and try to circumvent it by restraining themselves from intervening. We observed this in the second dissenting opinion of *Heung-Sun Park and Mi-Ja Park* where two Justices stated, "[T]he decision on the scope of customs concerning family relationship that should be legalized and coerced belongs to the category of legislation policy. Accordingly, unless the legislative decision is deemed to be evidently irrational, we cannot declare it unconstitutional."[12] As we can see here, judges can exercise judicial self-restraint and try not to intervene in the decision of the other governmental branches. On the contrary, the lack of self-restraint in judges results in active judicial intervention. For example, during the period from 1890 to 1937 in the United States, the lack of self-restraint on the part of conservative judges functioned as the biggest obstacle to progressive economic regulation.[13] Judicial self-restraint is usually exercised on the pretext of procedural errors rather than on the substance of the case. Strict adherence to judicial self-restraint limits the participation of judges in social change that the judges otherwise might be interested in. However, self-restraint by judges and social change are not completely incompatible in the cases where the major innovations come from the legislature and the Court's function is simply to legitimize such actions.[14]

Furthermore, even when the court rejects a challenge of unconstitutionality by citing judicial self-restraint, it does not mean that the court endorses the government action it upholds. According to Professor Choper, it just means that the court is affirming that the branch acted within the constitutional boundary with clear and convincing evidence: "Technically, the court decides only that the conduct is within constitutional boundary and, especially because of the powerful presumption of constitutionality

12. See note 7.

13. Joel B. Grossman, "The Supreme Court and Social Change," in *Law And Social Change*, ed Stuart S. Nagel (Beverly Hills: 1970), 63.

14. Professor C. Thomas Dienes expresses the judicial self-restraint as "literalist approach" and emphasizes that it will put more burden on the Congress: "A literalist approach to the interpretative function, a limited perspective on the role of the courts in constitutional decision-making, or an active use of abstention techniques will act to place a greater burden on the legislature." C. Thomas Dienes, "Judges, Legislators, and Social Change," in Nagel, ed., *Law And Social Change*, 40.

generally accorded in the Federalist Era, the court's rulings there usually say no more than that the national political branches had some rational or perceivable basis for their decision to exercise the delegated power."[15]

Second, the court helps majoritarian institutions by fixing their failures within the structure of democracy. Professor Martin Shapiro explains this with blacks and the potential failure of voting process to choose the representatives of the people. He starts with the assumption that the electoral process is normally a self-correcting mechanism and continues with the explanation of failure of the voting process with respect to blacks: "If racism among the majority White people keeps Blacks from voting or forming coalition with Whites that would bring some political victories, then the electoral mechanism cannot fix itself. It cannot achieve fairness to Blacks in the electoral process." According to Professor Shapiro, this is the very time that the court should intervene: "Then the Supreme Court is justified in engaging in judicial intervention to increase the Black political capacities so that the Black interests can be represented in the normal electoral and representative political process." In addition, when the voting process fails to reflect the widely held interests because they are too diffuse, the court should intervene to protect those interests: "Certain widely held values or interests such as those in freedom of speech, are too diffuse to be reflected in voting and so are never adequately represented in elected legislatures." Professor Shapiro states that this "correcting-the-failures-of-democracy" rationale is the narrowest democratic justification for judicialization of politics.[16]

The majoritarian institutions can induce the court's "correcting-the-failures-of-democracy" rationale by willfully delegating some decisions to the court at times. This appears to happen when the political costs of dealing with an issue are too great to risk, turning the issue into a no-win game for the elected decision-makers. In other words, the judicialization of politics occurs when majoritarian institutions decide that they do not wish to have the burden of making the final decision on certain issues. For instance, many U.S. state legislatures have seemingly been more than will-

15. Choper, *Judicial Review*, 233.

16. Martin Shapiro, "The United States," in *The Global Expansion of Judicial Power*, ed. C. Neal Tate and Torbjörn Vallinder (New York: 1995), 60.

ing to leave abortion policy in the hands of the courts due to the estimated political costs of taking any action on the issue.[17]

The Court as an Anti-Majoritarian Institution

Courts can also function as an anti-majoritarian institution. This happens when courts intervene and invalidate what the majoritarian institutions did. With respect to the theme of this research, the character of the courts as anti-majoritarian institution becomes clear when the courts assume an aspect of judicial activism.

At a minimum, the courts are a non-majoritarian institution because the members of a court are generally not elected by the will of majority of people. Therefore, the courts are responsive to the minority than are majoritarian institutions. When a legislative dispute involves a right, the forum of the dispute can be shifted from where the majority's right to rule is accepted, to one where the minority's right against the majority are acknowledged by non-majoritarian institutions like the courts.[18] Here, the courts become something more than just a non-majoritarian institution: they become an *anti*-majoritarian institution.

In reality, interpreting law and making law are difficult to distinguish from one another. Under the separation of power doctrine, it seems highly probable that the judges who are decision-makers in a constitutionally independent and co-equal branch would be fit to assert themselves in policy-making against the legislative and executive branches. But we should also keep in mind that the formal duty assigned to judges in the separation of power system is not to make, but to interpret the laws. However, distinguishing the act of interpreting the law from making it is difficult, as many judges themselves and socio-legal scholars recognize.[19]

Concerned with social change, judicial policy-making has an important meaning with respect to the legislature. In policy-making, policy can be formulated in such a manner to accommodate contending parties because negotiation and compromise are characteristics of the legislative process.

17.   C. Neal Tate, "Why the Expansion of Judicial Power?," in Tate and Vallinder, 32.
18.   Ibid. at 31.
19.   Ibid. at 29.

When the legal system deals with complex social or economic change presenting a wide range of legal issues, legislative—rather than judicial—resources assume more importance. However, even if the legislature were to intermittently review its actions in terms of change in social conditions, the disapproving parties in society would likely pursue judicial interpretation or a determination of the legislative enactment's constitutionality. At that time, the manner in which the courts exercise their prerogative in statutory interpretation, constitutional determination, and procedural abstention[20] will have a critical effect on the character of the legal response to social changes, influencing not only the role of the judiciary in the process but also that of the legislature.[21] Furthermore, when a new legal problem generated by social change arises, the court is required to act without the traditional guidance supplied by precedent or statutes. This maximizes the strain on the resources of the courts while simultaneously providing an excellent opportunity for judicial creativity.[22]

In some situations, the minority *and* the majority of the public will have faith in the power of judicial policy-making. When the public views the majoritarian institutions as powerless or even corrupt, it is not surprising that they would accord power to the policy-making of the Judiciary, which has a reputation for rectitude and can have as much legitimacy as that of the Executive or Legislature. This tendency should only be expedited when the courts are given more respect and legitimacy than the other

20.   In social change by judicial decisions, policy directives are more important than we think. Of course, the Court cannot have any influence over social change if it refuses to issue appropriate policy directives. However, the mere issuance of those directives is frequently not enough of a force to bring about such change, except where the policy requires change only in legal doctrine and without behavioral or attitudinal change where the policy is directed only at the workings of the federal judiciary or where the policy is a post-hoc legitimation of changes already accomplished. Grossman, "The Supreme Court and Social Change," 68.

21.   According to Professor Choper, a law is "not a law but only a tentative, pressure-wrought statement of policy until judges in court subject it to judicial process and render formal judgment." Choper, *Judicial Review*, 239.

22.   When a judge is required to decide such a dispute, he weighs the balance between the need for change and the desire to maintain stability and continuity with the past. If he decides to innovate, he preempts the function that properly belongs to the legislature.

government institutions.[23]

As we have seen above, the Legislature can willfully delegate some decisions to the Court. According to Robert A. Katzmann, the essential problem is that "congress has been deliberately vague and knew full[y] well that they would want the courts to step in and resolve some sensitive issues."[24] The usual pattern is that Congress does not want to deal with its responsibilities but would rather blame the court for its decisions later. The major reason for this seems to be the general unwillingness of the legislature to act, especially in the new area that is changing—a 'wait-and-see' attitude born of political reservation.[25]

In addition to filling in the gaps left by the legislature, the courts also respond to the broad delegation of decision-making authority by the legislature. Because they are standing in for the legislature, courts should try to behave as a good legislature would.[26] Occasionally, an irritated judge has lamented that the bulk of the court's workload consists of trying to fill in the black holes in legislation.[27] As for U.S. Supreme Court decisions, the assumption that members of Congress are paying attention to the hundreds of judgments made by the federal courts each year and that they act on them is misguided. It is true that Congress has reversed numerous statutory interpretations; but, more often, the Congress ignores them.[28]

---

23.   Tate, "Why the Expansion of Judicial Power?," 31–32.

24.   Fred Barbash, "Congress Didn't, So The Court Did," *Washington Post*, July 5, 1998, at C01.

25.   See Dienes, "Judges, Legislators, and Social Change," 38.

26.   John Hart Ely, *Democracy And Distrust: A Theory Of Judicial Review* (Cambridge, Mass.: 1980), 67–68.

27.   For instance, according to Fred Barbash, "[T]he late Chief Justice Warren E. Burger was so frustrated by it that he proposed a court impact statement to be issued by Congress whenever it wrote a law, so it would understand the latest burden placed on the court to divine what the legislative branch really meant." Barbash, "Congress Didn't, So The Court Did."

28.   Among the most frequently deployed techniques for assessing congressional desire is a kind of repetitive taste test. The Court interprets legislative language in a certain way and waits to see if Congress chokes on it. If it does not, the Court then assumes that Congress likes it. According to this approach, the more often the lawmakers do nothing about an interpretation and acquiesce in it, the more they approve of it.

Although courts work hard to respond to the broad delegation of decision-making authority as well as fill in the gaps left by the legislature, they are condemned no matter how they do their job. Regardless of their efforts, courts remain extremely vulnerable to condemnation by those who are motivated to discover their shortcomings.[29] In particular, when the U.S. Supreme Court actively intervened in state governments' acts, there was widespread enmity toward the Court. In Virginia, the state legislature called for the creation of a new tribunal to resolve constitutional issues of federal versus state power.[30] The accusation from the Conference of State Chief Justices was one of the strongest ones against the federal judiciary: the Conference thought it was unproductive of federal judicial decisions "to press the extension of federal power and to press it rapidly."[31]

The enmity toward the courts came not only from state governmental branches but also from other *federal* governmental branches. This enmity against overly active judicial intervention appeared to contradict the theory that the legislature does not truly speak for the people's values but the court does.[32] Alexander M. Bickel, who saw the court's role largely as one of responding to a consensus accurately reflected by the legislature, was greatly critical of the Warren Court's efforts to render legislatures more responsive.[33] Some commentators like John Hart Ely tried to set a limit on

29.   According to Professor Choper, for example, "in the apportionment field, *Baker v. Carr* was assaulted because it afforded no meaningful guidelines to lower courts and legislatures while *Reynolds v. Sims* was discredited because its boldly stated standard was found to be too rigid and inflexible." Choper, *Judicial Review*, 136.

30.   In Tennessee, a newspaper wrote, "[T]his Court, above the law and beyond the control of public opinion, has lately made a decision that prostrates the state sovereignty entirely and that must sooner or later bring down on the members of it the execration of the community." Ibid., 231.

31.   "The Report and Resolution of the National Conference of Chief Justices Conclusions of the Report of the Committee on Federal-State Relationships as Affected by Judicial Decisions, *Massachusetts Law Quarterly* 43 (1958), 87, cited ibid., 232.

32.   Tate, "Why the Expansion of Judicial Power?," 68.

33.   Alexander M. Bickel, *The Least Dangerous Branch: The Supreme Court at the Bar of Politics*, 2nd ed. (New Haven: 1986), 247–54.

judicial intervention.[34] In addition, Professor Choper emphasized that active judicial intervention should not be wasted in trying to expand federal power vis-à-vis the states, but instead it should be performed in the cases where a minority's rights are at stake:

> In deciding questions of the scope of national authority *vis-à-vis* the states, the [c]ourt needlessly risks losing the public's confidence because the constitutional interests at stake are forcefully and accurately represented in the national political arena. Thus, the Federalism Proposal is offered to conserve the [c]ourt's precious capital for those cases in which it is really needed—where poorly represented and unpopular individual rights are at stake.[35]

Professor Choper thinks the court's authority to exercise its most vital function of protecting individual rights depends on the public's willingness to accept the court's anti-majoritarian decisions.[36] Among the current Justices in the U.S Supreme Court, Justice Scalia warns against the excessive judicial intervention. He trusts the political process over the judicial process to lead social evolution in the United States. He believes the court should not invalidate the results of the democratic process just because the court does not agree with the majority's political values; rather, the court should overrule the majoritarian process only when government enacts a law that is not consistent with a right explicitly protected by the Constitution or a specific legal tradition. In effect, Justice Scalia believes that it

34. The limit he set up is as follows:"as long as judges do not decide on competing values and political concepts and as long as they control legitimate processes instead of legitimate outcomes, judicial review is compatible with democracy." Ely, *Democracy and Distrust*, 68.

35. Choper, *Judicial Review*, 258.

36. According to Professor Choper, Madison believed that each government possessed a different defensive armor that served as a means of preventing or correcting unconstitutional encroachments by the other. He claims that the defensive armor of the states was the political process and that of the national government was the judicial process. The thesis of Professor Choper's book is: "The Court should hold that the judicial power of the United States does not extend to the resolution of constitutional questions that the Court—through the use of the functional, but substantively neutral and non-opportunistic factors that have been previously explored at length—finds to be unnecessary for the preservation of genuine personal constitutional freedoms and subject to fair and effective resolution in the national political process." Ibid., 414.

should be the citizens of the United States who act through their elected representatives, that make the difficult choice necessary in recognizing social change.[37]

On the other hand, there is an opposite position thoroughly advocating for broad judicial intervention. It emphasizes the purpose of a statute in its interpretation, greater acceptance of the political role of the court in constitutional decision-making, and the need for a greater role of the courts as a coordinating branch in the policy-making process.

There is an adage on judicial self-restraint: "not to decide is to decide." In choosing not to intervene or not to substitute their own policy rationales with those of others, judges affirm existing policies, including the policy of "no policy," just as surely as if they had imposed those existing policies from their own will. In this sense, judges cannot evade their policy-making role.[38] However, judicial activism implies a more affirmative policy role than that involved in a judicial non-decision.

This position advocating for judicial intervention emphasizes that court decisions have direct and crucial effects on citizens in a symbolic way. Some available evidence indicates that American citizens are not knowledgeable about the Supreme Court. Hence, we would expect that American understanding of the Court's decisions would be primitive in symbolic terms. This being the case, we might infer that to the extent the court can afford effective symbolic representation of certain values, the Court is likely to have some influence[39] in promoting the behavior that these symbol-

---

37.   Justice Scalia has stated, "[I]f the Constitution were... but a novel invitation to apply current societal values, what reason would there be to believe that the invitation was addressed to the courts rather than to the legislature? One simply cannot say... that it is emphatically the province and duty of the judicial department to determine its content. Quite to the contrary, the legislature would seem a much more appropriate expositor of social values." Timothy L. Raschke Shattuck, "Justice Scalia's Due Process Methodology: Examining Specific Traditions," *Southern California Law Review* 65 (1992), 2786.

38.   Peter Bachrach and Morton S. Baratz, "Two Faces of Power," *American Political Science Review* 56 (1962), 947–52, cited in Tate, "Why the Expansion of Judicial Power?," 33.

39.   Professor Bradley C. Cannon makes a number of interesting distinctions that may be helpful in analyzing the problems of the impact of a judicial decision. He distinguishes between a person's "psychological reaction" to a decision, which he calls an "acceptance decision" and the person's "behavior response," or what the person actually does in

ic values may represent.[40] This position claims that the role of the courts could be enhanced by active judicial intervention.

However, this does not mean that there is no obstacle to active and creative judicial action. In handling exceedingly complex socio-legal problems, courts can only deal with specific aspects of the problem as they are presented. Of course, the language of an opinion can anticipate questions and give rather substantial clues as to the court's future disposition, but this type of language falls under the obscure classification of *dictum*. Even if the courts over time could shape a comprehensive policy through case-by-case decisions, the rate of change in modern society challenges the appropriateness of this process. The judicial activist would require extensive data on the social consequences of legislatively constructed policy, the possible social impact of suggested policy revisions, and the possible reactions of other legal actors which might produce a response directed at the court itself. However, it is questionable whether the courts currently have the ability to process such data adequately even if it were available.[41] The legislature's alleged superiority of information has often led judges to give deference to legislative judgment and is often cited as the main obstacle to effective judicial action.[42]

The timing of judicial decision-making is also an obstacle. A court tends to respond slowly to demands and thus, lacks the strategic element of "timing" in its policy-making. Events over which the court has no control

---

response to a decision. Professor Cannon also divides the consequences of a decision into three broad categories which he calls "compliance," "implementation," and "broad impact." "Compliance" refers to "whether lower courts or implementers such as the police obey the decision." "Implementation" refers to the "degrees to which agencies such as the police and school systems are taking the necessary steps to meet the decision's real goals." In other words, "compliance is carrying out the letter of the decision and implementation is fostering its spirit." "Impact" is a broader concept. For Cannon, it can mean "every event that can be traced to a judicial decision or policy." But he applies the term primarily to mean "second-order consequences of a decision." In other words, "impact" includes all the ripple effects of a decision. It is surely the most difficult aspect of a decision to measure. Bradley C. Cannon, "Courts and Policy: Compliance, Implementation and Impact," in *American Courts*, ed. Charles Johnson and John Gates (Washington, D.C.: 1991), 440–57.

40.   Grossman, "The Supreme Court and Social Change," 65–66.

41.   Dienes, "Judges, Legislators, and Social Change," 40.

42.   Ibid., 37.

commonly change the realities of a case, but the court may feel responsible to decide the case as it was in its original form. The Court cannot always act when needed, as, for example, in the ongoing litigation over the constitutionality of capital punishment.[43] Many governmental policy decisions come in response to some kind of demand and are limited by the exigencies of time. However, the court is presumably even more restricted in its function, and its capacity for bringing about change is limited accordingly.[44]

REASON FOR THE EXISTENCE OF THE CONSTITUTIONAL COURT OR SUPREME COURT

If we view the above bases of the court as a pro- or anti-majoritarian institution from a different angle, we can see the reasons behind the existence of a Supreme Court or Constitutional Court that performs judicial review. The reasons can be summarized as follows.

First, the Court exists to protect the minority's rights against the majority's willpower. As we have seen above, the legislature and executive are majoritarian institutions elected by the majority and represent the majority's will.[45] We could understand Tocqueville's proposition in this context: the legislature "represents the majority and implicitly obeys it" and the executive is "appointed by the majority and serves as a passive tool in its hands."[46] Between the two majoritarian institutions, the legislature can operate particularly undemocratically, even though it is traditionally under-

---

43.   Some point out that, similarly, legislative institutional response to rapid social change arguably tends to lag behind social change because the organization needed to obtain even a hearing takes time to develop. According to them, courts arguably cannot refuse to hear a dispute because "the job is hard, or dubious, or dangerous." K. N. Llewllyn, *The Bramble Bush* (New York: 1930), 35.

44.   Grossman, "The Supreme Court and Social Change," 63.

45.   An analysis of the factors affecting access to the legislative process indicates that unorganized, inarticulate interests such as those of individuals in either unorganized or weakly organized groups, or individuals who do not have full knowledge of their needs, can give little incentive for legislative response. They are minority groups.

46.   A. De Tocqueville, *Democracy In America*, ed. Mentor (New York: 1956), 115.

stood to be the most representative of all government institutions.[47] As a result, judicial review becomes necessary and judicial intervention becomes an important issue. When the Court exercises the power of judicial review to declare legislative, executive, or administrative action unconstitutional, it rejects the popular will by denying policies made by representatives, congressmen, or the elected members of the Executive branch. The dilemma here is that the Court actually has no direct political responsibility and has the weakest links to popular will. This means that a Court that lacks democratic justification is proclaiming that the will of the majority, expressed through the elected representatives or appointees within the majority's control, must be ignored. Judicial review appears to be not merely anti-majoritarian, but squarely against traditional democratic philosophy.[48]

The Court actively and creatively interprets the Constitution's open-ended provisions in order to protect the rights of minority groups against the actions of the majority. It makes no sense to employ the prevalent value judgments of the current majority to protect minorities from value judgments of the majority.[49] Here, the smaller the allegedly aggrieved group (or minority) is and "the more intense the felt need or the contempt of the majority, the greater the necessity of judicial review for the preservation of personal liberty."[50] In this sense, the U.S. Supreme Court is the most effective protector of the unpopular interests of an unrepresented minority because it is the most politically isolated judicial body. Except for the nearly politically impossible recourse of constitutional amendments, the Supreme Court's constitutional decisions are held to be final and the law of the land. This protection of the minority becomes more tenuous among the judges of the inferior federal courts although they share the same constitutional prerequisites as the Justices of the Supreme Court.[51]

---

47. Professor Choper points out the problem of the U.S. Congress: "It is not that far-reaching that laws promulgated by the legislative system are opposed by a predominant segment of the populace, but rather that Congress too often refuses to ordain solutions supported by national majorities." Choper, *Judicial Review*, 26.

48. Ibid., 6.

49. Ely, *Democracy and Distrust*, 68–69.

50. Choper, *Judicial Review*, 69.

51. Professor Choper points out the judges' relationships with the local community and their wish to keep the courts' prestige in their districts as the reason."Because

Second, the Court fosters democracy. As Martin Shapiro noted, on certain occasions democracy is not self-correcting without judicial intervention. The Court corrects the failure of democracy caused by the malfunctioning of the other majoritarian branches. In other words, the Court makes up for the failures of, and solidifies, democracy. Korea is a racially homogeneous nation while the United States is heterogeneous. Accordingly, in Korea, there is no distinction of minority and majority based on the race, at least. There are just interchangeable minority and majority positions in terms of political and economic power based on the issues. Therefore, in *Heung-Sun Park and Mi-Ja Park*, the Korean Constitutional Court played not the role of protecting minority rights against the majority's will, but rather that of fostering democracy by fixing a certain failure of the other governmental branches.

What then is the failure of Korean democracy demonstrated in *Heung-Sun Park and Mi-Ja Park*? I think the failure lies with the Korean Congress rather than the Korean Executive. The Korean Congress failed in representing the broad national sentiment of the Korean people. Rather, a local sentiment has been over-represented in the arena of Korean Congress. Here, as we have discussed in Part II above, the broad national sentiment of current Korean people is that the marriage limitation system is no longer suitable to modern Korean society.

Meanwhile, the opposite contention that the marriage limitation system is still a powerful Korean tradition and should be observed by the Korean people and protected by the Korean Civil Code and Constitution is not the national sentiment in Korea. This argument is now only supported by a small number of Confucian groups in Korea. Confucianism had been the social, political, and religious ideology at the center of Korean life before modernization. However, as Korean society became industrialized and modernized, Confucianism lost its position as the guiding ideology and has been reduced to one that the new Korean generation does not believe fits into modern Korean society. Now, Confucianism is barely holding

---

of their long and strong personal and professional relationships with the local community and bar and their desire to sustain the prestige of their courts within their respective districts, the front-line federal judges are often more constrained to observe politically popular local rules and customs and more loath to invoke community disapproval and hostility." Ibid., 69–70.

onto its existence with the support of some of the older generations in Korea. Since many of the older generations in Korea live in rural areas, many of the remaining Korean Confucianists reside in rural areas rather than urban ones. Therefore, in the case of *Heung-Sun Park and Mi-Ja Park*, this opposing argument supported by the small number of Confucian groups can be classified as one confined to rural areas.

The problem here is that the rural sentiment has been over-represented on the floor of Korean Congress. Congressmen want to be re-elected, so they are always concerned about their constituents' propensities. If a congressman is from a rural area where a big portion of the eligible voters are Confucian, the congressman may be reluctant to agree with the abolition of the system prohibiting marriage between persons of same surname and family origin, regardless of his own personal beliefs. Because this rural congressman does not want to lose the votes from the Korean Confucian groups, he will at least try to appear that he would not vote for the abolition of the marriage limitations.

As we have seen above, there have been several attempts in Korea since the early 1950s to repeal the marriage limitation system by revising the Art. 809, Sec. 1 of Korean Civil Code. Feminist groups have vigorously pressured Congress through developing social movements favoring family law revision and by intensively lobbying for congressional revision of the Civil Code. However, the more intensely the feminist groups put pressure on Congress, the more fiercely the Confucian groups fight back. The Confucian groups regard the feminist actions as a serious challenge to the Confucian tradition in Korea and as a threat to the basis of their existence. The Confucian groups put counter-pressure on Congress by holding frequent rallys in front of the Congress building and by lobbying each and every congressman through his or her family members that happen to be Confucianists of old age. For these reasons, the proposed revision bills could not pass through the Korean Congress.

At least in Congress, the rural sentiment fiercely supported only by the old Confucianists has prevailed over the broad national sentiment. A silent majority of Korean people think the marriage limitation system is not appropriate in contemporary Korean society. The intensity of the Confucianist resistance has enabled the Confucianists to overcome their inferiority in numbers; this leads to an an "over-representation" of sorts in Congress.

The famous 1954 *Brown vs. Board of Education* case[52] in the United
States is similar to *Heung-Sun Park and Mi-Ja Park* on the point of over-representation of local sentiment against broad national sentiment. *Brown*, in
Kansas, was just one of four companion cases. The four individual cases
coming from the states of Kansas, South Carolina, Virginia and Delaware
were consolidated because they were dealing with common legal questions.
The Court said, "they are premised on different facts and different local
conditions, but a common legal question justifies their consideration together in this consolidated opinion."[53] In each of the cases, black children
had been denied admission to public schools attended by white children
under laws permitting or requiring segregation solely based on their race.
The black children's and the white children's schools had been or were being
equalized with respect to buildings, curricula, qualifications and salaries of

---

52.   The case name in the official record is *Brown et al. v. Board of Education of
Topeka, Shawnee County, Kan., et al., Briggs et al. v. Elliott et al., Davis et al. v. County
School Board of Prince Edward County, VA., et al., Gebhart et al. v. Belton et al.*, 347 U.S.
483 (1954). There was another *Brown v. Board of Education of Topeka* case held in 1955. For
convenience, *Brown v. Board of Education of Topeka* in 1954 is called "Brown I" and *Brown v.
Board of Education of Topeka* in 1955 "Brown II." By pronouncing official segregation to be
a violation of equal protection, the Court in *Brown I* did not do much to modify the actual
educational patterns of Kansas or any other state by the pronouncement alone. A significant reduction in school segregation had been realized by a long series of implementation
decisions that followed *Brown I. Brown II*, decided one year after *Brown I*, was the first of
these implementation decisions. In *Brown II*, the Court gave the federal district courts
the primary responsibility for supervising desegregation due to their proximity to local
conditions and the possible need for further hearings. The Court also directed the district
courts to use general equitable principles for carrying out desegregation without giving
any precise guidelines. *Brown II* authorized the district courts to take into account the
public interest in eliminating desegregation in a systematic and effective manner because
it feared chaos and violence that might develop when instant desegregation was attempted,
and the lower courts were ordered to implement desegregation "with all deliberate speed,"
an order now infamous for its vagueness. *Oliver Brown, et al., Appellants, v. Board of Education of Topeka, Shawnee County, Kansas, et al., Harry Briggs, Jr., et al., Appellants, v. R. W.
Elliott, et al., Dorothy E. Davis, et al., Appellants, v. County School Board of Prince Edward
County, Virginia, et al., Spottswood Thomas Bolling, et al., Petitioners, v. C. Melvin Sharpe,
et al., Francis B. Gebhart, et al., Petitioners, v. Ethel Louise Belton, et al.*, 349 U.S. 294 (1955).

53.   *Brown*, 486.

teachers.[54] The unanimous opinion of the Court by Chief Justice Warren explicitly rejected the "separate but equal" doctrine formulated in *Plessy v. Ferguson* in 1896[55] and which remained law until 1954, saying:

> Segregation of children in public schools solely on the basis of race, even though the physical facilities and other tangible factors may be equal, deprives the children of the minority group of equal education-al opportunities, in contravention of the Equal Protection Clause of the Fourteenth Amendment."[56]

The Court's reasoning could be summarized in the following three points. First, even where all-black and all-white schools were equal in terms of tangible factors such as buildings, curricula, and qualifications and sal-aries of teachers, intangible factors inevitably prevented children who were restricted to all-black schools from having equal educational opportuni-

---

54. In the Kansas case of *Brown v. Board of Education*, the plaintiffs were black children of an elementary school in Topeka. They brought this action in the United States District Court for the District of Kansas to enjoin enforcement of a Kansas statute that permitted cities of more than 15,000 population to keep separate school facilities for white and black students. Based on that authority, the Topeka Board of Education elected to establish segregated elementary schools. However, other public schools in the community were operated on a non-segregated basis. The three-judge District Court found out that segregation in public education has a detrimental effect upon black children, but denied relief on the ground that the white and black schools were substantially equal in regard to buildings, transportation, curricula and educational qualifications of teachers.

55. *Plessy v. Ferguson*, 163 U.S. 537 (1896).

56. The Equal Protection Clause does not apply to the federal government. Nev-ertheless, on the same day as *Brown* was decided, the Court held that the federal govern-ment could not be permitted to operate racially-segregated schools any more than the states could in *Bolling v. Sharpe*, 347 U.S. 497 (1954). The Court held the racial segregation of the District of Columbia public schools to be in violation of the Due Process Clause in the Fifth Amendment. It meant that the Due Process Clause of the Fifth Amendment in-corporates the Equal Protection Clause of the Fourteenth Amendment. It was explained by Chief Justice Warren in terms of judicial unwillingness to hold the states to a higher constitutional standard than the federal government. "In view of our decision that the Constitution prohibits the states from maintaining racially segregated public schools, it would be unthinkable that the same Constitution would impose a lesser duty on the Fed-eral Government." *Bolling v. Sharpe*, 500.

ties.[57] "Our decision cannot turn on merely a comparison of these tangible factors in the Negro and White schools involved in each of the cases. We must look instead to the effect of segregation itself on public education."[58] Second, segregation of white and black children in public schools has a detrimental effect on black children because the policy of separating the races is usually interpreted as denoting the inferiority of black children, and a sense of inferiority has negative effects on children's motivation to learn. "To separate them from others of similar age and qualifications solely because of their race generates a feeling of inferiority as to their status in the community that may affect their hearts and minds in a way unlikely ever to be undone."[59] In order to prove this, the Court relied on the findings of psychologists and educators. Third, separate facilities are inherently unequal and such facilities deprive black children of their right to equal protection of the laws. "We conclude that in the field of public education the doctrine of 'separate but equal' has no place. Separate educational facilities are inherently unequal."[60]

With respect to *Heung-Sun Park and Mi-Ja Park*, the important point in *Brown* is that local sentiment in the southern states had been over-represented in Congress before the decision in *Brown*, as was the situation in Korea. In a sense, *Brown* could be characterized as a case of conflict between the national majority and the local majority in southern states on the matter of racial segregation in public school. According to Martin Shapiro, *Brown* means the intervention of a national court into the conflict in order to achieve unified national norms on racial segregation in public education. Before the *Brown* decision, this unified norm had been supported, "albeit perhaps at low intensity levels by [the] national majority." However, it had been "thwarted by local norms, often with high intensity, by local majorities or by local elites."[61]

In the United States, the South is different from the North in many

57.   Under the "separate but equal" doctrine, the Court thought that equal treatment is accorded when the races are provided substantially equal facilities, although these facilities are separated.

58.   *Brown*, 492.

59.   Ibid., 494.

60.   Ibid., 495.

61.   Shapiro, "The United States," 47.

aspects. When it comes to matters of education, the South was slower in its development compared to the North due to the rural character of the South and the different regional attitudes toward state assistance for public education. For example, "although the demand for free public schools followed substantially the same pattern in both the North and South, the development in the South did not begin to gain momentum until about 1850, about twenty years after that in the North."[62] The Civil War virtually stopped all progress in public education in the South. The low priority of Negro education in the South was serious both before and immediately after the Civil War. As of 1868, when the Fourteenth Amendment was adopted, "the movement toward free common schools, supported by general taxation, had not yet taken hold [in the South]. Education of White children was largely in the hands of private groups. Education of Negroes was almost nonexistent, and practically the entire race was illiterate. In fact, any education of Negroes was forbidden by law in some states."[63]

Racial prejudice and antipathy towards blacks had not completely disappeared in the South. Furthermore, the financial situation of southern state governments was poor after the Civil War. Because Southerners could not afford to fund public education itself, they were more likely to ignore the education of black children. Under these circumstances, many of southern states sustained racial segregation in public education and adhered to the old "separate but equal" doctrine of *Plessy* since the late nineteenth century.

Plessy approved the standard of separate but equal in the South. Presumably, it had been based on the shared moral values of the white majority in the South. Accordingly, *Plessy* had been able to win the approval both of its time and a half-century into the future. The majority of white southerners thought that the "separate but equal" doctrine was itself a neutral principle. For these reasons, local sentiment in southern states just before *Brown* was not in favor of racial desegregation in public school.

However, national sentiment on racial segregation in public education was different. By 1954 when *Brown* was decided, most Northerners

---

62. Cubberley, *Public Education in The United States* (1934), 288, cited in *Brown*, 490.

63. *Brown*, 489–90.

condemned "separate but equal." The majority of Northerners thought that *Plessy* had been morally wrong.[64]

This conflict between broad national sentiment and local sentiment in the South moved to Congress. Congressmen from the southern states fiercely objected to a bill requiring racial desegregation in public facilities even though desegregation was in accord with broad national sentiment at that time. Although southern congressmen were a minority, they objected to the revision bill so aggressively that they were able to overcome their numerical inferiority, just like the Korean Confucianists. Due to the strong resistance by congressmen from the South, the bill for racial desegregation was not able to pass the Congress..

Therefore, the Court intervened in *Brown*, just like the Korean Constitutional Court intervened in Korea. Where the Court decides a case so as to resolve an intensely divisive controversy, its decision has a unique dimension that resolution of noncontroversial cases does not usually carry. The Court's interpretation of the Constitution called both sides of the national controversy to end their conflict by accepting the common mandate rooted in the Constitution. In short, the principle announced in *Brown* was the prohibition of disadvantaging African Americans by law. It was inevitable that the adoption of this principle would entail disagreement among some white southerners. However, the Court approved broad national sentiment rather than local sentiment, and showed its strong will to carry on the spirit of *Brown I* in *Brown II*, where issues about the implementation of *Brown I* were clarified by the Court. It was not Congress, but the Court, which ended the conflict between the national majority and local majority,[65] just like in the Korea.

---

64.   For details on the difference of national and local sentiment in the southern states on racial segregation in public education, see Bickel, The *Least Dangerous Branch*, 76, 197.

65.   However, there also are those who are skeptical about the active role of the Court in the civil rights movement. According to Gerald Rosenberg, before Congress and the executive branch acted, courts actually had no direct effect on ending discrimination in the key fields of voting and education; that is, the court changed nothing. Only when Congress and the executive branch acted in tandem with the courts, did change occur in those key fields. Rosenberg points out, "In terms of judicial effects, then, Brown and its progeny stand for the proposition that courts are impotent to produce significant social

We can tell from the two cases that both in the Korean Congress[66] and the U.S. Congress, there were—and may still be—a minority barrier. The minority in Congress can obstruct the passage of a bill supported by the majority. There will often be vital regional interests represented by the minority in Congress. Indeed, the desires of certain recognizable groups of the country have been, and will be, periodically submerged by the force of competing groups. However, on some occasions, the regional interests represented by the minority in Congress may surface and block the bill supported by the majority, not with their numbers but with the intensity of their opposition.

Sometimes, even the local interest represented by the minority of congressmen tends to be against the interest of its party, despite the fact that the power of political parties in both the Korean and American congresses is very strong.[67] These circumstances seem to generate parochialism in Congress. Congressmen in both countries reflect and embody local

---

reform. Brown is a paradigm, but for precisely the opposite view." Gerald Rosenberg, "The Hollow Hope," in *Law and Society: Readings on the Social Study of Law*, ed. Stewart Macaulay, Lawrence M. Friedman and John Stikey (New York, 1995), 589. To support his argument, Rosenberg shows historic evidences concerned with the Civil Rights Act in 1964 and ESEA (the Elementary and Secondary School Act) in 1965."The decade from 1954 to 1964 provides close to an ideal setting for measuring the contribution of the courts *vis-à-vis* Congress and the executive branch in desegregating public schools. For ten years, the Court spoke forcefully while Congress and the executive did little. Then, in 1964, Congress and the executive branch entered the battle with the most significant piece of civil rights legislation in nearly ninety years. In 1965, the enactment of ESEA made a billion dollars in federal funds available to school districts that did not discriminate in accord with Title VI [of the Civil Rights Act of 1964]. This history allows one to isolate the contribution of the courts. If the courts were effective in desegregating public schools, the results should have showed up before 1964. However, if it was Congress and the executive branch, through the 1964 Civil Rights Act and 1965 ESEA, that made the real difference, then change would occur only in the years after 1964 or 1965." Rosenberg, 579–80.

66. The Korean legislature is based on a unicameral system and is different from the United States legislature, which is based on a bicameral system, having a Senate and a House of Representatives.

67. For the details on the rule of political parties in the Korean Congress and its problems, see Joogab Kim, "Jungdangui Yoksajeok Baldal [Historical Development of the Political Party]," *Jungdangkwa Heonbubjilseo [Political Party and Constitutional Order]*, ed. Byunghoon Lee et al. (Seoul: 1995), 64–113.

opinions in Congress and are exceedingly sensitive to local concerns. Congressmen generally choose to act and vote in accord with their perceived regional interests even when the interests are in conflict with those of their political parties. To congressmen, the local interests of their constituents are the priority because they want to be re-elected. Accordingly, it is natural that they care so much about the local interests of their electoral district.

In the United States, according to Professor Choper, "the most genuine disputes concerning regional interests, historically and contemporarily, revolve around economic matters."[68] For example, certain regions are more closely associated with manufacturing or the lack of it, while others are associated with agriculture or lack of it. Besides economic matters, he continues, the primary issue of regional conflict has been "race." According to him, the rights of blacks has intensely divided congressional opinion along geographic lines and clearly put uniform national norms in opposition to diversity among the states. Professor Choper claims that this trend to give priority to local interests of constituents has remarkably decreased since 1960 among American congressmen, and the Court has strengthened this change in priority through its decisions.[69] However, at least until *Brown* was decided in 1954, the trend to give the high priority to local interests had been prevalent among the American congressmen.

In Korea, the control of the political party over every congressman is very strong. By and large, the congressmen vote not according to their own will but according to a decision already made by the leaders of their party. The process of making the decision is not democratic. It depends almost entirely on the leaders of the party rather than the whole body of congressmen of the party. That is possible because the inner structure of political parties in Korea is hierarchical, and the parties are not based on the masses but rather are composed of politicians who congregated around

68. Choper, *Judicial Review*, 192.

69. Choper explains this with the concept of political and judicial process in his book. "In the 1960s, when the majority of the states' national representatives finally prevailed in the political process and decreed a monolithic solution, the Court, relying on several sources of congressional authority, unreservedly upheld the national power to do so. Despite the highly uneven impact of the new federal laws on the separate states, the issue of constitutional federalism was properly held to rest outside the judicial process." Ibid., 192.

the notable politicians.[70] For this reason, the control of congressmen by political party is so strong that, in my opinion, it has taken precedence over local interests in Korea.

Today, however, some signs of change are starting to appear little by little. On some occasions, some congressmen voted against the will of their party in order to follow the local interests of their constituents.[71] But by and large, the Korean congressmen still act more according to the will of their political party than local interests of their constituents.[72] For the issue of *Heung-Sun Park and Mi-Ja Park*, which concerned the abolishment of the Civil Code provision on the marriage limitation, the conservative political party leaders in Korea were reluctant to take the risk of losing support from the Confucian groups by actively supporting the revision bill led by feminist groups. The party leaders decided to remain inactive on the revision efforts without making their position clear. By remaining inactive and unclear, they hoped that both the Confucian and feminist groups would think the political party is on their side, or at least is not on their enemy's side.

Inactivity meant supporting the Confucian groups, however, because the revision bill could not pass the Congress merely with the votes of active pro-feminists. To pass the revision bill, the attendance of a majority of congressmen and the concurrent vote of majority of the members present were necessary.[73] Meanwhile, congressmen who came from the rural areas with

70.   For the problems on the structure of Korean the political party and reform proposal for its democratization, see Jibong Lim, *Jungchijageumui Kyujeye Kwanhan Hunbunjeok Kochal [A Constitutional Study on the Regulations of Political Funds]* (Dissertation for Master's Degree, Seoul National University, 1993), 78–85; Suntak Kim, "Jundangui Minjoohwaleul Wihan Bubjeok Bangahn [Legal Schemes for the Democratization of Political Party]," in *Jungdangkwa Heonbubjilseo [Political Party and Constitutional Order]*, ed. Lee et al., 282–302.

71.   For instance, any congressman would fiercely oppose the establishment of a nuclear waste dump site in their electoral district. That is because the residents in proximity of the proposed site are his constituents, and they would obviously object to it.

72.   For the details on reality of the control of congressmen by political parties in Korea and its problems, see Sowhan Choi, *Uihwoejungchiui Ironkwa Silje [Theory and Practice in Parliamentarism]* (Seoul: 1994), 332; Chongheum Park, *Uihwoehaengjungron [Congress Administration]* (Seoul: 1998) 644–46.

73.   Article 49 of Korean Constitution provides the general quorum necessary to pass a bill: "Except as otherwise provided for in Constitution or in law, the attendance of a

a big population of Confucianists fiercely opposed the revision bill.

Both the local interests from rural areas where Confucianists mainly reside and the ambiguous decision of the conservative political party leaders to remain inactive contributed to the outcome of the case. Therefore, the two factors raised a barrier against the passage of the revision bill in Korea before the decision of Korean Constitutional Court in *Heung-Sun Park and Mi-Ja Park* came out on July 16, 1997.

In order to further examine how a minority group of congressmen blocked the passage of a revision bill in Congress in Korea and the United States, we would need to understand the internal processes for the passage of a bill by the Congress in the two countries. First, in the United States, the committee chairman has disproportionate power, which tends to make it possible for the minority to interfere. In order to pass in plenary session, a bill must initially pass the committee with jurisdiction over the contents of the bill. The bill is supposed to be investigated by and discussed in committee. The committee can revise and even reject a bill if necessary. This bill-filtering process in the committee is called a "pigeonhole." The committee chairman wields great power over the committee decision. The chairman presides over the committee discussion and investigation, and has control over the selection of a bill and its priority for investigation and discussion. He also has the power to revive a bill that is abandoned by the committee in "pigeonhole." This means that he can restore the bill from death. Here, if the committee chairman is in favor of local and minority sentiment rather than the national and majority sentiment due to the decision of his political party, his own political propensity, or his electoral district's situation, the committee chairman's influence can form a great minority barrier against the bill.

However, this does not apply to the Korean Congress. In Korea, the committee chairman does not have such enormous power over passage of a bill. As in the United States, a bill must pass the committee's's[74] investiga-

---

majority of the total members, and the concurrent vote of a majority of the members present, shall be necessary for decisions of the Korean Congress. In case of a tie vote, the matter shall be regarded as rejected." The passage of revision bill for a unitary law or its provision, like that of the Civil Code provision in this case, depends on this general quorum.

74.   There are two kinds of committees—standing committees and special committees—in the Korean Congress, and when it comes to the Committee, it usually means

tion and discussion prior to the plenary session in Korea.[75] The committee can revise and even reject the bill, like a "pigeonhole" in the United States; however, the committee chairman in Korea has no power to save a bill abandoned by the committee. Only thirty or more congressmen can revive and bring back an abandoned bill before the plenary session,[76] and a discharge of a bill from committee can be done only by a certain number of congressmen.[77] The committee chairman cannot restore the bill from the death. He can just "externally represent the committee, expedite the committee proceedings, maintain order in the committee session [and] supervise the office work of the committee."[78] In addition, he decides the schedule of the committee session after consultation with the executive secretaries in the committee representing their respective political parties.[79] In short, he has formal but insignificant powers in the committee session as a committee chairman. He has no additional power that comes from his position as a committee chairman, and cannot form a minority barrier by himself.[80]

---

the standing committee. Art. 35 of Korean Congress Act prescribes,"The committees of the Korean Congress shall be divided into standing and special committees." For details on the role and operation of standing committees in Korean Congress in practice, see Jai Chang Park, *Korean Legislative Administration* (Seoul: 1995), 158–67. When more expert review is needed for a bill, each committee can have subcommittees. As a matter of fact, in Korea, once a subcommittee is composed, substantial review for the bill is usually performed by the subcommittee. For more details on the subcommittee and its real function in the legislation process, see Tongseo Park and Kwangwoong Kim eds., *Hankukui Uih-woekwachungron [Congressional Process In Korea]* (Seoul: 1992), 56.

75.   Article 93 of Korean Congress Act.

76.   Article 87 of Korean Congress Act.

77.   Actually, there is "discharge of committee" in the U.S. as well, which is just like that in Korea; it can be achieved by a petition of the congressmen. However, the number needed for it in the U.S. is much larger than that in Korea.

78.   Article 49, Section 1 of Korean Congress Act.

79.   Article 49, Section 2 of Korean Congress Act. For the practical powers of committee chairman in Korea, see Park, *Korean Legislative Administration*, 134.

80.   I think one of the reasons that the committee chairman cannot have more substantial power than the ordinary congressman is explainable by the way he is chosen. According to Article 41, Section 2 of Korean Congress Act, the chairman is elected among the standing committee members elected under Article 48 (1)-(3) at the meeting of the National Assembly (herein after referred to as "plenary session"). However, in the real world, the committee chairmen are chosen through deals between the whips from each political

Second, in the United States, there is vote trading between the two big parties, either between Republicans and Democrats or among groups of congressmen. Through vote trading, the two parties come to an agreement before voting for the bills. If group A agrees to vote in favor of a bill that is led by group B, the congressmen in group B promise to vote for a bill supported by group A in return. It is a give-and-take game. Generally, vote trading is made at the party level. However, it sometimes takes place beyond the political party realm. Depending on the issue, some groups of congressmen often trade votes regardless of the political party to which they belong, due to the difference in degree of the preference on a bill between the groups that participate in the trade. For example, gun control is a controversial issue in American society. A relatively small number of congressmen are strong supporters of unrestricted gun possession, while most congressmen are somewhat in favor of gun regulation. Many of these congressmen will vote against anti-gun legislation in exchange for the votes of the pro-gun congressmen on other issues about which they feel strongly. Pro-gun congressmen stand ready to trade their votes on things they care about less in exchange for supporting votes by other congressmen on gun control bills.

More importantly, the same phenomenon can take place among constituents. A Democratic congressman may win over his Republican opponent by a margin of 51% of the votes to 49% of the votes. If 80% of the voters in his district favor gun control laws but only mildly care about other

party and the election is just a nominal procedure. Therefore, the positions are usually filled with the seniors of each political party, who are controlled by their own political parties. They cannot have substantial power and political influence that is independent from the political parties they belong to. In addition, Article 41, Section 3 provides the time of committee chairman election, Section 4 on the term of the committee chairman, and Section 5 on resignation procedure of the committee chairman. "Section 3. The election as referred to in Paragraph (2) shall be held within three days from the first day of the meeting held after the general election of the members of the National Assembly, and if the term of the first elected chairman of the standing committee expires, it shall be held by the day on which his term expires; Section 4. The term of the standing committee chairman shall be the same as that of a standing committee member; Section 5. The standing committee chairman may resign from his chairmanship with the consent of the plenary session. Provided that when the National Assembly is out of session, he may resign with the approval of the Speaker."

things and 20% say that they care so much about guns that they will vote against their congressman in the next election if he votes for gun control laws, the congressman will not vote in favor of gun control. If he does he is not sure he will gain any votes while he is sure that he will lose the votes of all the gun supporters who voted for him in the last election. Since he cannot afford to lose those votes, he will not vote for gun control.

In Korea, as the rule of political party over the Congress becomes more intense, vote trading has started to become more prevalent among political parties,[81] but not between groups of congressmen beyond their party lines. The abolition of the National Security Act and the repeal of Article 241 of Korean Criminal Code on Adultery and Section 1 of Korean Civil Code Article 809 invalidated in *Heung-Sun Park and Mi-Ja Park* were the hottest political and social issues in Korean society and their repeals generated great controversy.

First, abolition of the whole National Security Act was led by the opposition party because dictators had historically taken advantage of the Act to oppress their political rivals who were judged to be "communists," "spies," "subversive forces," and "disturbing forces" against national security. Some of its provisions were revised but the Act itself has not been abolished yet.

Second, there were several attempts to repeal the adultery provision in Article 241 of the Korean Criminal Code but they were all faced with fierce resistance from feminist groups. While adultery is an issue in tort and family law in the United States, it is dealt with by the Criminal Code in Korea. Whereas adultery can yield disadvantage in calculation of alimony in the United States, in Korea both parties involved in adultery are put in jail unless the accusation is withdrawn. In many cases, when the husband committed adultery, the wife could accuse and put her husband and the adulteress into jail. After that, the wife would withdraw her accusation and in return, receive financial payment from her husband. The withdrawal of accusation would automatically result in divorce. Here, the money played the role of alimony. Some conservative groups in Korea tried

81. In 1997, when *Heung-Sun Park and Mi-Ja Park* was decided, there was one big majority party and two opposition parties in Korea. The second opposition party played a particularly important role in the voting trade.

to repeal the provision on the ground that the adultery provision had lost its original purpose—maintaining sexual morality in married life—and was taken advantage of by women to extort money from their husbands after their marriage was practically over. However, the repeal effort soon confronted enormous resistance from feminist groups and could not pass Congress.

Third, the repeal movement of the Civil Code provision on marriage limitation, as detailed above in *Heung-Sun Park and Mi-Ja Park*, was led by feminist groups, fiercely objected to by Confucian groups, and ultimately could not pass Congress. Both the major political parties and individual congressmen could easily calculate that their votes in favor of the repeal legislation would gain only a few votes while losing far more. Congressional votes in favor of repealing the marriage limitation statute would have cost a substantial number of Confucianists' votes, perhaps even enough to lose some of the rural districts where conservative Confucianists were concentrated. Congressional support of repeal would have gained only a thin scattering of votes because most non-Confucianist votes would be based on many other issues far more important to them than the marriage law.

As a result, the Korean Congress repealed none of the three until 1997, when *Heung-Sun Park and Mi-Ja Park* was decided. The vote trading between the majority party and opposition parties interfered with the repeal of the National Security Act; opposition parties sacrificed abolition of the National Security Act in return for the support of the majority party for other bills. On adultery, the congressmen who agreed with the feminist groups that fiercely lobbied against the repeal were also a minority in numbers. On the marriage limitation issue, the congressmen who agreed with the Confucian groups were a minority in numbers in Congress as well, but the Confucian groups, despite being a minority in numbers, vehemently lobbied the congressmen. On the latter two occasions, the minority congressmen fiercely lobbied by the minority interest groups traded votes with the majority group in return for sacrificing their positions on other bills and succeeded in interfering with the passage of the revision bills. The process of vote trading is same as that in the United States that we have seen above.

The Korean Constitutional Court finally invalidated the Civil Code provision on marriage limitation in 1997. Though Congress failed due to vote trading, the Korean Constitutional Court intervened and corrected the failure in democracy. The other two—the National Security Act and Adultery provision in the Criminal Code—remain in place.

Therefore, at least in *Heung-Sun Park and Mi-Ja Park*, the Korean Constitutional Court actively intervened in failures of democracy within the Korean Congress. This failure had derived from the over-representation of local sentiment in rural areas and fierce minority obstruction led by the Confucianist groups. Other problems in the internal decision-making process of the Korean Congress, such as vote trading, made it possible for the minority to prevail. Meanwhile, in *Brown*, the U.S. Supreme Court also intervened actively to correct the failure of democracy in the U.S. Congress, whose failure had originated from over-representation of local sentiment from the southern states. Intense minority obstruction supported by Southerners was made possible by the problems in the U.S. Congress's internal decision-making process, such as disproportionate power of committee chairman and vote trading.

CONCLUSION

So far, we have seen the degree and the specific forms of judicial intervention in policy-making through the decisions of the Korean Constitutional Court and the U.S. Supreme Court. The Judiciary is not elected by the people but is instead appointed by the other governmental branches. Nonetheless, the Judiciary invalidates laws proposed and made by the other branches. In addition, through its active and creative interpretation, the Courts can effectively create new law based on existing law, although their main duty is to interpret and apply the law in a specific case. These judicial interventions, which seem to misappropriate the authority of the majority, are excused on two grounds: first, they protect minority interests from majority will; and second, they foster democracy by correcting internal procedural failures of the other governmental branches and their electoral systems, which could not be corrected by the branches themselves. In the U.S. Supreme Court, such judicial intervention has been actively tried and expanded over a long period of time; in Korea, it is a comparatively recent phenomenon, beginning with the establishment of the Korean Constitutional Court in 1988.

The Korean Constitutional Court demonstrated active judicial intervention in the name of democracy by correcting the failures of the Korean Congress in *Heung-Sun Park and Mi-Ja Park* and answers the question that has been posed at the beginning of this article—that is, why it should not be the Korean Congress but the Korean Constitutional Court that takes the lead in abolishing the system prohibiting marriage between persons of same surname and family origin. Active judicial intervention in policy-making is synonymous for judicial activism in the sense that active intervention in policy-making means being actively against the decisions made by the Executive, the Administrative and the Legislative branches.

The Justifiability and Limits of Judicial Governance

Hong Sik Cho[1]

The Decline of Legislatures and the Rise of Judicial Governance

The power of the judicial branch is expanding. It is not a phenomenon unique to Korea, but a global one. Even the United Kingdom, where the Parliament holds sovereign power, has seen conspicuous development in administrative law since the 1980s,[2] and the House of Lords has ruled that European Court of Human Rights decisions will prevail over British law made by the Parliament.[3] Expansion of judicial authority can also be witnessed among new-born or recently democratized nations, including Caribbean states, New Zealand, Israel, Saudi Arabia, and the "Third Wave" democratic states of Russia and Eastern European nations formerly in the

1. National University of Korea. This essay translates a revised version of my article printed in 趙弘植 [Hong Sik Cho], 司法統治의 正當性과 限界 [*The Justifiability and Limits of Judicial Governance*] (2009), chapter 1. I would like to give special thanks to Professor Laurent Mayali and John Yoo both of whom were instrumental for steering my attention to this project by inviting my contribution to the book co-edited by them. I also thank Mr. Sejong Yoon and Goya Choi for their sincere assistance in translating the article. Needless to say, any fault found in this essay is mine.

2. See Susan Sterett, *Creating Constitutionalism? The Politics of Legal Expertise and Administrative Law in England and Wales* (Ann Arbor: 1997).

3. *R. v. Secretary of State for Transport, ex parte Factortame Ltd.* (No. 2) [1991] 1 A.C. 603.

Soviet bloc.[4] In effect, many of these countries are not entirely democratic, yet they are willing to brand themselves as democracies because the word democracy has some normative power in the international community. Likewise, the fact that these states have incorporated judicial review into their constitutions, even when it is not properly practiced, shows the normative power of constitutionalism and the concept of judicial review.[5]

The proactive role of courts does not appear foreign to contemporary eyes, but in fact, expansion of judicial power is a remarkable event in political history. In the early phases of modern political philosophy, there was no such thing as "judicial power." If we take a look at the early designers of democracy in England, John Locke placed little importance in courts.[6] And to Albert V. Dicey, the legislature was entitled to unchecked sovereign power.[7] The French took it even further. The Court took no part in Rousseau's "general will" of the people, because the people hold sovereign power, and the general will of the people does not allow challenges from judicial elites. Rousseau's theory and the defensive position of French Courts during the Revolution resulted in a long-lasting tradition of judicial distrust in France,[8] which eventually led to the establishment of the Conseil d'État in 1872.

The rise of the Courts strikes a contrast against the fall of parliamentary sovereignty, which has long been recognized as the core of democracy in modern political society.[9] Parliamentary sovereignty is comprised of two principles: 1) the popularly elected legislature plays the main role in making decisions of the State and 2) the decisions of the State are made

4.   *The Global Expansion of Judicial Power*, ed. Neal Tate and Thorsten Vallinder (New York: 1995).

5.   Tom Ginsburg, *Judicial Review in New Democracies: Constitutional Courts in Asian Cases* (New York: 2003), 6–9.

6.   For a related discussion, see 趙弘植 [Hong Sik Cho], "The Court from the Perspective of Contractarianism: Standing to Sue in Civil Suits of Environmental Groups," 比較實務研究 [*Studies on Comparative Law and Practice*] VIII (2006), 383–445.

7.   For Dicey, the legislature has the right to enact and abolish any laws. According to English law, no person or organization has priority over or the right to abolish parliamentary acts. Albert V. Dicey, *Introduction to the Study of the Law of the Constitution* 8th ed. (1924).

8.   See Alec Stone, *The Birth of Judicial Politics in France* (New York: 1992).

9.   For the sovereignty of parliament, see Jeffrey Goldsworthy, *The Sovereignty of Parliament: History and Philosophy* (Oxford: 1999).

in accordance with majority rule. However, by the late twentieth century, the idea of parliamentary sovereignty seemed to have lost its original form. Judicialization of governance or judicial governance is one of the concepts that aptly describe this situation. With the judicialization of governance, 1) the judicial branch rises to take part in governing the state and 2) "practical reasoning" gains power over majority rule in making decisions.

The Concept of Judicial Governance

Judicialization

Judicialization is a multi-faceted concept.[10] It refers to the increase of judicial or quasi-judicial procedures in government decision-making and other newly emerging areas of the society. Further, the idea also refers to juridification,[11] where judicial discourse and procedure permeates into areas that were conventionally unfamiliar with law. However, the most apparent change is always found in the intervention of the Court in public policy. Although establishment and implementation of public policy had been considered a job for politicians or bureaucrats, the frequency and depth of Court intervention in this area is expanding.[12] This is what we call "judicialization of governance," or "judicial governance".

10. For the concept of judicialization, see Alec Stone Sweet, *Governing with Judges: Constitutional Politics in Europe* (Oxford: 2000); John Ferejohn and Pasquale Pasquino, "Rule of Democracy and Rule of Law," in *Democracy and the Rule of Law*, ed. Jose Maria Maravall and Adam Przeworski (Cambridge: 2002); Martin Shapiro and Alec Stone Sweet, *On Law, Politics, and Judicialization* (Oxford: 2002); John Ferejohn, "Judicializing Politics, Politicizing Law," *Law and Contemporary Problems* 65 (2002), 41; Richard H. Pildes, "The Supreme Court, 2003 Term: Foreword: The Constitutionalization of Democratic Politics," *Harvard Law Review* 118 (2004), 29; Ran Hirschl, "The New Constitutionalism and the Judicialization of Pure Politics Worldwide," *Fordham Law Review* 75 (2006) 721–53.

11. Hirschl, "New Constitutionalism," 723; idem, "The Political Origins of Judicial Empowerment through Constitutionalization: Lessons from Four Constitutional Revolutions," *Law and Social Inquiry* 25 (2000), 91. Cf. Jurgen Habermas, *The Theory of Communicative Action*, trans. Thomas McCarthy, (Boston: 1984) vol. 2, 356–73. Habermas describes "juridification" as changing a social problem which has been informally regulated to one that is regulated by laws, and thus a "colonization of the world of life". Ibid., 357.

12. Tate and Vallinder, *The Global Expansion of Judicial Power*.

To properly grasp the meaning of judicialization of governance, one must begin by identifying the difference between political process and judicial process. Sally F. Moore, an anthropologist who sought understanding of legal systems through studying African tribal communities, suggested that mankind employs two different ways to settle disputes: judicial process and political process.[13]

In a purely judicial process, the judge bears the authority and responsibility to make an executable decision in accordance with the established norms. In a purely political process, on the other hand, dispute is not settled by a third person, such as a judge. Instead, the dispute is settled by balancing the social power of the parties. The stronger acquires the power to enforce its will, but the power would still be limited by the influence of the other party. In a purely political process, norms play little direct role.

As Moore explains, judicialization of politics is a change from a two-party relationship to a three-party relationship.[14] While a two-party relationship is defined by relative negotiating power, a three-party relationship is defined by mutually agreed rules.

According to Yoshio Hirai, two-party conflict is either resolved by the stronger ("organization conflict"),[15] or through trade, negotiation, and compromise when one party cannot prevail over the other ("interest conflict").[16] The reason why interest conflicts can be solved without physical force is because the parties have some values and valuations in common with each other, and these valuations diversify and develop through the course of negotiation. When parties have no common value or valuation, a compromise acceptable to both parties cannot be reached because there is

13. Sally Falk Moore, *Law as Process: An Anthropological Approach* (London: 2000), 181–82. Cf. Hans Kelsen, *What is Justice? Justice, Law, and Politics in the Mirror of Science* (Berkeley: 1957).

14. See also Shapiro and Sweet, *On Law, Politics, and Judicialization.*

15. 平井宜雄 [Yoshio Hirai], 法政策學: 法制度設計の理論と技法 [*A Theory of Legal Policy Making*], 2nd ed. (1995), 15. In a organization conflict involving an interdependent relationship, the relationship between the two will be structured according to the hierarchy whereby the ranks are determined. Norms are created to justify the position of the higher rank. In case an interdependent relationship does not exist, submission and subordination are created through the exercise of physical force.

16. Ibid.

no "common" standard to determine who should prevail ("value conflict").[17] Therefore a "value conflict" can only be settled peaceably by the intervention of a third party whom both parties deem impartial. Hirai claims that the way the third party makes a decision in value conflicts is the paragon of "legal decision-making."[18]

Meanwhile, the third party bears the responsibility to justify its decision because without such justification, the opposing parties will refuse to accept the result.[19] Therefore, legal decision-making essentially requires a set of rules, and these rules form a normative structure that guides future actions. The normative structure creates discourse on rules and norms, and this discourse forms the basis of the practical and strategic decisions of each individual. Now, interaction between parties with potential conflict takes place in consideration of the normative structure, and conflicts and their resolutions feed back into the structure. The whole set of processes, which refines and calibrates the normative structure, is called the process of judicialization.[20]

Political Implications of Judicial Governance

Governance refers to the process of deciding upon a state's direction and implementing necessary policy measures. In a state ruled by its people, i.e. a democratic state, the government must reflect as much preference of the people as possible. The representatives are elected by the people and are asked to act on behalf of the majority. This is how "rule of the many" as in *demo*-cracy is achieved. On the other hand, the Court in a democratic state functions in an undemocratic role.[21] Judges are appointed, not elected. The Court is expected to protect rights, not to make public policy. In modern "liberal" states, a right is a shield from abuse of power, a negative right,

---

17. For values and valuations, see Cass R. Sunstein, *Free Markets and Social Justice* (New York: 1999), chapter 3, "Incommensurability and Valuation in Law."

18. Hirai, *[A Theory of Legal Policy Making]*, 16.

19. For justification of a judge's judicial decision, see infra Section V. 3.

20. Tom Ginsburg, "Judicialization of Administrative Governance: Causes, Consequences and Limits," *National Taiwan University Law Review* 3/2 (2008), 1.

21. For example, see Antonin Scalia, "The Doctrine of Standing as an Essential Element of the Separation of Powers, *Suffolk University Law Review* 17 (1983), 894.

and the power belongs to the majority in a democratic state. Therefore, the Court, the guardian of rights, is the guardian of the minority. The Court must protect the minority against impositions of the majority to secure democracy from the illiberal risk of majoritarian excess.[22]

With judicialization of governance, the Court intervenes in the formation and implementation of public policies. It means that the Court, the guardian of the minority, takes part in deciding the policies that are supposed to be designed by the majority. The Court, by participating in policy making, seeks to assume "the even more undemocratic role of prescribing how the other two branches should function in order to serve the interest *of the majority itself.*"[23] The judicialization of governance contradicts the idea of liberal democracy where the majority realizes its preference through politics and the minority is protected by the judicial system.

Of course, the Court never openly declares that it is making policy decisions. Such a role can only be given to the Court under *juristocracy*.[24] Also, it is rare to find a complaint filed against a government policy without anyone claiming harm to one's right. In such rare cases, the plaintiff would argue that the policy violated the law, and such illegality must be corrected to uphold the rule of law. But in fact, the law represents the interest of the majority as it was created through majority rule. Therefore, one who raises legal claims against the government's actions or omissions is the beneficiary of the law and her grievance is that of the majority, unless the plaintiff is the very object of the law's requirement or prohibition. The plaintiff is in effect making complaints about the government's failure to act upon the objectives of the law, which reflect the majority's preference.

For instance, imagine the government decides not to enforce environmental standards in consideration of the failing economy. One who raises legal claims on this omission is not the object of the environmental regulations, but a beneficiary. The environmental regulations were put in place

---

22. See Larry Alexander, "Illiberalism All the Way Down: Illiberal Groups and Two Conceptions of Liberalism," *Journal of Contemporary Legal Issues* 12 (2002), 625.

23. Scalia, "Doctrine of Standing," 894 (emphasis original).

24. See Ran Hirschl, *Towards Juristocracy: The Origins and Consequences of the New Constitutionalism* (Cambridge, Mass.: 2004); *From Democracy to Juristocracy? The Power of Judges: A Comparative Study of Courts and Democracy*, ed. Carlo Guarnieri and Patrizia Pederzoli (Oxford: 2002).

because the majority wanted environmental protection. It means that the plaintiff, in asking for its strict enforcement, is not the minority who needs judicial protection. Rather, the ones whose property rights are limited by environmental regulation are the minority. Conventionally, a beneficiary can only raise legal claims when he or she proves that there is a special form of harm that cannot be recovered through the political process and can only be remedied by the Court. If not, one can only persuade others to implement stronger environmental initiatives through a political forum. Contrary to this view, judicialization of governance enables the Court to decide on public policies on behalf of the majority, a truly revolutionary idea to the structure and principles of all liberal democratic states.[25]

Two Aspects of Judicial Governance

Judicialization of governance is mostly discussed in the context of constitutional issues. This is often referred to as the "judicialization of politics,"[26] where the Court increasingly has the final say on politically significant issues. Constitutional review of legislation is the most apparent example of this phenomenon. One dramatic example can be found in the U.S. presidential election of 2000, where the U. S. Supreme Court practically decided the winner of the election.[27] In Korea, the Constitutional Court denied the motion for the impeachment of the President which was presented by the National Assembly in 2004,[28] and in the same year, the congressional plan to relocate the capital was frustrated by the Constitutional Court.[29]

25. A question could be raised. In other words, if everything is done according to the discussion of the paper, in cases where important legislative intent decided by the parliament is disregarded and not implemented by the administrative branch, should the court be passive in taking any action if none of the minority's right is affected? For this question, see 趙弘植 [Hong Sik Cho], "Standing in Litigations with Dispersed Legal Interest," 判例實務研究 [*Studies on Case Law and Practice*] IV (2000), 439.

26. See e.g. 許盛旭 [Seong Wook Heo], "Politics and Law: An Empirical Study on the Function of Court's Legal Interpretation," *Seoul National University Law Journal* 46 (2005), 344.

27. *Bush v. Gore*, 531 U.S. 98 (2000).

28. Constitutional Court of Korea decision of May 14, 2004 (2004Hun-Na1).

29. Constitutional Court of Korea, decision of October 21, 2004 (2004Hun-Ma554,566 [consolidated]).

In all of these events, the issue was politically very important and sensitive, and also had traditionally been discussed and resolved within the political process, not through intervention of a third power such as the Supreme Court or the Constitutional Court. Judicial settlement of political issues is conspicuously increasing.

The second aspect of judicialization of governance is the "judicialization of administration," which is related to administrative law. This aspect has not gained as much attention as judicialization of politics from the public or academia. Nevertheless, it holds great importance, since administrative law applies to regulations which directly influence people's everyday lives.[30] When the judge reviews administrative decisions, administrative law guarantees public participation in the decision-making process through administrative procedures and regulates whether and how the regulatory interest—e.g. clean environment or welfare benefits—should be protected as a right. In this light, administrative law defines the relationship between the government and individuals, or more broadly the state and the people.

Judicialization of Administration and Standing in Administrative Litigation

Judicialization of administration is rapidly progressing in essentially all European, Anglo-American and Asian jurisdictions. Despite differing legal systems and theories, the trend shows "guarantee of fair procedures" and "guarantee of administrative litigation" as a common trait.[31] The possibility of administrative litigation is widening as the Court is getting more generous to requirements for justiciability in general, and the standing of private parties to bring administrative litigation in particular.

Korea is not an exception from this trend. The Korean Supreme Court proposed an amendment bill to the Administrative Litigation Act in 2002, attempting to broaden standing in administrative litigation. The

---

30.   Tom Ginsburg, "The Regulation of Regulation: Judicialization, Convergence, and Divergence in Administrative Law" in *Corporate Governance in Context: Corporations, States and Markets in Europe, Japan and the U.S.*, ed. Eddy Wymersch et al. (Oxford: 2006), 321–38.

31.   Ibid. See also Tom Ginsburg and Robert Kagan, *Institutions and Public Law: Comparative Approaches* (New York: 2005).

Court is a passive power by nature, since it can only act when a complaint is filed. Broadening standing will allow more people to file complaints on administrative actions, and it will lead to wider judicial review of administrative decisions. For this reason, the scope of standing is crucial in determining the role of Courts.[32] To prevent an over-judicialization of the processes of self-governance,[33] we must look carefully into the subject of standing.

In order to understand the concept of judicial governance, this essay analyzes the issue of standing in administrative litigation. Judicial governance is not limited to Constitutional review of legislation and courts' interpretation of Constitutional provisions on governing structure and fundamental rights. Judicial governance can also be found in judicialization of administration, i.e. procedural and substantive control of administrative actions by courts' legal judgments in administrative litigations. And standing is what determines the scope of administrative litigations. Although standing has not received much attention because of its technical nature, it plays a pivotal role in balancing the power of political and judicial processes. Also, by understanding this concept in the context of judicial expansion, one can acquire a different perspective on the judicialization of governance more generally.

POLITICAL CONDITIONS OF JUDICIAL GOVERNANCE

As seen in preceding chapters, judicialization of governance is an on-going process taking place on a global scale. However, a closer look into each jurisdiction reveals that despite general convergence, considerable differences do exist between jurisdictions. For instance, constitutional review in Austria and Germany is performed by constitutional courts, while it is done by general courts in United States.[34] The breadth of standing requirement differs from jurisdiction to jurisdiction.[35] Why do courts show different attitudes? And more fundamentally, under which conditions does judicial power expand? These questions can be answered by looking into

32. See Cho, "Standing in Litigations."
33. Scalia, "Doctrine of Standing," 881.
34. For details, see Ginsburg, *Judicial Review in New Democracies*.
35. See Cho, "Standing in Litigations," at 474.

the cause of judicial expansion, and it will also help us design a tailored model for a specific jurisdiction.

There are mainly two explanations why a democratic state implements constitutional review: the "demand theory" and the "supply theory."[36] The demand theory suggests that elevated rights awareness, or rights ideology of the people, is the cause.[37] As democracy or liberalism prevails, individuals tend to become more sensitive about their rights, and the Court, the guardian of rights, gains more power. On the other hand, the supply theory explains that judicial expansion is intended by the power elites to prolong and maintain their political and economic advantage.[38] According to this theory, when a political party in power is unlikely to win the next election, it attempts to preserve the political gains acquired during its term. It seeks to realize such attempt through legislation with the expectation that the law will be enforced by the people and the courts. In this light, judicial expansion is kind of an insurance plan made by political parties in order to safeguard themselves from political persecution and reversal.[39] For instance, the single five-year presidential term limit stipulated in the current Korean Constitution reflects the common interest of the political leaders who wielded power at the time of its drafting in 1987. Supply theory suggests that constitutional review becomes more active when the power is fragmented, because there is higher need for insurance under a divided power. Fragmentation of power means more room for the Court. In the past, the Court's attempt to decide on a political issue was either ex ante blocked by political pressure or corrected by legislation ex post. With judicial expansion, these measures are no longer available for politicians.

This theoretical framework can also be applied to the field of administrative law. Each theory offers explanations for why Korea has de-

---

36. See Ginsburg, *Judicial Review in New Democracies.*

37. See generally Charles Epp, *The Rights Revolution* (Chicago: 1998).

38. J. Mark Ramseyer, "The Puzzling (In)Dependence of Courts: A Comparative Approach," *Journal of Legal Studies* 23 (1994), 721. See also Ramseyer and Minoru Nakazato, *Japanese Law: An Economic Approach* (Chicago: 1999).

39. The expression "insurance model of judicial review" by Ginsburg, *Judicial Review in New Democracies.* For comments on the insurance model of judicial review, see Tom Ginsburg et al., "Roundtable: Judicial Review in New Democracies: Constitutional Courts in Asian Cases," *National Taiwan University Law Review* 3/2 (2008), 143, 156–58.

veloped strict administrative procedure law. The demand theory gives a "bottom-up" approach arguing that increasing rights awareness towards the government led to the legislation specifying such procedures. The supply theory suggests a "top-down" approach wherein the administrative procedures are substitute measures for controlling the bureaucrats as the authoritative regime gave way to a democratic system.[40] Political power uses ideology and bureaucratic hierarchy to control its agents, the bureaucrats. However, with democracy and post-ideology, political competition increases and the average terms of political power are shortened, resulting in fragmentation of power. Under these changing terms, politicians need to have control over bureaucrats more than ever, as "the agency problem" arises where bureaucrats begin to act in their own interest.[41] In addition, the free flow of international capital accelerates judicialization in individual states by changing the economic environment,[42] and also turns these changes into an irresistible global trend.[43] In other words, judicialization of administration is initiated by the political conditions, and is fortified by economic and international factors.

Supply theory may appear unfamiliar to lawyers, since legal theorists are used to normative approaches. However, if what this theory suggests holds truth, its implications are enormous. Lawyers generally have always believed that constitutional review, administrative procedures and litigations protect the rights of the people. But if these institutions fundamentally serve the interest of the ruling elites, as supply theory argues, the justifiability of the system will be seriously marred, and understanding the risks and dangers of this system will be an important task.

The Korean Supreme Court's attempt to amend the Administrative Litigation Act in 2004 was a test case for a grander plan to intervene in political and administrative processes. Korea and Japan both sought to

40. Tom Ginsburg, "Dismantling the 'Development State': Administrative Procedure Reform in Japan and Korea," *American Journal of Comparative Law* 49 (2001), 585.

41. Mancur Olsen, *The Logic of Collective Action* (Cambridge, Mass.: 1971).

42. Curtis Milhaupt, "A Relational Theory of Japanese Corporate Governance: Contract, Culture, and the Rule of Law," *Harvard International Law Journal* 37 (1996), 3.

43. Judith Goldstein, Miles Kahler et al., "Introduction: Legalization and World Politics," *International Organization* 54 (2000), 385.

revise their administrative litigation laws at a similar time, but the contents were not quite the same. While the Korean Supreme Court suggested broader standing, the Japanese amendment of the Administrative Litigation Act made no changes on the issue of standing. "Principal-agent theory" offers an explanation of why the two states responded differently to a similar challenge. In terms of political economy, administrative litigation provides a means by which ruling elites control bureaucrats, rather than a rights protection mechanism. Politicians intend to have more efficient control over bureaucrats by allowing the people and the Court to monitor the bureaucrats through broader standing. The fact that the Korean Supreme Court itself suggested an amendment to the Administrative Litigation Act demonstrates that the Korean judiciary is "politically active" enough to act on its own political gains. For politicians, the Court fighting for its political power is not easy to control at all. In other words, the "agency cost" is so large that politicians would never trust the Court to control the bureaucrats for them, and that is why the Supreme Court's amendment bill will not be accepted by the legislature.

Institutional Limits of Judicial Governance

If fragmentation of political power is the cause of judicial governance, as supply theory argues, the justifiability of judicial governance would be in question. However, before moving on to the normative assessment of judicial governance, there is one remaining issue, whether the Court has the institutional competence to decide on the matters regarding national policies. Assessing the justifiability of judicial governance is a process of finding the right role of the Court. And before exploring the right role of the Court, first we need to identify and verify the ability of the Court since normativity cannot impose impossibility on the people.

One of the important social backgrounds of judicial expansion is suspicion of the political and legal results of unfettered democracy.[44] Likewise, expanding the role of administrative litigation means there is distrust of the administrative system. The government has two grounds for justifying its authority to decide on public matters: democratic legitimacy and exper-

44.   John H. Ely, *Democracy and Distrust* (Cambridge, Mass.: 1980).

tise. Government bureaucrats function as a "transmission belt,"[45] carrying out the will of the legislators elected by the people. Thus, they also hold democratic legitimacy conferred by the legislature, and ultimately by the people. Also, specialized knowledge and expertise is essential to carry out specific tasks governments perform today, and such expertise is efficiently developed and utilized through a professional bureaucratic class.

However, the reality of administrative regulation calls justifications for administration into doubt. Bureaucrats are captured by rent-seeking interest groups,[46] and as a result, people recognize regulations as serving the interest of specific groups instead of the public. Public policies are always vulnerable to the influence of interest groups. Small groups with bigger stakes tend to be much more engaged in decision-making processes than general consumers or taxpayers.[47] The reality of administration makes it very difficult to justify the democratic legitimacy of administrative bureaucrats.

The same logic applies to the expertise of administrative bureaucrats. In the era of "postnormal science,"[48] facts become ambiguous, and value conflicts demand prompt decisions. As shown in problems of nuclear waste, human cloning, and genetically modified organisms, uncertainty and risks dramatically increase and social consensus seems all the more unlikely.[49] These problems cannot be solved by preaching science and telling people to trust expert opinions, but by communication and building mutual agreement in the decision-making process.

How about the Court? The Court is not free from this problem, and

45. See Richard B. Stewart, "The Reformation of American Administrative Law," *Harvard Law Review* 88 (1975), 1677, 1675, 1684. Concerning the "transmission belt" model, see Elena Kagan, "Presidential Administration," *Harvard Law Review* 114 (2001), 2245, 2260–62.

46. For example, see generally Daniel A. Farber and Philip P. Frickey, *Law and Public Choice* (Chicago: 1991); Jerry L. Mashaw, *Greed, Chaos, and Governance* (New Haven: 1997).

47. Olsen, *The Logic of Collective Action*, 40.

48. For "postnormal science", see Thomas S. Kuhn, *The Structure of Scientific Revolutions* (Chicago: 1962).

49. For such risks and legal actions, see 趙弘植 [Hong Sik Cho], "Risk Law," *Seoul National University Law Journal* 43/4 (2002), 27–128.

furthermore it can cause greater concerns. In the modern era, it is true that the judiciary has made remarkable achievements in protecting the rights of minorities. Can we further expand the judicial role to permit the Court to decide on what is best for the majority? According to U. S. Supreme Court Justice Antonin Scalia, the answer is no. Scalia argues that there is no guarantee that the Court can carry out such a task, and in fact, judges are in certain ways intended to be inadequate for these sorts of tasks.[50] Regardless of jurisdictions, judges are appointed among the most highly educated elites, and they are not politically liable for their decisions. Also, judges are trained to value abstract principles over concrete results. The judicial branch is purely designed to protect the rights of the minority against the majority.[51]

However, this is only true when the political process is properly functioning. When the political process is manipulated by a handful of interest groups, the Court stands as the last resort. Most people support the idea of environmental regulations or consumer protection, but the actual regulations are often different from what people want. People distrust the politics and the administration for a reason. And this is why many argue that the Court and the people are the only ones capable of correcting the government's failures.

However, the Court is not free from the flaws of political process, and in certain ways, judicial failure can be even more devastating. Judicial governance is founded on the Court's "moral superiority" over politics and "institutional confidence" that the Court is capable of overcoming democratic shortcomings shown in the "Condorcet Paradox" and "Arrow's Theorem."[52] But the decision-making process of the Court has the same risk of failure that the political process commits in collecting individuals' preferences. The structure of judicial decisions is not communicative, but strategic in nature because litigations adopt an adversarial system where two opposing parties are represent their own positions before a judge, who attempts to determine the truth of the case. In litigations, no other person than the parties to the dispute is allowed to participate in the procedure,

50. Scalia, "The Doctrine of Standing," 896.
51. See Cho, "Standing in Litigations," at 450.
52. See generally Dennis C. Mueller, *Public Choice III* (Cambridge: 2003).

which inherently institutionalizes interest group politics. This structure is vulnerable to manipulation by the minority. According to social choice theory, furthermore, the multi-member court is also exposed to path-manipulation when it makes its own decisions.[53] A proper understanding of the risk of judicial governance requires a positive study that exceeds the scope of this essay. Without such effort, it would be risky to conclude that judicial governance could be an adequate remedy for political failures.

JUSTIFIABILITY AND LIMITS OF JUDICIAL GOVERNANCE

The Court's strategic position in political forums and its limits in decision-making process do adversely affect the justifiability of judicial governance. However, this does not mean that what exists is necessarily what should be. As Immanuel Kant pointed out, what ought to be is all the more morally valuable when conditions do not allow it to be.[54] Legal conflicts are mostly "value conflicts", where opposing parties cannot reach a mutual consensus because they do not share common values or valuations. In this chapter, after briefly exploring the discussions on the justifiability of judicial governance, the philosophical aspect of justifiability of judicial governance will be analyzed with consideration of "value."

Social Utility of Judicial Governance and Procedural Fairness

Judicial governance refers to the policy decisions made by the Court. The core question of policy decisions is, "What is public interest?" There are a number of opposing views on the adequacy of judge-made public interest decisions. First, some argue judicial intervention will enhance the quality of regulations while some argue it will only increase the regulation cost.

53.   For a detailed discussion, Maxwell L.. Stearns, "Standing Back from the Forest: Justiciability and Social Choice," *California Law Review* 83 (1995), 1309; 趙弘植 [Hong Sik Cho], 司法統治의 正當性과 限界 *[Justifiability and Limits of Judicial Governance]* (2009), ch. 3.

54.   Immanuel Kant, *Groundwork of the Metaphisics of Morals*, ed. Mary Gregor (Cambridge: 1998).

The former suggests that the possibility of judicial review forces regulators to provide better reasoning and results, but the latter rebuts that view
with comparative law studies that show that, as regulation becomes more
complicated and expensive, its effectiveness remains unchanged.[55] Robert
Kagan points out that the cost of judicial governance is larger than it may
seem, and the U.S., for instance, is going through excessive procedures
and creating unnecessary conflicts because there is simply too much "due
process". So-called "adversarial legalism" causes excessive judicialization
and increases legal uncertainty, since parties in interest will try to exhaust
every single remedy available. Pluralization of decision-making authority
and diversification of decision-making process increase legal uncertainty.
Because regulatees tend to avert high-cost unpredictable risks, the regulators become stronger, and it becomes harder to control administrative
discretion.[56] Even worse, "adversarialism" will prevail in the society where
individuals seek remedy through confrontational rights claims instead of
compromise and negotiation. This behavioral tendency will be met with
more defensive regulations, enormously increasing the social cost.

On the other hand, Michael Dorf argues that judicial intervention
will improve the contents and procedures of regulations.[57] Collective decision-making in a democratic state is required to meet certain standards
to be normatively justified. If it is agreed that democracy should not be
limited to the simple aggregation of preferences, but should reach to the
discovery of common good through deliberation, administrative litigation
can be considered as a part of the democratic institution that facilitates discussion and deliberation. The Court has a unique structure that promotes
discourse, experimentation, and reflection, and adding administrative litigation to the democratic forum can improve the procedural fairness of de-

55. Robert Kagan and Lee Axelrad, "Adversarial Legalism: An International
Perspective," in *Comparative Disadvantages: Social Regulations and the Global Economy*, ed.
Pietro Nivola (New York: 1997).

56. Robert Kagan, *Adversarial Legalism: The American Way of Law* (Cambridge,
Mass.: 2002); "Adversarial Legalism and American Government," *Journal of Policy Analysis
and Management* 10 (1991), 369.

57. Michael C. Dorf, "Legal Indeterminacy and Institutional Design," *N.Y.U.
Law Review* 78 (2003), 875-981; Michael C. Dorf and Charles F. Sabel, "A Constitution of
Democratic Experimentalism," *Columbia Law Review* 98 (1998), 267.

cisions. This view argues that because judges have the specialized ability to form public discourse and execute the "public reason,"[58] the court can offer better-reasoned policy decisions.

While it is true that the potential cost of judicial governance has been overlooked, as Kagan points out, Dorf's argument on the merits of judicial governance also holds truth. The cost and benefits of judicial governance would only be properly measured by positive research and analysis within specific jurisdictions, which exceeds the scope of this essay. For now, this essay will continue to focus on the normative aspect of the justifiability of judicial governance.

Raz's Service Conception of Authority

Judicial governance means that the Court asserts itself as an authority in policy decisions. In judicial governance, the Court asks the people and other state institutions to act in accordance with its public interest decisions instead of their own. In principle, one should be free to choose how to live her life, since humans possess practical reason and are inherently free to use it. Meanwhile, "governance" means individuals voluntarily subject themselves to the commands of the authority. If individuals choose their own reason over authority, it will lead to "philosophical anarchism."[59] This creates a tension between individual reason and the authority of the state, and the classical answer to this dilemma has been to justify the State by contrasting it with the chaos of anarchy.[60] The more chaotic the anarchy is, the more the state can be justified.[61] Likewise, judicial governance can only be justified when it is proven that the society is better off with the Court's authority than without it.

58. John Rawls, "The Idea of Public Reason Revisited," *University of Chicago Law Review* 64 (1997), 765.

59. Kant originated the notion of philosophical anarchism. In a paper entitled "What is Enlightenment", Kant emphasized how important it is to "Dare to be Wise (*Sapere aude!*)." For Kant's philosophy of enlightenment, see Manfred Geier, *Kants Welt* (Reinbek: 2003), chapter 5.

60. See generally Thomas Hobbes, *Leviathan*; John Locke, *Two Treatises of Government*; Jean J. Rousseau, *The Social Contract*.

61. For a comparison of the state of nature for Hobbes, Locke and Rousseau, see Hyo Jong Park, *Democracy and Authority* (2005), chapter 2, "The Social Contract," 231–364.

Joseph Raz's two theses of the "service conception of authority" have been widely accepted on the issue of justification of authority.[62] First, the reason one must follow the directives of the authority is because the subject has an independent reason to do so. The fact that the directive was made by the authority is a good reason to follow it, but the subject has a separate reason. Authority is binding because its directives are dependent on reasons which apply to the subjects.[63] In other words, law cannot claim authority unless it claims to be based, at least in part, on these dependent reasons. This is the "dependence thesis."

Secondly, the subjects are normally justified in following directives of the authority despite their own reasons because following the authority is more likely to lead them to comply with reasons which apply to them. This is what Raz calls the "normal justification thesis." For instance, people listen to the weather forecast in the morning and take an umbrella with them, not because the weather service told them so but they do not want to get wet in the rain. The directives of the weather service are not based on its own reasons, but are based on the reasons of the subjects. And the weather service is more likely to be correct about the weather than ordinary people. This is how the authority is justified.

Again, judicial governance means that the Court declares its own authority in policy decisions. To justify the Court's authority, first, the Court's decisions must be based on the reasons of its subjects, the people. And second, the people must be able to make better choices when following the Court's decisions.

In the dependence thesis, political conditions and institutional limitations of judicial governance do not seem to allow the Court to claim that its decisions are based on the reasons of the people. The status of the Court in the political forum is too weak to reflect the will of the people, and the decision-making process of the Court cannot guarantee proper reflection. However, an empirical analysis would still be required to determine wheth-

---

62.   For Raz's service conception of authority, see Joseph Raz, *The Authority of Law* (Oxford: 1979); Joseph Raz, *The Morality of Freedom* (Oxford: 1986). For "dependence thesis" and "normal justification thesis", see ibid. at 38–57. Raz responded to certain criticisms concerning the service conception of authority in "The Problem of Authority; Revisiting the Service Conception," *Minnesota Law Review* 90 (2006), 1003.

63.   Raz, *The Morality of Freedom*, 47.

er the possibility of such judicial failure is greater than government failure. For now, let us ignore the possible differences in political institutions and courts in terms of the dependence thesis, and assume that judicial decisions are just as based on people's reasons, and continue on with the normal justification thesis.

Internal Justification and External Justification of Legal Decisions

There are two streams in discussions on the justification of legal decisions. "Internal justification" investigates whether certain legal conclusions are logically inferred from the premises. "External justification" asks whether the premises used in the internal justification can be justified.[64]

(1) A judge is obliged to remain impartial.

(2) Mr. Kim is a judge.

(3) Mr. Kim is obliged to remain impartial.

The syllogism above shows that legal conclusion (3) is a logical inference of the major premise (1) and minor premise (2). When a statement is logically inferred from its premises, it is internally justified. However simple it may sound, internal justification is powerfully persuasive. Internal justification demands logical reason from the decision-maker, and establishes that "like cases are treated alike", thus comporting with the principle of equality.[65] Also, it secures legal stability, since internal justification indicates that the premises warrant the conclusion. If participation of parties is guaranteed in establishing the major premise, it also corresponds with the principle of self-determination.[66]

However, logical inference is not the only source of legal decisions, since cases arise where the major premise has to be determined first. In the above example, if it is unclear whether a judge is obliged to remain impartial or not, the rest of the logical process is meaningless. Also, to a trained

---

64.　沈憲燮 [Heon Sup Shim], 分析과 批判의 法哲學 [*Analytic and Critical Legal Philosophy*] (2001), 207, 263.

65.　Ibid. at 212. This is a principle of universalizability, and also a principle of formal justice. Ibid. at 266–67.

66.　The principle of self-determination allows the "principle of being bound by law" in legal decision-making. This is because the principle of self-determination demands "citizen-made law" to be major premise in legal reasoning. Ibid. at 212.

lawyer, determining the major premise is often much more challenging than the logical inference.[67] Therefore, external justification is the core of justification of legal decisions. Law contains many indeterminate terms, general clauses, discretional terms, flaws, and contradictions. The Court makes policy decisions with such indeterminacy of the major premises. The justifiability and limitations of judicial governance can be defined by these questions: Can the Court itself determine the major premise instead of respecting the decision of other institutions? And if it can, under what circumstances?

Value and Valuation in Law

Some historic quotes appear puzzling to us. Patrick Henry's "Give me liberty, or give me death!" is not entirely "rational," since one must be alive to enjoy liberty. However, it is after we learn the historic background of this statement that we come to understand the commitment of the speaker to an idea or value and the motivations and meanings which explain such a declaration. The rationality model,[68] which explains human decision-making with the aim of establishing universal rules based on causal explanations, is too simple to embrace all the various beliefs of different individuals. On the other hand, the normative belief of a political subject constitutes its situation awareness and determines its actions.

Value is the fundamental element of normative beliefs of individuals. People hold dear different values. When we ask children what they want to be in the future, we enjoy a colorful spectrum of diverse answers. There is not a universal standard to determine which dreams are more "valuable" than others. That is because we cannot reduce all these dreams to a higher category of value. For example, if we try to put "happiness" as a higher

---

67. "A person with sound mind does not suffer from the risk of deduction, but from the risk of decision… The person will not making any deduction errors… However, the risk of error and difficulty lies on the establishment of premises." Ibid. at 267–68.

68. The rationality model stems out from pure objective rationality model proposed by Max Weber in *Soziologische Grundbegriffe* (1921). It is used to deduce the actions of a rational individual based on the individual's knowledge concerning the individual's inclination, purpose and situation. See generally 鄭政吉 [Jung Kil Jung] et. al., 政策學原論 [*Principle of Policy*] (2003), 473–85.

category of value, it will be a mere tautology of asking "what is your future happiness?" instead of "future dream." This is a plurality of values.[69] Furthermore, these values have no common and objective standard to compare to one another. This is called the incomparability of values.[70]

Most of the challenges we encounter today in our society are a result of conflicting values between individuals. Left wing vs. right wing, pro-choice vs. pro-life, preservation vs. conservation of wildlife, and controversy over the risk of "mad cow disease" are prominent examples. In all of these controversies, people argue and claim the superiority of their values. The reason why they cannot reach a middle ground and settle is not because they lack proper practical reasoning, but because their practical reasoning stems from their values and the values they hold are plural and incomparable.

To put it simply, balancing arguments can solve the conflict between comparable values, and cost-benefit analysis based on a single metric can solve the conflict between comparable and commensurable values. Furthermore, when there is a higher category of value that encircles all the values at stake, logical deduction starting from such a higher category of value will offer a solution. However, when opposing values are incomparable, all we can do is to choose one over the other.

One is free to make value choices in private matters. But what happens in the public domain cannot be entirely left to individuals because we often need collective action. Since the values of each member of a society are incomparable, it is impossible to infer a conclusion that is acceptable to everyone through practical reason. This means a society is forced to make value choices, and the real question is, "How do we make value choices?"

Coordination Problems and Public Goods

A "coordination problem" arises where most people act according to what they expect others would do in the same situation.[71] Korea and Japan are geographically close but have different traffic rules. While Koreans drive on the right side of the road, Japanese use the left side. Let us imagine the roads before these rules were implemented. Drivers facing each other

---

69.   Sunstein, *Free Markets and Social Justice,* 70.

70.   Ibid.

71.   Raz, *The Morality of Freedom,* 49.

would try to figure out which side of the road the other driver is trying to use to decide which side to drive on. If their guess turns out to be wrong, a collision would be inevitable. In this situation, it would be immensely useful for both drivers if they had agreed upon a rule in the first place. As seen in Matrix. 1, both Driver A and Driver B acquire a payoff of positive 1. The bottom line of the coordination problem is that it is the existence of a rule, not the contents, that matters.

Matrix 1. Coordination Problem Payoff Matrix

		Driver B	
		Left Side	Right Side
Driver A	Left Side	(1, 1)	(0, 0)
	Right Side	(0, 0)	(1, 1)

Of course, there are cases where people have differing interests in the contents of the rule. For instance, say a couple on a date is talking about what to do on a lovely evening. The boyfriend wants to go to a baseball game, and the girlfriend wants to see a ballet. As seen in Matrix 2, the players in this game have different payoffs according to the choice. The boyfriend would acquire more benefit watching the game, and the girlfriend with ballet. However, either choice would still pay more than doing each activity on their own because, obviously, they are in love. This is the "battle of the sexes game".[72] This model aptly shows the underlying driving force that holds people together in a society despite the conflict and the challenges.

Matrix 2. Battle of the Sexes Payoff Matrix

		Girlfriend	
		Baseball	Ballet
Boyfriend	Baseball	(2, 1)	(0, 0)
	Ballet	(0, 0)	(1, 2)

72. Douglas G. Baird, Robert H. Gertner and Randal C. Picker, *Game Theory and the Law* (Cambridge, Mass.: 1994), 41–42.

If we go back to the drivers' coordination problem, while it is true that any rule is better than no rule, people would still have certain preferences such as left side over right side. For this reason, most of the coordination problems tend to take the form of the second matrix, where the parties are not indifferent to which outcome is agreed upon.

Public goods also face a coordination problem. Distribution and production of public goods is one of the most important functions of a modern administrative state and also an important basis for justifying the authority of the state. In fact, most administrative law serves the purpose of supplying public goods. Public goods, such as police, fire control, and national defense, are distinguished from private goods and services because they are both non-excludable and non-rivalrous. In short, the benefits of these goods can be enjoyed regardless of payment. Under such conditions, any rational person would choose to free-ride on the payment of others. As a result, with no one willing to pay, no one would supply these goods and services. To correct this situation, the incentive structure has to be reformed by finding and punishing free-riders.

However, free-riders are difficult to get rid of where individuals act upon their own initiatives. The famous "prisoner's dilemma" succinctly depicts the difficulty of social cooperation. As seen in Matrix 3,[73] the best interest of each individual leads to the worst interest of the society.[74]

---

73. Raz, *The Morality of Freedom*, 48–51.

74. Assume that there are two soldiers guarding a bunker. If both soldiers attack the enemy, they will be able to fight off the enemy, but both will suffer some minor injuries. Both soldiers gain a benefit of 2, therefore making the matrix (2, 2). If both the soldiers try to escape, they will be captured, but their lives will be spared, making the benefits gained (1, 1). If one soldier launches the attack, while the other escapes, the other soldier will be able to make it out of the warzone without suffering even a minor injury, while the soldier who makes the attack dies. The soldier who escapes receives a benefit of 3, while the dead soldier gets 0, thus making the matrix (3, 0). As a whole, an attack launched by both soldiers is the best option, because a matrix of (2, 2) provides the best choice (2+2=4). However, from the perspective of a soldier individually, this is not the best alternative. Let's look at the situation from the viewpoint of soldier A. If soldier B launches an attack, escaping (matrix of (3, 0)) is a better alternative than launching an attack together (matrix of (2, 2)), and if soldier B escapes, escaping (matrix of (1, 1)) is a better choice than fighting the enemies alone (matrix of (0, 3)). Therefore, whatever soldier B chooses, betraying soldier B and escaping is a more rational choice for soldier A. The same analogy applies to soldier B. As

Matrix 3. Prisoner's Dilemma Payoff Matrix

		Prisoner B	
		Cooperation	Betrayal
Prisoner A	Cooperation	(2, 2)	(0, 3)
	Betrayal	(3, 0)	(1, 1)

State and legal norms are justified by the need for social cooperation. The State coordinates the interactions between individuals through substantive law and supplies public goods. In this light, the problem of public goods is also a coordination problem that demands coordination by the authority.[75]

The Moral Coordination Problem and Positive Law

Individuals make their own value decisions according to their own valuations in moral areas. However, policy decisions or rules cannot afford to have such indeterminacy caused by different values of individuals, and therefore demand a "knot," or an agreement on social issues. In this view, conflicting values on a social issue can be seen as a "moral coordination problem". In moral coordination problems, it would be more "moral" to follow the decision than to question its validity once the "knot" has been tied.[76] Not only would continuing debate on such questions lead to endless

---

a result, both soldiers are captured while escaping (matrix of (1, 1)). This example is shown in E. Ullmann-Margalit, *The Emergence of Norms* (Oxford: 1977), 30.

75. John Finnis includes the prisoner's dilemma in the broad sense of the coordination problem. In other words, he uses the term in a broad sense that includes situations where the constituents of a society collectively pursue an interest instead of pursuing their own respective interests. He argues that this broad sense of the coordination problem explains and justifies the law. In the long run, since an individual's position constantly changes, it is important to discover a solution even in situations where the interests are in conflict. John Finnis, *Natural Law and Natural Right* (Oxford: 1980), 255. Marmor also includes the prisoner's dilemma and the coordination problem within the scope of collective action. Andrei Marmor, *Interpretation and Legal Theory*, 2nd ed., (Oxford: 2005), 89.

76. David Lewis, *Convention: A Philosophical Study* (Cambridge, Mass.: 1969); William S. Boardman, "Coordination and the Moral Obligation to Obey the Law," *Ethics* 97 (1987), 549–55.

battles of conflicting values, but, further, expectation and reliance the community has on these knots deserve respect, and therefore it is more moral to respect them.

Most of what people consider and recognize as "law" is coordination. To David Hume, even property, the very essence of democracy and the market economy, was no more than a coordination to facilitate social cooperation.[77] As shown in the example of the traffic rules, recurring coordination problems can be solved by autonomous social convention or by the authority of the state. While convention played a major role in small communities in the past, it is difficult to figure out what the convention is in the contemporary world. The most important function of positive law is to offer a set of rules that people can refer to whenever conflicts arise in the course of social interactions.[78] Let us take property for an example. There would not be a single *a priori* rule that prescribes what should belong to whom. However, it would not be wise to leave possession of goods to individual decisions either, since there would evidently be continuous conflict. In this situation, choosing a set of rules among possible options is in the best interest of each individual and the society as a whole.

Practical Authority and the Political Process

The State takes care of the coordination problem not because the state has superior knowledge of the matter than the people, but because of its "position."[79] The State has a "salient" position because of the fact that people are subject to its existence and that it has been resolving collective problems. The special characteristic of coordination where "there is no right answer" demands that "someone has to determine what should be the law."[80] In

77. David Hume, A Treatise on Human Nature, bk. III, pt. II, sec. ii; Thomas W. Merrill & Henry E. Smith, "The Property/Contract Interface," *Columbia Law Review* 101 (2001), 794.

78. Ullmann-Margalit, *Emergence of Norms*; John Finnis, "Law as Coordination," *Ratio Juris* 2/1 (1984), 97–104. Gerald Postema, "Coordination and Convention at the Foundation of Law," *Journal of Legal Studies* 11 (1982), 165; Leslie Green, *The Authority of the State* 89–121 (1988); 長谷部恭男 [Yasuo Hasebe], 比較不能な價値の迷路 [*The Labyrinth of Incomparable Values*] (1999), 3-6.

79. Hasebe, [*Labyrinth*], 8.

80. Shim, [*Analytic and Critical Legal Philosophy*], 114.

moral areas, most people believe that there cannot be a "moral expert"[81] and
that people can make proper moral decisions upon reaching a certain age
of moral maturity. Therefore, the authority in moral decisions should be
given to a "better situated" person.[82] Since the State holds the most salient
position, people would expect the best results by following the directive of
the State once the decision is made. Such expectations promote compliance to the State's directives and fortify the salient position of the State.
In short, in coordination problems, it is authority, not truth, that creates
law.[83] Now, which state institution holds the most salient position to coordinate? In democracy, the political sector, namely the legislature and the
administrative branch headed by the president, would hold superior democratic legitimacy and thus the more salient position. It is all the more so
when considering that democracy demands that the majority perform the
coordination function. It also aligns with other components of democracy,
such as self-governance and "oneness of the ruler and the rulee."[84] When
absolute truth cannot be found, majority rule at least guarantees the "least"
harm, since it allows the most people to freely choose their actions.[85] It
leads to the conclusion that the political sector, especially the legislature,
should have the authority to decide moral coordination problems. And this
is why the Court should respect the decisions made through the political
process.

The Role of the Court

Then what should the Court do? Why can't the Court be engaged in coordination problems? The answer can be found in the nature of value conflicts, the source of coordination problems. The Court's decision in judicial

81.   Ibid., 137.

82.   Marmor, *Interpretation and Legal Theory*, 134.

83.   This is a famous statement made by Thomas Hobbes. Shim, *[Analytic and Critical Legal Philosophy]*, 113.

84.   Carl Schmitt, *Die Geistesgeschichtliche Lage heutigen Parlamentarismus*, 3rd ed. (Berlin: 1961), 28–29; 長谷部恭男 [Yasuo Hasebe], 憲法の理性 *[The Reason of the Constitution]*, 167 (2006).

85.   Hans Kelsen, *Vom Wesen und Wert Der Demokratie*, 2nd ed. (Tübingen: 1929); Hasebe, *[Reason]*, 169. For arguments justifying majority rule, see Robert Dahl, *Democracy and Its Critics* (New Haven: 1989), chapter 10.

governance is essentially a "value decision for the State." In moral coordination problems where incomparable values clash, there cannot be a "right" answer. If the Court "second guesses" the political decisions on coordination, the situation would regress to the pre-coordination state. In the subjects' position, this would appear as a "collision of authorities," which will lead to confusing unpredictability.

Such uncertainty brings much concern when considering the possibility that the political sector may try to again reverse the Court's decision. As Condorcet pointed out, this would lead to an endless cycle of ping-pong coordination between politics and the Court. As a result, the society will deteriorate to a state of indeterminacy. As Raz aptly stated, if authority is justified by the need for coordination, the directives of the authority must be accepted as an "exclusionary reason" to act accordingly.[86] An authority can settle coordination problems only when the subjects follow the directives of the authority without challenging it with their own practical reason.

Therefore, the Court must respect, not challenge and intervene against, the coordination made by the political sector. The task for the Court can be found in areas i) where coordination has not been performed by politics despite its necessity and ii) where people hold homogeneous values so the coordination problem does not arise.

To elaborate on the first area, almost all important decisions on coordination are made into positive law through the political process. However, because it is neither possible nor desirable for law to prescribe a resolution for every possible variation of cases, people often are not sure what the political decision demands in a given situation. In this area, the Court should be able to make detailed coordination on concrete cases that arise in real life. The "rule of law" entitles the Court to be in a salient position to coordinate the "remaining" problems.

It is still important that these coordinations be made consistent with the framework decisions made by the political process. And the judge must take a "one case at a time" approach[87] based on "incompletely theorized agreements".[88] In contemporary society, where a myriad of incomparable

86. Raz, *The Morality of Freedom*, 50–51, 56.

87. Cass R. Sunstein, *One Case At a Time* (Cambridge, Mass.: 1999).

88. Cass R. Sunstein, "Incompletely Theorized Agreements," in *Legal Reasoning and Political Conflict* (New York: 1996).

values compete, it is impossible to devise a grand theory that incorporates all principles, rules and precedents. If there were a judge capable of such a Herculean task, he or she should not be allowed to do so because it would challenge the authority of the political sector in coordination problems.

The second area for the Court is where coordination is not needed because people share the same values. Slavery is a good example because no one in the contemporary civilized society would support slavery. However, we are well aware this has not always been the case in the history of mankind.[89] Today, slavery is disapproved of because it destroys the core of individual autonomy. After ages of commitment to the value of "liberty," we have come to universally internalize the value of autonomy so deeply that we do not need any coordination on the matter.

Matrix 4 describes the situation concerning a universal value. The payoff matrix is precisely the opposite of the Prisoner's Dilemma in Matrix 3. The Prisoner's Dilemma equilibrates at mutual betrayal, while in the universal value game, mutual cooperation forms the equilibrium point. For example, if Citizen B takes a slave despite Citizen A's disapproval of slavery, Citizen A would acquire 3 while Citizen B acquires nothing. This is because Citizen B would be socially condemned for the act, and the "reputation cost" will exceed the benefits of slavery.

Matrix 4.

		Citizen B	
		Cooperation	Betrayal
Citizen A	Cooperation	(2, 2)	(3, 0)
	Betrayal	(0, 3)	(1, 1)

89. A. Leopold, who first came up with the notion of land ethics, discussed Greek society to explain the error of the concept of land possession with respect to ecological ethics. While Greece with its democracy depended on a slave economy in the past, it would be absurd to assume that slavery still exists in Greece at present. Leopold predicts that the absurdity one feels about our attitude towards land will be equivalent to the absurdity one feels about the slavery of the past. A. Leopold, *A Sand County Almanac* (1949). Anyway, the point is that the various judgments concerning slavery in the past have changed so much that all people now agree to object to slavery.

Let us look into the equilibrium of the universal value game. As shown in Matrix 4, when Citizen A cooperates with the disapproval of slavery, Citizen B acquires 2 cooperating together and 0 by betrayal.[90] If Citizen A chooses to betray, Citizen B acquires 3 by cooperating and 1 by betrayal.[91] No matter which position Citizen A takes, it is better for Citizen B to cooperate with the universal value, and the same applies to Citizen A. The equilibrium of this game is a state of mutual cooperation.

Mutual cooperation is the equilibrium point because disapproval of slavery is a strongly shared value in this society. What this society needs is not coordination, but identification of the traitors. Acts against universal values will be met with negative evaluation from the society, and this functions as a very efficient punishment. Unlike the Prisoner's Dilemma, universal values do not require any reformation of incentive structures or political initiatives. All it needs is a "confirmation" that the act in question is a disgrace to the cherished value of the community. That is why the Court, an institution without democratic legitimacy, can perform this task. The task does not even need the ex ante approval of the majority.[92]

90.   In cases in which Citizen A cooperates, why is the benefit 2 when Citizen B cooperates, while the benefit is 3 when Citizen B betrays Citizen A? This is because the moral evaluation of Citizen A's cooperative action becomes higher when Citizen B betrays Citizen A, instead of cooperating. Be advised that it is turbulent age, not peaceful time that does make a hero.

91.   A society where Citizen A approves of slavery and Citizen B opposes slavery (0+3=3) is more virtuous than a society where both Citizen A and Citizen B approve of slavery (1+1=2). In the case in which Citizen A approves of slavery, why is the reward 0 when Citizen B opposes, and 1 when Citizen A also approves? This is because the moral criticism with respect to Citizen's A approval about slavery becomes harsher when Citizen B opposes the system, instead of approving it. It is axiomatic that a crow looks blacker when it is with white-colored herons than when it is with other crows.

92.   If the societal values are unified, wouldn't a court system be unnecessary, since every individual in the society would abide by the unified values? In other words, one could argue that the court will lose its authority when societal values are unified. However, this is not the case. Even when societal values are unified, betrayal acts still remain in the society. First, even in a society where values are unified, no one can be absolutely confident that the other party would cooperate. This is because there could be an individual within the society who is a wolf in lamb's clothing. Second, there could be people who mistakenly consider the universal value game as the "chicken game," thus asking for the impossible.

At this point, it is worth taking note of a historical fact. Constitutional review in Germany since the Second World War is a good example of judicial governance. However, the success of the German Constitutional Court is not attributed to its political power or the excellence of its reasoning. As Ernst-Wolfgang Bökenförde points out, German constitutional review could flourish because defeat in war and remorse for the Nazi Holocaust rendered German society unprecedentedly value-homogeneous.[93] In other words, the decisions of the Constitutional Court are supported because German society came to have a widely shared set of values. This means that the Constitutional Court was not the "driving force" that led post-war Germany. Rather, it functioned as an "alarm" that warns the driver when the train has veered away from the intended destination of its passengers.

PROPORTIONAL CONSTITUTIONALISM, TRUTH, POLITICS AND LIBERAL DEMOCRACY

Proportional Constitutionalism

To sum up the discussion so far, judicial governance refers to public policy decisions made by the Court. Public policies are value choices for the State, and a "value judgment" is subject to the valuation of the decision maker. Value judgments have no right answers, and are therefore "coordination problems" where a "knot" or a decision with coordinating force is needed. Knots matter because the society cannot be consolidated or maintained without overcoming the moral indeterminacy. The knot in coordination problems, in other words, the value choice of a state, at least if it is to claim democracy, must be made by democratic political process. Since there can be no expert in values, the choice must be made by the one holding the most

---

With respect to the chicken game, see Baird et al., *Game Theory and the Law*, 43–44. Even in a virtuous society, there will always be individuals who act like a wolf in lamb's clothing to make unjust gains from virtuous people. Reputation cost means nothing for these individuals. To them, gentle lamb is just a cowardly chicken. Cf. Hasebe, *[Labyrinth]*, 15–18.

93. Ernst-Wolfgang Bökenförde, *State, Society and Liberty*, trans. J.A. Underwood (New York: 1991).

salient position. Therefore, the first author of law in a democratic state is the political sector comprised of the legislature and the administration headed by the president.

Meanwhile, public policy decisions by the Court cannot be justified if they contradict with the value judgment already made by the political sector. Such review by the Court will return the problem to pre-coordination status, and the subjects will be confused by the collision of authority. The role of the Court lies in the "remaining" areas of coordination. Generally, linguistic rules and conventions are sufficient for understanding the text of law created by political coordination. However, the indeterminacy of language sometimes demands interpretation. Just as creation of text is coordination, its interpretation is also part of coordination. The rule of law justifies the Court's authority to perform the remaining coordinations. The Court is the second author of law that ties the knots that politics missed.

The Court's main domain is problems with universal values where the members of the community hold homogeneous values. If political decisions infringe universal values, the Court not only has the power but also an obligation to overturn the decision. This is the quintessence of the rule of law.

This is the outline of the proportional constitutionalism suggested in this essay. In short, state institutions should decide on coordinations proportionally to their democratic legitimacy while respecting the universal values of mankind.

Truth, Science, and Politics

What is the difference between proportional constitutionalism and conventional constitutionalism? Proportional constitutionalism emphasizes the importance of political process and demands self-restraint of the Court.[94] Metaphorically speaking, the political sector is the "locomotive with driving force" and the Court is the "guard rail for derailed wheel."

Universal values determine the boundaries of the role of the Court. When the society shares a wide variety of values, it is possible that the role of the Court exceeds the role of politics. In other words, the domain

94. For the importance of political process, see Jeremy Waldron, *The Dignity of Legislation* (Cambridge: 1999).

of the Court is determined by the question, "What are universal values?" The answer to this question, at this point, is that not so many values seem to be universal.

Life, liberty, property, political fundamental rights, and the right to equality have risen to receive universal support. The Korean Constitution has incorporated other fundamental rights such as social rights. It also provides that rights and liberty should not be neglected on the ground that they are not enumerated in it. However, it is noteworthy that the Constitution has also left the contents of the social rights to legislation, which means the concretization of social rights is a coordination problem. This essay claims that universal values should be limited to the "essential part" of life, liberty, property, political fundamental rights, and the right to equality. The Korean Constitution has articulated the "essential part" in the exception clause (the Constitution of Korea, Article 37 (2)) which stipulates that even for the purpose of national security, public order, and public welfare, the essential part of rights and liberty cannot be limited.

The grounds for this claim are, of course, the plurality and incomparability of values. To reiterate, not many values have unanimous support and thus warrant robust judicial protection. In fact, there would be many different opinions on whether a value has acquired such status or not. It also means that distinguishing coordination problems from universal value problems is not an easy task either.

Another justification of judicial restraint is the characterization of judicial judgment as politics as opposed to science. The implication of this characterization for the Court is that judges cannot "discover" universal values just as scientists find natural truth through research. This is because universal values are different in nature from scientific "truth," and what judges perform is closer to politics than science.

From a value-oriented perspective, the State exists to produce and distribute values. Politics is the process of choosing which values to pursue. In other words, politics pick the values to produce, and distribute them according to certain rules.[95]

---

95. The commonly accepted concept of politics is probably the definition given by David Easton, which is the authoritative allocation of values. David Easton, *The Political System* (New York: 1953), 126–130.

Geoffrey Brennan and Jammed M. Buchanan explain the nature of politics in comparison with science.[96] According to their theory, science is defined as "a social activity pursued by persons who acknowledge the existence of a nonindividualistic, mutually agreed-on value, namely truth, and who, furthermore, accept this value as the common goal of all participants in the enterprise." The scientific community is "a society of explorers,"[97] and individual scientists share a common goal: pursuit of truth. In this community, it is generally accepted that "it is not legitimate for an individual scientist to claim respect for his own beliefs merely because they are his own."

Science also values consensus, but only in an epistemological context. Consensus between learned scientists does not render anything true, because consensus is no more than a verification process. Truth itself exists apart from the individual or common beliefs of scientists. For this reason, even if a statement gains unanimous consensus from the scientific society in a given moment, the truth value of the statement can be overturned at any time. Earth was widely believed to be flat in medieval times, but is understood to be round today. Earth did not become round because all contemporary scientists believe it to be so. It only means that the best available verification method at the time supported that the earth was flat, and today's verification supports the earth being round. In science, it is accepted that reality exists entirely independently from individual or collective belief.

Now let us look the Court's decision on universal values. Are judicial judgments a scientific activity? Do judges make decisions about truth? Here, I suggest that the answer is no. Judicial decisions are different from politics,[98] but it does not necessarily mean they are closer to science. Technically, judicial decision is closer to politics than science. Scientists express their beliefs on the truth of a certain statement, but they do not confer personal value to the statement. A scientist is an observer, always one step

96. Geoffrey Brennan and James M. Buchanan, *The Reason of Rules* (Indianapolis: 2000), chapter 3, "The Myth of Benevolence." The following is a summary of their argument. The author will not include footnotes for parts that are not emphasized.

97. This is a famous expression by Michael Polanyi; ibid., 47.

98. The differences between a political process and a judicial process are the existence of norms and a third party who makes a decision based on the norms. See Moore, supra note 12.

away from her object of research. A scientist asks whether a statement is an accurate description of an objective truth or not, rather than whether a statement is good for her or the society at large.[99] Analogically speaking, the question for a scientist is essentially different from "is surplus apple good for me?" or "is surplus apple good for both apple farmers and consumers?"

On the other hand, a judge is not an observer but a participant who lives with, modifies, and forms the object of her study. A judge does not ask "what is" but "what ought to be." Of course, the perspective of the judge and the perspective of the society are separate. It is possible to distinguish how the judge thinks the society should be and how the rest of members of the society think the society should be. For this reason, a natural law theorist may deem judicial decisions similar to the scientific finding. In the viewpoint of natural law, a judgment is a collaborative effort to "discover" the "common good" beyond individual preferences and values. The "common good" is the Holy Grail waiting to be discovered, and the quest resembles the scientific society's pursuit of truth.

However the mechanism of judicial judgments differs from that of science. As H. L. A. Hart aptly points out,[100] cognition of legal matters requires not only collection of externally observable data, but also understanding of the internal meaning of the data to the participants of the matter. To study the traffic rules of a society, one should understand what the red light means to the drivers as well as the stopping rate of passing cars at a red light. Cars stop at a red light because the driver not only comprehends the meaning of the signal but also accepts the command as a normative standard for herself and others. That is to say, the cognition of law is incomplete unless one acquires the participants' point of view [until the participants recognize it as law.] To an observer, a traffic signal is no more than a clue about people's reactions, just as dark clouds indicate plausible rain. With an observer's viewpoint, one may figure out 'going against the traffic signal may result in sanctions' but he or she will never reach the conclusion 'drivers have an obligation to comply with the traffic signals.'[101]

99.   Brennan and Buchanan, *Reason of Rules*, 48.

100.   H. L. A. Hart, *The Concept of Law*, 2nd ed. (Oxford: 1994), 89–91.

101.   Ibid. at 90.

Raz has distinguished the view of participants into two categories.[102] One is the "committed point of view," which is the view a judge typically takes. A judge is committed to the law in the sense that the judge believes the law is morally just, and therefore it is a valuation. The other one is the "detached point of view," usually taken by lawyers and law scholars. In this view, the participant is not committed to the moral justifiability of the law. The detached point of view stands on the precondition "if current positive law is just and binding," and therefore is an objective cognition. The statement "A has an obligation to pay one thousand dollars to B" would be a committed statement if sentenced by a judge in court, and a detached statement if made by a lawyer in a consultation.

This is another reason why judgments should not be understood in the science model. Even if the parties in the judicial process take an observer's view, there has to be considerable difference between the collected data. If the parties take participant's view, there would be another layer of gap between the meanings parties take from the data. Further, if the parties take a committed view, there would be a contrasting difference in the valuation between the parties.

For such reason, a legal positivist would argue that it is inappropriate to ask whether legal statement A promotes the common good better than legal statement B. This is because the common good is not exogenic, but is constructed within the society through processes including judicial process. Instead, a legal positivist would ask the participant if a legal statement is in her interest. Or even more adequate question would be whether a legal statement serves the best interest of the public according to her judgment.

To conclude, the judicial process is a dispute process where respective parties seek to persuade each other according to certain procedural rules by competing with their own value decisions, and the judgment is the final agreement concluded among the participants of the process.[103]

---

102.   Raz, *The Authority of Law*, chapters 7 and 8.

103.   For instance, this is the mainstream theory of interpretation concerning civil law taken by Japanese scholars. For details, see 瀬川信久 [Nobuhisa Segawa], "民法の解釈 [Interpretation of Civil Law]," 民法講座 [*Lectures on Civil Law*] 別巻 (1990), 1, 1, 72.

Revisiting Liberal Democracy as a Touchstone Concept

Let us review the discussion so far with liberal democracy as a touchstone. History reveals that all wars were caused by extreme conflicts of values. Man is a social animal and it cannot survive on its own. The only option is to figure out the principles for constitution and maintenance of society by which we can enjoy the benefits of communal life while preserving our own values and valuations. Liberal democracy is a product of this effort.

Liberal democracy proposes two principles. First is the distinction between law and morality. There are many types of norms that govern social living. The distinction between law and morality specifies the rules of which violation is met with sanctions, and allows individuals to acknowledge these rules before they act. People are able to plan their lives with predictability and also keep their moral norms without violating the law. Before the modern era, people's fates were dependent upon unpredictable value judgments of monarchs. Since the rise of the modern state, legal norms are established by the value judgments of the majority. Democracy made it possible to distinguish law from morality, and this distinction emancipated people from the "value judgments of the absolute power." The second principle is the distinction between private and public. The distinction between public and private does not intend to expand the public domain or emphasize the public. Rather, it was proposed to protect individual autonomy in private matters. While the distinction of law and morality protects individuals and allows them to freely act in the public domain, the distinction of public and private ensures freedom in private domain. And private freedom is protected by rights, the greatest invention of the modern era. Rights freed individuals from the value judgments of the majority in private matters.

The structure of modern liberal states corresponds to the principles of liberal democracy. Law protects the private domain of individuals by entitling them to the rights to life, liberty, and property (personality and property law), by supporting the exchange and trade of these rights (contract law), and by acting as a guardian when a right is infringed (tort law). Also, the Court has provided legal protection from the harms done by the majority through legislation and administration. On the other hand, the decisions regarding the public domain where no identified rights are dispositive have been left to the political process. The Legislature and the Executive hold democratic legitimacy that realizes self-governance by the people. Dictatorship of the majority is a possible concern. However, this concern can be settled by the fact that the majority is equally subject to the law and that the constitution of the majority continuously changes with issue, time, and circumstances.[104] The judiciary lays the foundations of properly functioning political process by securing the equality, freedom of speech, and fair opportunity to participate.

The structure of the liberal democratic state demands that the Court must remain the guardian of the minority from the tyranny of the majority and should not attempt to assume the "undemocratic role"[105] of telling the legislative and executive branches how to serve the interest of the majority. Therefore, in liberal democracy, the Court can intervene in democratic decisions and their execution only when the right of the minority is violated. Judicial governance in administration means that Court intervention is not limited by this trigger.

The dynamics of power today are quite different from the time when Montesquieu first suggested the separation of powers. Political power and judicial power interact, and the boundary between politics and judicial decisions is becoming vague. However, the State can properly operate only when the powers adhere to their proper roles. Proportional constitutionalism is a principle devised to prevent excessive judicialization of politics. Many principles have been established to prevent politicization of the judicial process. However there has not been sufficient discussion on judicialization of politics. This is why we must stand vigilant and attentively assess the state of judicial governance and propose proportional constitutionalism as a legitimate and constraining framework.

104. See generally Ely, *Democracy and Distrust.*
105. Scalia, "Doctrine of Standing," 894.

The State of Fundamental Rights Protection in Korea

Dai-Kwon Choi[1]

INTRODUCTION

This article explores the problems of how fundamental rights have been manifested in positive law for their protection and how they have evolved in reality and speculates on their future development in South Korea (hereinafter simply Korea). Fundamental rights are basic entitlements that legally assure individuals that they are free to develop and realize their physical, mental and moral humanity. Fundamental rights are rooted in the ideas of natural law and natural rights that individuals are endowed with dignity and worth as human beings from the moment they are born. In relations with power in the real world, fundamental rights are embodied in and protected by positive laws (constitutional law, international law, etc.). However, this does not mean that fundamental rights cannot exist without positive laws on the sole ground that they are created by the positive laws. The concept of fundamental rights is antecedent to that of the positive laws. Fundamental rights guaranteed by a constitution are simply those that are materialized into legal norms by the positive constitutional law.

The ideas of natural law and natural rights[2] were first developed by

---

1.   Professor Emeritus, Seoul National University; Distinguished Professor, Hadong University.

2.   We may well object to the idea that natural rights are of the ancient origin just as natural law is. Perhaps, the ideas of natural rights are a modern invention. See Lynn Hunt,

Greek and Roman Stoics, Roman law scholars, and Christian scholars, who were succeeded by the U.S. Constitution and the Declaration of the Rights of Man and of the Citizen of France in modern times. In the nineteenth century, they were enshrined in the declaration of fundamental human rights protections in the constitutions of various countries. After the two world wars, especially the Second World War, the ideas of fundamental human rights were internationally revived. Although the Charter of the United Nations does not have specific articles on human rights, its very existence is founded upon the respect for human rights. The world-wide aspirations for the protection of fundamental human rights were manifested in the Universal Declaration of Human Rights in 1948. The ideas of fundamental human rights on a global level are materialized in positive international laws, including the International Covenant on Civil and Political Rights and many other human rights-related international treaties and conventions.

The free democratic Republic of Korea was born in 1948 with the blessing of the United Nations, having been liberated from the 36 years of harsh suppression and exploitation by Japan following the tragic end of the Daehan (Korean) Empire by imperialist invasion. Naturally, the Republic of Korea in Chapter Two of its Constitution provides for and proclaims the basic human rights protection provisions and their guaranteeing constitutional institutions based on the ideas of natural law and natural rights. Then, in 1990, Korea joined the International Covenant on Economic, Social and Cultural Rights (Appendix A), the International Covenant on Civil and Political Rights (Appendix B), and the Optional Protocol to the International Covenant on Civil and Political Rights, which were adopted by the United Nations in 1966 and entered into effect in 1976. Korea also joined many human rights related international treaties, including the Convention on the Prevention and Punishment of the Crime of Genocide, the Rome Statute of

---

Inventing Human Rights: A History (New York: Norton, 2007). It may also be interesting to note that Roman and old English legal systems were an action (*actio*)-centered system whereas modern legal systems (Civil Law and Anglo-American Law) are rights-centered systems. The concept of action is more a procedural one for realization of a claim, not necessarily a concept of modern day substantive right which entails a right to sue. In fact, the idea of natural rights is traceable only to the Enlightenment. See Eibe Riedel, "Universality of Human Rights and Cultural Pluralism," in Christian Starck, ed., *Constitutionalism, Universalism and Democracy: A Comparative Analysis* (Baden-Baden: 1999), 34–36.

the International Criminal Court, the Convention on the Elimination of All Forms of Discrimination against Women, the Convention on the Rights of the Child, the Convention Relating to the Status of Refugees, and the Protocol Relating to the Status of Refugees. In these ways, Korea has equipped itself with a number of positive law apparatuses for human rights.

This article will first examine the problem of how the positive law apparatuses for the protection of fundamental rights are constructed and organized in Korea, with the major focus placed on the Korean Constitution's fundamental human rights clauses and their related provisions, that is, the positive law framework guaranteeing fundamental human rights in Korea. The legal provisions alone, however, do not necessarily guarantee their full realization. Any ideal or normative system may not be fully realized in the actual world. There may be a gap between norm and reality. We will address the problem of how human rights protection has been evolving in the real world, that is, the problem of the current state of human rights protections in Korea, and then the problem of how they might progress, that is, the matter of their prospect in Korea. It may be worthwhile to explore those cognitive, evaluative and behavioral dimensions of human dignity and worth that affect the reality of the human rights protection to account for gaps and tensions between the formal law and the reality. In the process of our analysis, we will conduct a cautious exploration as well of whether the Confucian ideas and ethics that governed Far Eastern Asian societies for the past thousand years functioned similarly to Western ideas of natural law and natural rights in the West and if we can expect Confucian ideas and ethics to perform such a function.

CONSTITUTIONAL GUARANTEES OF FUNDAMENTAL HUMAN RIGHTS[3]

Enumeration of Fundamental Human Rights

From the very beginning in 1948, the Constitution of the Republic of Korea started with a comprehensive catalogue of the fundamental rights and their

---

3. About the fundamental rights in the Constitution of the Republic of Korea, see Dai-Kwon Choi, *Honbophak-kangui [Lectures on Constitutional Law]*, enlarged edition (Seoul: 2001), 181–298; Young-seong Kwon, *Honbophakwonron [Constitutional Law: A*

guaranteeing institutions incorporating the latest ideas on the protection of fundamental human rights that had been developed by mankind up to that time. Through a number of constitutional amendments thereafter, moreover, the catalogue of fundamental rights and guaranteeing institutions were further refined and upgraded. Consequently, the Korean Constitution now possesses quite an outstanding chapter on the fundamental rights and duties (Chapter 2), theoretically and in terms of constitutional provision. The Constitution has such modern political freedoms clauses as equal protection of law (Article 11), freedom of personal liberty and actions (Articles 12 and 13), freedom of residence and a right to move at will (Article 14), freedom from intrusion into the place of residence (and ensuing requirement for search warrant) (Article 16), privacy (Article 17), privacy of correspondence (Article 18), freedom of occupation (Article 15), freedom of speech and the press, and freedom of assembly and association (Article 21), the right to vote and the right to hold public office (Articles 24 and 25), freedoms of conscience and religion (Articles 19 and 20), and freedom of learning and the arts (Article 22). The Constitution also provides comprehensively for social rights that include the right of property (Article 23), an equal right to receive education (Article 31), the right to work (Article 32), the workers' right to independent association, collective bargaining and collective action (the so-called workers' three rights) (Article 33), the right to live a life worthy of human beings (Article 34), and the right to live in a healthy and pleasant environment (Article 35).

Moreover, the Constitution further encompasses "claimant's basic rights" clauses such as the right to petition (Article 26), the right to trial by the judge in conformity with the law (Article 27 Section 1), the right to a speedy and open trial, the right to claim just compensation in cases where a criminal suspect or an accused under detention is not indicted or acquitted, the right of a criminal victim to make a statement during the proceedings of the trial of the cases involved, and various other rights provided for

---

Textbook], revised edition (Seoul: 2006), 283–709; Chol-su Kim, *Honbophak-kyeron [Constitutional Law]*, 19th edition (Seoul: 2007), 335–1175; Nak-in Song, *Honbophak [Constitutional Law]*, 6th edition (Seoul: 2006), 229–667; Young-soo Jang, *Kibonkwonron [Theory on Fundamental Rights]* (Seoul: 2003); Jong-sop Chung, *Honbophakwonron [Constitutional Law]*, 3rd edition (Seoul: 2008), 355–767; Young Huh, *Hankukhonbopron [Korean Constitutional Law]*, 4th edition (Seoul: 2008), 201–600, etc.

a criminal suspect, an accused person or even a criminal victim (Article 27 Sections 3, 4 and 5 and Articles 28 and 30), and lastly the right of tort claims against the State (Article 29). These rights are those that are necessary or otherwise designed to realize the fundamental rights when they are violated. By nature, the aforementioned social rights can be realized only when they become legally positive through legislation and financial support in the budget. In any case, the catalogue of the fundamental rights provided in the Constitution leaves no doubt that the enumerated fundamental rights cover quite extensively various elements and aspects of human lives ranging from politics and economy to society and culture.

Nonetheless, it is significant that the Constitution has the overarching Article 10 providing for human dignity and worth and the right to pursue happiness at the beginning of Chapter 2 on the fundamental rights. Article 10 precedes the specific fundamental rights that follow. Needless to say, Article 10 is obviously the root provision or original source for the fundamental rights specified above. The specified rights are simply details or examples of the former, general provision on the guarantee of fundamental rights. And the notion that the fundamental rights specifically enumerated are mere example provisions of this general provision is also supported by Article 37 Section 1. In the Section, it is stipulated that "Freedoms and rights of citizens shall not be neglected on the grounds that they are not enumerated in the Constitution." Article 10 and Article 37 Section 1 are the reflection of the idea of natural law and natural rights manifested in the form of fundamental human rights in the positive law and naturally imply further that those rights specified in the Constitution are by no means "exhaustive" of fundamental human rights. Due to these two general provisions, therefore, the provisions of the individually designated constitutional rights as such are less significant in relative terms. The fundamental rights and their guarantees may be expanded and developed beyond those specified through evolutionary processes including interpretation of the Constitution.

Specific fundamental rights enumerated in the above-mentioned catalogue of fundamental rights feature those rights people have traditionally claimed against state power. The right to personal freedom is about freedom from intrusion by state power, and social fundamental rights are about protection by the state power or a claim to it. Today, however, we live not only in a society characterized by industrialization, urbanization and globalization but also in an organized or collective social environment where massive or large-scale organizations and groups have emerged. We live in a social environment of huge corporations, large media organizations, nation-wide political parties and social groups, labor organizations, NGOs and large-scale organized demonstrations. Therefore, individuals are not in the position to wield any significant influence without belonging to or leveraging these organizations or groups. In fact, violations or threats of violations of human dignity and worth may also be caused by the power of these huge or large organizations and groups. Therefore, the necessity to protect human dignity and worth has emerged not only in relations with the state but also with these large organizations and groups.[4]

Along with recognition of such phenomena, constitutional discussions about how fundamental human rights shall be claimed against these huge private organizations and groups have begun in Korea. This refers to discussions about the force of the fundamental rights as to a third person or the force against private parties (*Drittwirkung*) and discussions about state actions or state functions.[5] For instance, by their nature, the three labor rights or the right to a healthy and pleasant environment may be claimed judicially against not only the state but also against business enterprises. This claim is also somewhat applicable to the equal protection of law right. In the case of other fundamental rights, however, it is theoretically challenging to realize them through the administration of justice. That is

4.   Dai-Kwon Choi, "Kibonkwonui jaesamjajok hyoryok [The Force of the Basic Rights as to a Third Party]," in idem, *Honbophak: Bopsahoehakjokjopkun* [*Constitutional Law: Socio-Legal Approaches*] (Seoul: 1989), 154–188.

5.   Ibid.; Young-seong Kwon, *Honbophakwonron*, 324–331; Chol-su Kim, *Honbophak-kyeron*, 403–413; Nak-in Song, *Honbophak*, 260–264; Young-soo Jang, *Kibonkwonron*, 96, 109ff., 187–188; Jong-sup Chung, *Honbophakwonron*. 269, 293–330; Young Huh, *Hankukhonbopron*, 251–261. Perhaps, a series of "state action"/"state function"-related American judicial precedents such as *Smith v. Allwright*, 321 U.S. 649 (1944); *Terry v. Adams*, 345 U.S. 461 (1953); *Marsh v. Alabama*, 326 U.S. 501 (1946); *Amalgamated Food Employees Union v. Logan Valley Plaza*, 391 U.S. 308 (1968); *Pennsylvania v. Board of Trust*, 353 U.S. 230 (1957); *Burton v. Willmington Parking Authority*, 365 U.S. 715 (1961); *Shelly v. Kraemer*, 334 U.S. 1 (1948); *Barrows v. Jackson*, 346 U.S. 249 (1953) and others may be cited as an American version of or a functional equivalent to the doctrine of the force of the fundamental rights as to private parties.

an important reason why a claim on the force of fundamental rights to a third person tends to be realized more through legislation than by the courts. One good example is the Civil Rights Act in the U.S. or the Equal Employment Opportunity Act in Korea. There are other examples showing that the force of the fundamental rights to a third person is expanded and realized through legislation such as access to the press (e.g., a claim to correct reports)[6] which is realized in the press acts, in-party democracy in the Political Parties Act, union democracy and a right to live a life worthy of human beings in labor laws, and the protection of minority shareholders in the corporation act.[7]

The So-Called Institutional Guarantees

Meanwhile, the Constitution not only stipulates a number of provisions on fundamental rights in Chapter 2, but it also provides for the constitutional protection of several political, social and cultural institutions, which are called institutional guarantees in German constitutional theories. They include the plural party system (Article 8), freedom of the press (Article 21), the private property ownership institution (Article 23), family institution on the basis of individual dignity and equality of the sexes (Article 36), autonomy of universities (Article 31 Section 4), and local self-government (Articles 117 and 118). It is not difficult to notice that the constitutional guarantees of these institutions are closely associated with the protection of the freedom and rights of the people. The plural party system (in opposition to single party system) is closely related to freedom to establish and join a political party, while the private property ownership system is associated with the right to property (in opposition to state ownership system). Also, the family institution is related to gender equality, while the autonomy of universities is associated with academic freedom. And local autonomy is related to political freedom and the right to vote. What are constitutionally protected are these institutions/systems as such. The con-

---

6.   See Press Arbitration and Remedies Act, Articles 15–16, which provide for the right to correct and Article 17 for the right of reply.

7.   Dai-Kwon Choi, *Honbophak: Bopsahoehakjokjopkun [Constitutional Law: Socio-Legal Approaches]* (Seoul: 1989), 154–188; Dai-Kwon Choi, *Honbophak-kangui,* 195–200.

stitutional guarantees of these institutions have been discussed in Korea under the German scholarly influence.[8]

In Germany, however, these institutions have long history and tradition. They are defined as historically/traditionally formed institutions. For instance, the institutions of autonomy of universities or local autonomy may date back even to medieval Germany. Given this fact, we can notice that these institutions did not exist in Korea until they were adopted by the Constitution; thus we are trying to establish and constitutionally to protect these institutions in Korean society by incorporating them into the Constitution (1948) because their constitutional protection is crucial for the protection of related fundamental rights. Then, in Korea, those provisions of institutions should not be referred to as institutional guarantees; rather it should be regarded as a blueprint of the Constitution on political, economic, social and cultural institutions that need to be established along with the guarantees of fundamental rights in the Constitution.[9] In the case of the family institution, for instance, it should be one of an extended family that was indeed the historically established, traditional family institution in Korea, if we follow the German scholarly definition of institutional guarantee. The historical traditional institution of the extended family incorporates the principles of male-centered family headship in the family registry system and the ban on marriages between couples who have the identical surnames and the identical place of ancestral origin (such as Kim of Kimhae), both of which were recently ruled unconstitutional on the grounds of gender equality and others by the Constitutional Court.[10] However, the Constitution calls for the family institution that should be formed "on the basis of individual dignity and equality of the sexes" (Article 36 Section 1). Since the plural party system, the autonomy of universities, and local autonomy are institutions that were not recognized during the dynastic and the Japanese days before their adoption into the Constitution,

---

8.   Young-seong Kwon, *Honbophakwonron*, 187ff.; Chol-su Kim, *Honbophak-kyeron*, 357–362; Nak-in Song, *Honbophak*, 247–251; Young-soo Jang, *Kibonkwonron*, 22–23; Young Huh, *Hankukhonbopron*, 168–171, 230, 216–217, 416, 443, 476, 551, 777ff., 792ff.; etc.

9.   Dai-Kwon Choi, *Honbophak-kangui*, 43.

10.   Constitutional Court decision of February 3, 2005 (2001Hon-Ka9, etc.); Constitutional Court decision of July 16, 1997 (95Hon-Ka6, 13).

they are a blueprint for a new nation that should be realized along with such principles of the Constitution as the guarantee of fundamental rights. In the case of the private property system, it is also a constitutional guarantee of a blueprint system in the sense that it categorically denies the state property ownership of totalitarianism, and serves as the basis for a market economy in a situation where it is difficult to state that Korea had a well functioning market economy in the past, because of its extreme poverty and the wartime state-controlled economy under the extractive Japanese colonial rule.

The Constitutional Provisions of Public Duties

The Korean Constitution includes provisions on the duty to pay taxes (Article 38) and the duty of national defense (Article 39) in the same chapter on fundamental rights. Needless to say, the public duty clauses of the Constitution are significant in the sense that they clearly enumerate the financial and military foundation of the nation. At the same time, they are significant in that the citizens are required to perform these public duties "as prescribed by laws;" they are in fact designed to better guarantee the fundamental rights related to the duties of taxes and national defense such as a right to property and a right to personal freedom and actions. The stipulation of "as prescribed by laws" indicates that the imposition of the duties of taxes and national defense is placed first of all under the scrutiny of the National Assembly, the representatives of the citizens, and then, secondarily and lastly, under the judicial scrutiny of the Constitutional Court.

Restrictions and Limitations of Fundamental Rights

Article 37 Section 2 of the Korean Constitution concerns restrictions placed on fundamental rights. Inherently, one's fundamental right cannot be allowed to violate the same fundamental right of others, or the very existence of a national community which guarantees those rights. In the reality of political, economic, social and cultural life that we encounter every day, the question of the extent to which the fundamental rights are protected is in fact more important than that of what fundamental rights are protected. The Constitution clarifies the basic constitutional principles on the extent of the limitations placed justifiably on fundamental rights by way of Article 37 Section 2, which stipulates that

> the freedoms and rights of citizens may be restricted by laws only when necessary for national security, the maintenance of law and order or for public welfare. Even when such restriction is imposed, no essential aspect of freedom or right shall be violated.[11]

Comparatively speaking, this general clause of the restriction or limitation on the fundamental rights stipulated in the Korean Constitution seems unusual among many constitutional documents. Probably the reason for such an unusual clause may have to do with the necessity felt to clearly define the constitutional principles guiding the determination of what exercise of fundamental rights is or is not constitutionally allowed and to what extent, since Korea lacked experience in democratic political order and the constitutional guarantee of fundamental rights. In fact, in a country with a long history of democracy and guarantee of fundamental rights, the kind of constitutional principles on the permissible restriction on fundamental rights do exist in the form of actual political practices of many years, or judicial precedents by the highest court or the constitutional court, without such a written provision.

Article 37 Section 2 of the Constitution proclaims the following four requirements for constitutionally justifiable restrictions on fundamental rights. First, there should be a necessity to restrict fundamental rights. National security and the maintenance of law and order or public welfare are the constitution-provided examples of such a necessity. Second, the necessity for such a limitation alone is not enough; it must be unavoidable. When there is an alternative that can resolve such a necessity, then the proposed restriction on fundamental rights shall not be allowed. Third, even when the limitation on fundamental rights is unavoidable, it shall be minimal. Fourth, although the restriction is justified, it must be stipulated by law. Indeed, the purpose of Article 37 Section 2 of the Constitution is to clarify the principle that fundamental rights and freedom should be guaranteed to the maximum extent and their restrictions should be to the minimal extent.

Laws limiting fundamental rights in violation of these requirements are unconstitutional. The purpose of rigorous requirements for restricting

---

11.   Dai-Kwon Choi, *Honbophak-kangui*, 203–220.

fundamental rights in Article 37 Section 2 is to guarantee fundamental rights to the maximum extent possible, and to permit their restriction, to a minimum extent, only when there is an unavoidable public necessity. When ruling a statute or statutory provision unconstitutional, the Constitutional Court sometimes relies on the principle of proportionality or the principle of ban on excessive restriction in its determination of the matter, whether the second and/or third requirements described above is/are met. Furthermore, a constitutionally justified restriction should be stipulated by law passed by the National Assembly. For instance, restricting fundamental rights through other legislative means (e.g., presidential or ministerial orders or rules) without a definite constitutional authorization is basically unconstitutional. In addition, laws that restrict fundamental rights should be applied generally. They should not amount to an administrative or judicial action in the name of legislation (such as attainder); that violates the doctrine of the separation of powers. Furthermore, any law limiting fundamental rights should be clearly defined, or ruled unconstitutional. If the law limiting fundamental rights is unclear, ambiguous or too extensive, the exercise of fundamental rights may be unnecessarily contracted.

It is noteworthy that a statutory provision's unconstitutionality is first reviewed by the National Assembly, both the representatives of the people and the legislature of the nation. Only the secondary and final review is performed by the Constitutional Court in the legal process. Particularly since not every law or provision undergoes judicial review, a before-the-fact review of constitutionality by the National Assembly is naturally important. To that extent, it is clear that a National Assembly that works hard to fulfill such a function is definitely needed for the better guarantee of fundamental rights. And it would not be an overstatement to say that constitutional litigation in Korea almost entirely center around the interpretation of Article 37 Section 2 of the Constitution rather than around enumerated specific fundamental rights as such.

Constitutional Court

The picture of the constitutional framework for the guarantee of fundamental rights laid out in the Korean Constitution is completed by the description of the constitutional review of legislation performed by the

Constitutional Court. The Constitutional Court is probably the most successful institution among those brought about by democratization in Korea in 1987. It has proved itself significant for democracy and the protection of fundamental rights in Korea, as described later. The constitutional provisions of fundamental rights are only parts, albeit very important ones, of the written constitution. Therefore, the fundamental rights in the Constitution are ultimately protected by the institution of judicial review of legislation provided by the Constitution. In Korea, there has never been a time when the written constitution did not feature a constitutional review of legislation institution since the first Constitution of 1948, and even during the authoritarian period. The institutional patterns of constitutional review have varied, however, and the constitutional review institutions did not function well under the rule of past authoritarian regimes. Nonetheless, it is important that a constitutional review of legislation was never removed from the written constitution. We were aware that a constitutional review of legislation was essential to safeguard the Constitution and to protect fundamental rights.

In accordance with the Constitution, the Constitutional Court has jurisdiction over the following matters: 1, the constitutionality of a law upon the request for review by the courts; 2, impeachment; 3, dissolution of a political party; 4, disputes about the jurisdictions among State agencies, between State agencies and local governments, and among local governments; and 5, constitutional complaints as prescribed by law (Article III Section 1). Except for the single case of impeachment against the President, which took place in 2004,[12] however, cases on impeachment and the dissolution of a political party are rarely filed. And jurisdictional disputes are filed only occasionally. The more than 1,000 cases filed each year at the Constitutional Court mostly concern the constitutionality of legislation upon the request of the courts or constitutional complaints. Fundamental rights are placed under constitutional protection through the constitutional review of legislation function of the Constitutional Court.

The Constitutional Court performs the constitutional review function (Article 107 Section 1), 1, at the request of a court on its own initiative

---

12.   Constitutional Court decision of May 14, 2004 (2004Hon-Na1), in which the President was eventually acquitted.

or on the request of the parties of a case, when the constitutionality of a law is at issue in a trial (Constitutional Court Act Article 68 Section 1; or 2, when a constitutional complaint is filed by any citizen who claims his or her constitutionally protected basic rights have been violated by a governmental action or non-action (except for the judgments of the ordinary courts), or in the event that his or her request for constitutional review of law is rejected at the trial court (Constitutional Court Act Article 68 Sections 1 and 2). And no constitutional complaint is permitted unless a resort to other judicial redress has been exhausted. Over the constitutionality or legality of administrative decrees, regulations or actions, however, the Supreme Court has the final word when it is at issue in a trial (Article 107 Section 2).

REALIZATION OF FUNDAMENTAL RIGHTS

On the one hand, fundamental rights require for their realization embodiment as constitutionally protected provisions and constitutional guarantee institutions, such as a constitutional review of legislation, in the Constitution. On the other hand, we believe that they also require citizens' supportive consciousness or affirmative awareness toward the positive Constitution (that embodies the fundamental rights).[13] Without citizen support of the Constitution, which is a social-psychological element of the living Constitution, a gap can develop between constitutional norms and realities. And the constitutionally-guaranteed institutions would not operate without such citizen support. Despite the ideal of the constitutionally provided fundamental rights, such citizen consciousness of fundamental rights may not have fully developed under the dictatorship of the past due to the lack of previous experiences in democracy (a cultural lag phenomenon). The constitutional awareness of the citizens may not have developed because the disparity between constitutional norms and the political realities was justified on the grounds of situational inevitability or urgent national necessity. The past experiences of the disparities between constitu-

---

13.   Dai-Kwon Choi, *Honbophak*, 12–46, esp. 36. Here, the same phenomenon is analyzed with a concept of legal consciousness or social approval.

tional norms and political realities in Korea may well be understood with these behavioral variables.

Liberal Democracy and the Guarantee of Fundamental Rights

The Korean Constitution started with the proclamation of liberal democratic order and the guarantee of fundamental rights from the moment it was enacted and adopted in 1948, although the political realities did not fully follow its ideal afterward. It may be necessary to explain in the first place why the (South) Koreans for their political order decided to adopt liberal democracy and the guarantee of fundamental rights from the very beginning. Indeed, it would be worthwhile to explore the variables that might account for the Korean determination to adopt such an ideal liberal democratic order and the guarantee of fundamental rights when they did not have any previous experience in democracy or the guarantee of fundamental rights. At the time of the adoption of the first Constitution, Korea suffered extreme political confusion, frustration, and difficulties following the division into South and North, while their joy of liberation from Japanese rule at the end of the World War II and their hopes for founding an independent state were trampled. And the Korean people were also experiencing severe ideological confrontations between the left and the right under the military administrations by the Soviet Union in the North and by the U.S. in the South.[14]

Firstly, one most important factor that explains Korea's adoption of on free democracy and the guarantee of fundamental rights in 1948 was the desire for freedom and independence after many years under the Japanese rule of oppression and exploitation, following the previous monarchical ruler. When the Koreans founded their state, their strong desire for freedom and independence was expressed in their decision to embrace free democracy and the guarantee of fundamental rights. Take the examples of the rule of law, warrant system, ban on torture, privilege against self-incrimination, the right to request the court to review the legality of arrest or detention (habeas corpus), the right to prompt assistance of counsel, and the validity of confession as evidence, which were declared along with the

14.   Dai-Kwon Choi, "Constitutional Developments in Korea," *Review of Korean Studies* 6 (2003), 29–31.

provisions on personal liberty (Articles 12 and 13), freedom of speech and press and freedom of assembly and association (Article 21). These rights and freedoms are the opposite of what the Koreans had experienced in criminal procedures and other proceedings under Japanese rule. In addition, the provision that sovereignty rests with the people (Article 1 Section 2) repudiates not only monarchy, but also foreign rule; and the doctrine of self-determination was based on the experiences of the Korean people such as in the nation-wide uprisings against Japanese rule in 1919.

A second factor that may explain Korea's decision to adopt liberal democracy and the guarantee of fundamental rights is that the Korean Constitution was adopted by the Korean Constituent National Assembly, with the blessings of the United Nations with a number of resolutions of the UN General Assembly led by the U.S., itself a free democratic state, and the UN's monitoring of the first-ever election to form the Constituent National Assembly, along with the support of the American Military Government.[15] Consequently, for instance, the right to request the court to review the legality of arrest or detention, originating in Anglo-American habeas corpus law and initially introduced to Korea by the American Military Government, is provided now in the Constitution.[16] The "farmland-to-the-tiller principle," adopted in the Constitution for farmland reform (Article 86 of the First Constitution of 1948), is actually preceded by the American Military Government's distribution to landless farmers of the former Japanese-owned "enemy" farmlands controlled by itself.[17] The liberal influences

15. For the international and domestic circumstances under which the Republic of Korea was established with the adoption of its liberal democratic Constitution, as Korea's division initially started as an expedient military measure and then turned into a political line, see Dai-Kwon Choi, "A Legal Analysis of the Division, the Present State, and the Future Courses of Korea," in Myoung-Kyu Kang and Helmut Wagner, eds., *Korea and Germany: Lessons in Division,* (Seoul: 1990), 27–104, esp. 29–38.

16. For the evolution of habeas corpus law in Korea, see Su-Yong Kim, "Chaepo kusok jokbusimsajaedo e kwanhan honbopsajok yonku [A Study of Constitutional History on the Judicial Review of the Legality of the Arrest or Detention (Korean habeas corpus)]" (Master of Law thesis, Seoul National University, 2004).

17. For the Farmland Reform of Korea, see Song-ho Kim, Kyong-sik Chon, Sang-whan Chang and *Sok-du Pak, Nongjikyehyoksayonku [Study on the Farmland Reform History]* (Seoul: 1989); Song-chan Hong, ed., *Nongjikyehyokyonku [Study on the Farmland Reform]* (Seoul: 2001); Il-yong Kim, "Nongjikyehyokul dullossan sinwhaui haechae" [Dis-

deriving from exchanges with the free World including the US, and, in particular, the political leadership of the first President Syngman Rhee, an American-trained Ph.D, who was well accustomed to the American politics and legal culture, had greatly contributed to the adoption of the liberal Korean Constitution and to the founding of the Republic of Korea.

A third factor that explains Korea's decision to adopt free democracy and the guarantee of fundamental rights is the transformation of the North into a Stalinist totalitarian society and a satellite state of the Soviet Union, which it imposed there after the Korean liberation from Japan. The transformation of the North into a communist totalitarian state meant the entry of a rival system to the Republic of Korea on the international and domestic stages. Liberal democracy and the guarantee of fundamental rights were stark contradictions of the totalitarian principles upheld by the North Korean regime. Pluralism, in particular, the plural party system, the right to property (private ownership), freedom of speech and press, freedom of assembly and association, freedom of religion and conscience, freedom of election, the separation of power into administration, legislation and judicature, and the constitutional review of law institution are the major liberal democratic principles that refute the totalitarian constitutional principles pursued by North Korea. Farmland reform in South Korea rejected the compulsory seizure and distribution without compensation formula in North Korea and was instead based on the confiscation with payment and distribution with payment method that was in harmony with the private ownership institution. In addition, the Korean Constitution avowedly adopted the market economy based on the freedom of contract and private ownership institutions that reject the state controlled, centrally planned economy (command economy).

These three factors that could explain Korea's early decision to adopt liberal democracy and the guarantee of fundamental rights in its Constitution are in fact those that have continuously contributed to the political, economic, social, and cultural developments of Korea thereafter. We believe that those are the factors contributing significantly to Korean devel-

---

mantling the Myth on the Farmland Reform]," in Ji-hyang Pak, Chol Kim, Il-yong Kim, and Yong-hun Yi, *Haebangjonhusaui jaeinsik* [*Reappraisal of Ante-and Post-Liberation History*] (Seoul: 2006), 295–389; Hochul Lee, "Political Economy of Land Reform: A Historical Institutional Explanation" (Ph.D. dissertation, Rutgers, 1993), 125 ff.

opment as the only country in the world that successfully attained both free democracy and industrialization based on market economy among the numerous states founded after the World War II. The fact that a free democratic system is superior to a totalitarian one is indeed clearly attested by the South-North contest in the Korean peninsula and by the collapse of the former Soviet Socialist bloc globally. Everyone in a free democracy is provided with equal opportunity to develop his capacity to the fullest extent, so an entire society can perform far better by putting together individual successes than a totalitarian polity.

In the meantime, however, despite its written formal constitution that proclaimed the ideal of liberal democracy and the guarantee of fundamental rights, Korea underwent more or less authoritarian political realities from 1948 when the Constitution was adopted until its "democratization" in 1987. Thus, the Koreans had experienced a gap between a formal liberal constitution and a contrary political reality under authoritarian rule. Now, the question we face is how to account for the emergence of the gap between the free democratic constitutional norms and the authoritarian political realities in Korea.

Constitutional Norms and Authoritarian Political Reality

Indeed, a country does not immediately become a free democratic state where fundamental rights are guaranteed merely because it adopts a written constitution stipulating free democracy and the guarantee of fundamental rights. Since the adoption of the Constitution, Korea passed through the authoritarian phase in which the press, associations, opposition parties and the three major labor rights were suppressed while powers were concentrated in the hands of the executive, and then entered the free democratic era, following the "democratization" in 1987, when political practices became consistent overall with constitutional norms. Constitutions in which the political reality does not match formal democratic norms, as in the case of Korea, are referred to as "nominal constitutions" by Loewenstein[18] in contrast with "normative" constitutions, in which political realities are largely

18. Karl Loewenstein, *Political Power and the Governmental Process* (Chicago: 1965), 147–153.

consistent with constitutional norms. The term nominal constitution was once in vogue among Korean constitutional students during the authoritarian era. The question raised was why the political realities lagged behind the aspiration for free democracy declared in the written constitution. To their disappointment, Loewenstein only suggested such a classification and did not explain it. On the basis of Korean experiences, let us try to analyze the reason why the Korean Constitution had to remain a nominal constitution, that is, why authoritarianism emerged in Korea.[19]

One of the factors that helped to make political reality in Korea lag behind the written formal constitution may well be cultural. In fact, before the founding of the Republic of Korea, Koreans had never experienced democracy in their history. In particular, under the harsh suppression and exploitation of Japanese rule, Koreans were deprived even of the kind of benevolent administration bestowed by the previous royal dynasty on the basis of Confucian concepts of propriety and virtue, not to mention any concept of the guarantee of fundamental rights by the Constitution. Therefore, it is easily understandable that the old undemocratic ways of thought, behavior and political practice could not change overnight simply because a new age had arrived. Needless to say, it takes re-education and time to change customary ways.

A second factor may well have been the avowedly obscurantist policy of the Japanese rulers, which was intended to systematically eradicate the Koreans' self-governing ability to justify Japanese rule of Korea. Japan completely eliminated leadership and managerial education in activities and organizations necessary for living as a nation in the modern world, including science and technology. With few exceptions, Koreans were not trained for high management positions in government offices, the military, the police force, prisons, and even Japanese-run factories and business organizations. Koreans were hired only as low-ranking functionaries who needed instructions from their superior to carry out.[20] In the Army, for example, they were privates and non-commissioned officers, rarely commissioned officers. When the Republic of Korea was founded and trained personnel necessary

19.   Dai-Kwon Choi, "Constitutional Developments in Korea," 32–34.

20.   Un-kyong Pak, *Iljaeha chosoninkwalryo yonku [Study on Korean Officials under Japanese Rule]* (Seoul: 1999), esp. 37–39.

for running state organizations were very much demanded, those former low-ranking functionaries were inevitably highly placed to fill higher management positions and commanding posts.[21] This was because they were the only personnel trained at all then. This is one of the reasons why the pro-Japanese faction was not completely eliminated and thus debates concerning pro-Japanese elements continue to be held in Korean politics even today.

Thirdly, since those trained for low positions by oppressive governing authorities of Japan were appointed to high and low management and commanding positions in the newly established governmental agencies, and some even to the cabinet and other political office, it can easily be imagined that the customary undemocratic behaviors acquired under Japanese rule would show up in various ways in the newly established government institutions (administration, police forces, military, courts of justice, prisons, etc.). And their undemocratic ways of thinking were transmitted naturally to their newly appointed subordinates. Accordingly, anti-democratic, oppressive political behavior toward human rights had to linger on for a while even under the newly adopted Constitution which prescribed democracy and the guarantee of fundamental rights. Collective punishment in the military (called *danchaekihap*, meted to an entire unit for a wrong done by one or a few members), and torture during police investigations were notorious examples of the kind. It took years to eradicate those practices in democratic Korea.

A fourth factor may have been the urgent necessity to safeguard the Republic of Korea from the persistent, serious subversive activities by North Korea's communist regime and pro-North Korean communists very

---

21. This situation is vividly pictured by the example of 4 star general Paik Sonyob, the Korean war hero. He, an ex-lieutenant of Japan' puppet Manchurian army, began the Korean War as a division commander with the rank of Colonel and became one star general in the very early phase of the War at the age of 29. For example, he had to train his men for infantry-tank unit joint operations for the first time for him and his men while engaging in combat with enemy according to his Korean War memoir, *Kun kwa na [The Army and I]* (Seoul: 2009). Education and training while engaging in actual combat were the norm for the Korean military during the Korean War. This metaphor applies equally to many other areas of activities such as science and technology, university education, industrialization, and democratization during rapid development.

active in South Korea. North Korea's activities to overthrow, destroy and communize South Korea included various provocative actions launched by North Korea along the thirty-eighth parallel, overseas and in the South before, during, and after the Korean War. Such a tense atmosphere threatening the Republic's existence justified the appointment of even former pro-Japanese officials and the adoption of oppressive authoritarian practices to combat the subversive activities. Furthermore, the strong necessity not only to win in the competition of a political nature against North Korea but also rapidly to industrialize the state to escape from the structural poverty handed down from the Japanese colonial period provided a pretext to justify authoritarian politics suppressing human rights and the basic rights of workers. In fact, there exists a controversy over whether authoritarianism by President Chung-hee Park can be justified because of the necessity of economic development or whether economic development was necessary in order to justify his authoritarianism. However, no one today denies that his authoritarianism was instrumental in the takeoff of Korean economic development, justified to safeguard the South and to develop its economy. For poverty was and is a hotbed for communism.

Emergence of Normative Constitution as a Result of Democratization

Let us now examine how democratization was achieved from the authoritarian politics for which the various above-described factors account. When this issue is seen from the perspective of the constitution-supporting consciousness mentioned above, the disparity between constitutional norms and political reality may be considered less the result of lacking the cognitive aspect of the constitutional consciousness than that of the absence of its evaluative and/or behavioral aspects. Knowledge alone does not ensure law-abiding behavior. No doubt, the reason for the introduction of such a social psychological element as the constitution-supporting consciousness is again to better account for the politico-social changes that took place in Korea from the nominal constitution in the authoritarian past to the normative constitution today. The force of constitutional norm ultimately lies in the people's constitution-supporting consciousness that is expressed in such various ways as judicial decisions, votes, public opinions, etc. in peace time, and as resistance, even armed resistance, to illegal power in a coup

d'etat or revolutionary situation. There is no criminal sanction for violation of the constitutional norm as such beyond the constitution-supporting
consciousness. Interestingly enough, one of the pledges of the junta leaders
in 1961 was to safeguard the nation and free democracy from the threats of
subversion from the north. The formal free democratic Constitution was
maintained during the authoritarian period. The authoritarian leaders were
very much interested in the rule of law or its appearance to enhance their
legitimacy at home and abroad and to control public officials unless their
very political power was threatened. Thus, the partial rule of law and partial constitutionalism were plausible: there were regularly held elections,
plural political parties, free speeches, etc., although there were electoral ir-
regularities, and suppression of opposition parties, speeches, labors, etc. At
the same time, there had been incessant underground and overt democratic
movements led by liberals, clerics, workers, and university professors and
students who asserted nothing other than their constitutionally provided
rights and freedoms. These democratic movements culminated in the civil
uprising-like democratization in 1987. Thus understood, democratization
is simply the reflection not only of the cognitive element but also of the
evaluative and behavioral aspects of the constitution-supporting consciousness and awareness. Now, political practices have become more consistent
with the constitutional norms. Let us explore the factors that account for
the result in the achievement of democratization so as for the authoritarian
political practice to change to become, in a large measure, consistent with
the liberal formal constitutional norms.[22]

First, we believe that the one crucial factor that led Korea to democratization is the very existence of a free democratic written constitution
stipulating the guarantee of fundamental rights. Even during the period
of authoritarianism, the written constitution of free democracy had never been abolished, even at the time when it was reduced almost to nothing because of the contradictory, authoritarian political realities as indicated above. Moreover, the authoritarian politics that was in violation of
the formal liberal constitutional norms was rationalized as the necessary
measure to protect free democracy from communist subversion more than
anything. Korea maintained the plural party system and held regular

---

22.   Dai-Kwon Choi, "Constitutional Developments in Korea," 34–35.

elections. Democratization movements did not claim what was not stipulated in the Constitution; they focused on the fundamental rights of the people proclaimed in the Constitution, such as the freedom of the press and association as well as the worker's rights. Although it remained only a nominal constitution of free democracy, the very existence of the written liberal constitution, which served as a framework for the democratization movement, differentiates Korea's authoritarianism of the past from the authoritarianism of today in China. Although China is developing a market economy through reform, it does not have a multiple party system and still has a single Communist Party. Also, China does not hold elections regularly to select leaders and still lacks the freedom of the press, association and religion and worker's rights in contrast to Korea.

Furthermore, the existence of a written liberal democratic constitution and accordingly held elections had an enormous effect of educating the Korean people on democracy and heightening their constitution-supporting consciousness. Formal education on the written liberal constitution was provided through school, in particular, university. Thus, the people's constitution-supporting consciousness has steadily increased in its evaluative and behavioral as well as cognitive aspects. Paradoxically, anti-democratic behaviors of dictators such as unfair elections and oppressions of opposition parties and workers educated the citizens on democracy.

A second factor that enabled the realization of democratization might be the emergence of the middle class that grew along with industrialization. In Korea, industrialization acted as an important rationale justifying authoritarianism. And yet the very existence of the middle class that grew as a result played a significant role in achieving democratization in Korea. In that sense, the authoritarianism practiced in Korea was impregnated with its own demise (that is, democratization). At any rate, the middle class that flourished as a result of economic development has emerged as the educated class, along with improved availability of higher education made possible by economic resources. And the emergence of an educated and relatively affluent middle class has accompanied liberal effects (including liberal mores and trends) on the political system. Such liberal effects are likely to be amplified by active material and human exchanges at home and abroad. The global penetration of the Internet accelerated these effects. On the basis of the Korean experience, it is an interesting question whether the growth of the middle class in China will eventually bring about more or less similar liberalizing effects on the Chinese authoritarian system.

A third factor is the persistent democratization and labor movements led by students and intellectuals during the authoritarian period.[23] The theory on the democratization generation, the so-called 386 generation,[24] whose terminology is in vogue in Korea, is associated with these movements launched from the 1970s through 1980. Such democratization and labor movements led to the people's resistance movement (the exercise of the popular right to revolt) in June 10, 1987, which finally brought about democratization in the same year.

It goes without saying that these three factors above are closely interrelated to each others. In any case, the three factors as integrated had contributed to the democratization of Korea. We believe that the democratization brought about by those factors set a milestone that showed the growth of a civil society autonomous of the state power. Now it became a matter of commonsensical fact that excessive state intervention (e.g., in the form of regulations) not only reduces efficiency but also hinders further development. And the guarantee of fundamental rights institutions came to function as an important principle of balancing between autonomous civil society and the justifiable exercise of the state power.

23.   For those democratic and labor movements, see Won-soon Park, *Yoksaga idulul mujoero harira [History will Acquit Them, History of Advocacy for Human Rights in Korea]* (Seoul: 2003); Silrok Minchonghakryonundongkyesungsaophoe, ed., *1974 Nyon sawol: Silrok Minchonghakryon [April 1974: History of Democratic Youth and Students League]*, 2 vols., (Seoul: Hakminsa, 2003); In-sop Han, ed., *Jonguiuibop, yangsimuibop, inkwonuibop [Law of Justice, Conscience, and Human Rights]* (Seoul: 2004); "Minbyun baekso [Lawyers for a Democratic Society White Paper]," (Seoul: 1998).

24.   In the 1990's immediately following the democratization of 1987 when the military dictatorship had ended and the democratic stage was ushered in with the Constitutional Amendment of the year, the term 386 generation referred to those who were in their thirties (already in their forties now in the 2000s), attended colleges in the 1980s, and were born in the 1960s, They were regarded as largely responsible for democratization movements in the 1980s but also for the various progressive trends in Korean society today.

PROSPECTS FOR THE GUARANTEE OF FUNDAMENTAL
HUMAN RIGHTS—BY WAY OF A CONCLUSION

So far, we have reviewed how fundamental human rights have evolved in Korea from the time when the formal free democratic constitution was adopted for the first time in Korean history up to the present. Fundamental rights are an inseparable part of the living Constitution and are placed under the constitutional protection system in Korea. In the past authoritarian era, the fundamental rights existed only on paper as an ideal to be achieved while the political reality was different. Since democratization in 1987, the Korean Constitution featuring the guarantee of fundamental rights has become a normative constitution (that is, a living functional constitution). Now, what we face here is the question of how constitutionally provided fundamental rights are going to evolve under the newly achieved normative constitution. We will survey a few problem areas that have been emerging since 1987. They are all related to developments of democracy and concomitant constitution-supporting consciousness (civic culture) in Korea.

One outstanding problem with the fundamental rights provisions in Korea is how to improve the wretched state of the North Korean people in human rights protection. Constitutionally as well as in brotherly love of compatriots, North Koreans are also the citizens of the Republic of Korea according to the Constitution Art. 3. As a legislative gesture for the betterment of the North Korean human rights situation, the North Korean Human Rights Act has been proposed for years at the National Assembly but with no success thus far,[25] because of objection of the left-leaning opposition parties. Presently, there are around twenty thousand former North Koreans who managed to settle in the South following their escape from the North, which itself is *de facto* a large starving prison camp. A large number of North Koreans, estimated to be two to three hundred thousand, are currently living in China while hiding their identity, following their illegal entry to seek food, freedom, or a route to the South; many women are even sold to forced marriage or to prostitution. China system-

25. See the proceedings of conference on North Korean Human Rights Act *Pukhaninkwonbop baro algi [Due Understanding of North Korean Human Rights Act]* held on July 4, 2012 by Pukhanjayuinkwon kukminyonhap [Citizen Coalition for North Korean Freedom and Human Rights].

atically grants no refugee status to those North Korean escapees, whom the government sends back to North Korea when they are discovered. Back in the North, harsh punishment, even execution, awaits them. Recently it became known that South Korean human rights activists in China who work for North Koreans, especially those who help to extricate them from the North for their relocation in the South, are arrested and tortured, even by using electric rods.

As we have learned through our experience of the tragic Korean War (1950–53), there is no greater large-scale and organized violation of human rights than a war. Technically Korea is still in a state of war with the North because only a cease-fire agreement was entered into by the combatants (Armistice of 1953). The Korean peninsula has been one of the world's most volatile areas where war may break out in any time because of the belligerency of the North which incessantly provokes the South, including terror activities and limited armed attacks; the sinking of the *Chonan* navy ship and the shelling of Yonpyong island near the NLL, the dividing line, between two Koreas (2010) are only the latest. Prevention of war, not to mention peace-making, is indeed an invaluable action of protecting fundamental rights in our part of the world.

Unification[26] is no doubt the surest way to make peace in Korean peninsula. The Korean aspiration for unification is variously manifested in a number of constitutional provisions: the Preface, the territory clause of Article 3, the peaceful and free democratic unification clause of Article 4, the President's duty clause of Article 66 Section 3, the Presidential inaugural oath clause of Article 69, and the national referendum clause of Article 72. Installment of government's Ministry of Unification is another manifestation. The Korean Constitution started as the constitution that covered the entire Korea by providing for *de jure* sovereign power over "the Korean peninsula and its adjacent islands" (Article 3), despite the *de facto* division into two Koreas. Accordingly, the Constitution demands that fruits of free democracy and market economy, fundamental rights protection and economic prosperity, be so extended to North Koreans for them to share and enjoy as well through unification.

26. Dai-Kwon Choi, "Honbopjok kwanjomeso bon hankuk tongil [Korean Unification Seen from the Constitutional Perspective]," *Kongbop yonku* [*Public Law Studies*] 39/3 (2011), 11–19.

The Constitution of Korea equips itself with constitutional measures to defend free democracy from its own enemy ("defensive" or "combative" democracy). As one of the defensive measures, a political party whose purposes and/or activities are contrary to basic (free) democratic order may be ordered by the Constitutional Court to be dissolved upon the government's prosecution (Constitution Article 8 Section 4). An alternative or derivative party which is identical with or similar to thus dissolved one is also not permitted (Political Parties Act 40). The National Security Act which purports to restrict anti-state subversive activities and speeches has been consistently declared constitutional by the Constitutional Court,[27] although it has been incessantly challenged by the left-leaning liberals and politicians and also by the North. No doubt, the Act is justified on the basis of Constitution Article 37 Section 2. In a constitutional challenge, the Act's Article 7, one of the most controversial, which proscribed subversive speeches, was declared constitutional by the Court to the extent that they amounted to be "clearly" subversive either to the free democratic order or to the lawful government (in a well-known "limited" constitutionality ruling in 1990).[28] The Act was accordingly amended to accommodate the ruling. And yet challenges to the Act continue.

A noticeable right-left ideological polarization has developed in recent years. This ideological division is much complicated by the variety of attitudes and policies held by South Koreans toward the North, its people (their compatriots), eventual unification, the National Security Act, and other related matters. Those who are designated as leftists include not only people who want to engage the North in various ways but also those who align themselves to the North Korean regime and/or its policy lines because of their socialist and/or ultra nationalist solidarity or of their suspected or known special ties with the North. The term North loyalists-leftists (*jongbuk jwapa*) is widely used to describe the latter elements these days. A few North loyalists-leftists entered the National Assembly

27.   Constitutional Court Decision of June 25, 1990 (90Hon-Ka11); Constitutional Court Decision of January 16, 1997 (92Hon-Ba6); Constitutional Court Decision of 1997 (89Hon-Ma240); Constitutional Court Decision of April 25, 2002 (99Hon-Ba27), etc.

28.   Constitutional Court Decision of April 2, 1990 (89Hon-Ka113). Concerning the ruling, see Dai-Kwon Choi, *Saryejungsim Honbophak [Case-Centered Constitutional Law]*, expanded ed. (Seoul: 2001), 333–348.

as the result of recently held general election 2012. Naturally, the conservatives voice their demands for the government's action to prosecute some North loyalists-leftists on the charge of National Security Act violation, even to prosecute a political party on the far left for its dissolution,[29] and to take various other necessary actions to defend the state from the loyalists-leftists' subversive activities (including disqualification procedure against those who became National Assemblymen). They also demand the government enact special legislation to dissolve at least those North loyalist-leftist organizations and groups that were previous ruled by the court to be anti-state and/or subversive on the basis of the National Security Act and yet are still active, modeled after the legal principles applying to an alternative or derivative political party whose original party was dissolved by the Constitutional Court's decision.[30] There are some signs that the North loyalists-leftists groups are declining with the failure of the North as a polity at the same time. In any case, the ideological polarization is further complicated by the widened gap between the haves and the have-nots and by the accompanying increases of non-regular workers and unemployed youths, although the Korean economy continues to grow, becoming the world's twelfth largest by overcoming the Asian financial crisis of 1997, the effects of American financial crisis of 2008, and those of current European crisis. Recently, various populist policy proposals, particularly, expanded welfare programs, are very much rife for politicians to grab as their party's public pledges for their election victory.

An issue of livelihood recently raised in relation to "non-regular employment" is also a human rights issue when looked at closely. However,

29. See a monthly magazine's article on the matter, Jin-yong Pae, "Minjunodongdangun haesanhaeya hal wihon jongdanginka [Is the Democratic Labor Party an Unconstitutional Party that Should Be Dissolved?]," *Wolkan Chosun*, October 2011, 114–121.

30. See daily newspaper editorials, for example, *Chosun ilbo*'s editorial dated on August 15, 2012 "'Ijok' pankyolulbadun danchae haesansikilsu itke bop gochoya [Law Should Be So Revised As To Be Capable of Dissolving Those Organizations Judicially Designated As Being Subversive]". See also *Pankukgadanchae·ijokdanchae, idaero bangchihalkosinka? Pankugadanchae·ijokdanchae haesanipbop bangan [Should Anti-State and Subversive Organizations Be Left Alone? Legislative Device for the Dissolution of Anti-State and Subversive Organizations]*, Proceedings of Conference held on August 13, 2012 by Kukgajongsanghwachujinwiwonhoe [Committee for Restoration of National Normalcy].

problems with the violation of these human rights are also an issue of politics and economy that goes beyond the legal-judicial framework of guaranteeing fundamental rights which we analyzed above. It is certainly true that the areas covered by laws (international and domestic laws) have broadened in our lives over time when we look back upon the history of either mankind or Korea. The issue of the pursuit of peace has become at the same time a part of international laws in which the United Nations is involved and a part of domestic laws such as the Constitution (Articles 4 and 5 of the Constitution). The issue of livelihood, which once depended on individuals in the by-gone era of *laissez-faire*, has now become a legal issue (Livelihood Protection Act in Korea).

Let us explore further the function of parliament for the protection of human rights as mentioned tangentially along with Constitution Article 37 Section 2. Comparatively speaking, the U.K. does not have a written constitution (except for an 800-year-old Magna Carta, etc.), a written catalogue of fundamental rights and a constitutional review of law institution. However, no one describes the U.K. as a country that does not protect human rights nor support democracy. (In other form, however, it conducts judicial review of legislation deemed in violation of the guarantee of fundamental rights by having joined the European Convention of Human Rights). In the U.K., therefore, those issues that would be resolved through constitutional amendments or constitutional litigations in Korea are handled through decisions by Parliament. A dissolution of the Parliament with an important issue pending before its term expires works like a national referendum. For instance, after the dissolution of the Parliament with the issue on joining the EU pending, if the government of the party that won the majority in the election decides to resolve the issue (joining the EU) as reflecting the majority opinion of the people, the government's decision concludes the issue. The situation is somewhat similar in the case of Japan, on a somewhat different ground. It has a constitution that stipulates fundamental rights, but issues are concluded practically with parliamentary decisions made by the Diet. This is only because a judicial ruling of unconstitutionality in constitutional cases is very rare and hardly ever found in reality, because of Japan's extreme judicial restraint.[31] These kinds

31.   Dai-Kwon Choi, "Bikyo sahoe-munhwajok munmaekeso bon sabopjokukju-ui

of comparative case studies clearly show that an issue of fundamental rights is an issue of internal politics and law as well.[32]

The point stood out dramatically in 2004 when the Constitutional Court ruled the Capital Relocation Act unconstitutional,[33] and when a case on the impeachment of the President was filed and an acquittal decision was made.[34] There arose hectic debates over whether judicial (constitutional) review was in violation of democracy when a decision made in a democratic manner (by the parliamentary majority) was ruled unconstitutional or invalid by a few un-elected judges. Debates over such a conflict between democracy and the rule of law have originated in the U.S. and have been a old topic there.[35] Nonetheless, the U.S. invented a judicial review institution with an experience of 200 years and, in particular, inspires a number of newly independent and/or democratized states with the institution. In the case of the U.S., however, such a debate over the conflict between democracy and the rule of law carries some point of relevance in that it invented and operated a judiciary review system without explicit authorization in its written constitution. In the case of Korea whose Constitution explicitly authorizes a constitutional review of legislation institution, however, the debate over the conflict between democracy and the rule of law does not carry as much relevance, unless we dare to challenge the legitimacy of the Constitution, the very foundation of the Republic of Korea.

Moreover, as long as we accept free democracy (the Korean Constitution is based on free democracy!), in which the majority rule and the protection of the minority are the key features, a judicial (constitutional) review of legislation institution is understood as a crucial device to check

---

wa sabopsokukju-ui: hana ui tamsaek [Judicial Activism/Passivism in Cross-Socio-Cultural Contexts: An Exploratory Inquiry]," *Seoul Law Journal* 46/1 (2005), 19–39.

32. Dai-Kwon Choi, "Minjujuuiwa bopchijuui: Honbopjaepanui jongchihak [Democracy and the Rule of Law: the Politics of Constitutional Litigation]," *Honbopronchong [Journal of Constitutional Law]* 19 (2008), 199–205.

33. Constitutional Court decision of October 21, 2004 (2004Hon-Ma554–566).

34. Constitutional Court decision of May 14, 2004 (2004Hon-Na1).

35. Robert A, Dahl, *Pluralist Democracy in the United States: Conflict and Consent* (Chicago: 1967), 143–170; Robert A. Dahl, *How Democratic Is the American Constitution?* (New Haven: 2001), 55–56, 152. And Tim Koopmans, *Courts and Political Institutions: A Comparative View* (Cambridge: 2003), 104–108.

and balance the majority rule for the protection of the minority. In fact, the Constitutional Court of Korea has been regarded as one most successfully settled and successfully functioning institutions since democratization was achieved in 1987. Now the Constitutional Court has become an indispensable, established institution of Korean democracy as the annual number of constitutional cases filed has exceeded 1,000 long ago. In fact, the primary focus of the fundamental rights in the Constitution is on the protection of the rights of minorities in the process of politics. And constitutional complaints, which account for over the two-thirds of the total constitutional cases, are significant in the sense that they allow individual citizens to directly petition the Constitutional Court for relief without going through other institutions when their fundamental rights are infringed upon.

When looking comparatively into the constitutional history of a country (e.g., Korea) which has a constitutional review of legislation and into that of the U.K., we can notice that the role of a parliament and citizen trust in it do act as a relevant factor. In the constitutional history of the U.K., the Parliament played a major role in the democratization of the country. In the case of Korea, rather the citizens have played a major role in democratization process in the form of exercising their right to resistance (e.g., "the April 19 Revolution" in 1960 and the June 10 Civil Uprising in 1987) more than the National Assembly did. Frankly, the National Assembly did not have enough achievements nor carry the sufficient trust of the citizens in its ability to protect the freedom of the citizens (fundamental rights). To popular disappointment, the National Assembly has continued to fall short in performance and gaining the people's trust even up to the present.

The Constitution clearly states that the guarantee of fundamental rights depends for its successful realization on the performance of the National Assembly and on the citizen's trust in it as much as on the expectations and reliance placed on the judiciary including the Constitutional Court. The purpose of the Article 37 Section 2 of the Constitution is to make sure that the National Assembly, the representative of the people, is primarily an important institution responsible for guaranteeing fundamental rights, as mentioned above. The judiciary, particularly the Constitutional Court, becomes only secondarily the institution for guaranteeing the fundamental rights. The Constitution dictates the National Assembly to monitor closely its legislative deliberation process to see if a certain bill unjustifiably infringes or restricts fundamental rights. Above all, the National Assembly is the representative body of the people and the legislative body (Article 40 of the Constitution). The National Assembly is the state organ that speaks for the various opinions and interests of the people and performs the tasks of integrating those opinions and interests into the general will of the state (e.g., legislation) through debates, deliberations and compromises. The people's constitutional expectations of and trust in the National Assembly rest on those functions.

However, the behaviors displayed by the National Assembly for years look more like the behaviors of an agency representing the partisan interests of particular political parties and/or political forces than those constitutionally expected of the National Assembly. Thus parliamentary agreement is hard to obtain. The kind of parliamentary failures (or crisis)[36] shown in the legislative process of the National Assembly is most likely to be reflected eventually in the constitutional review of the legislation process.[37] Legislation involved in partisan politics in the legislature is most likely to be referred by opponents to the Constitutional Court's constitutional review process, especially when it was passed by the numerical majority without a consensus. This is one reason why there are so many constitutional litigations in Korea. Perhaps, this phenomenon can be the evidence that Korean democracy (constitutional democracy)[38] is dynamic. Consequently, we ought to pay attention to the dynamic interrelations of the National Assembly, the judiciary, and the people beyond the nominal conflict between democracy and the rule of law.

36. Dai-Kwon Choi, "Hankukui uihoeju-uiwa ku munjaejom [Parliamentarianism of Korea and Problems]," *Uijongyonku [Journal of Legislative Studies]*, 1 (1995), 87–106. See also Carl Schmitt, *The Crisis of Parliamentary Democracy*, trans. Ellen Kennedy (Cambridge, Mass.: 1985).

37. This is what happened in the so-called Media Integration Acts litigation at the Constitutional Court. See Constitutional Court decision of October 29, 2009 (2009Hon-Ra8–9–10). See also Dai-Kwon Choi, "Urinara bopchiju-ui mit uihoeju-ui-ui hoegowa jonmang [The Rule of Law and Parliamentarianism in Korea: Retrospection and Prospect]," *Seoul Law Journal* 49/4, esp. 231–239.

38. For constitutional democracy, Dai-Kwon Choi, *Bochiju-ui wa minjuju-ui [The Rule of Law and Democracy]* (Seoul: 2012), 286ff.

In any case, the central role of the National Assembly prescribed by the Constitution is for it to be the supreme representative and legislative body to perform the functions of representing the various interests and opinions of the people and of integrating (e.g., by exercising statesmanship) them into the general will of the state (e.g., legislation)[39] in the three-way inter-relations of the National Assembly, the judiciary and the people.[40] When inter-party agreement is not reached in the parliamentary decision-making process, the opinions of the majority should prevail to become the general will of the state according to the rule of majority votes and a decision made based on the majority vote should be put to the confidence vote of the government party in the next general election.

In political reality, however, the ruling and opposition parties would clash even physically over every major legislative agenda critically important to the national interest for their passage or obstruction and thus waste valuable time by means of refusal to attend sessions, occupation of the National Assembly building, and/or the obstruction of proceedings,[41] unless consensus is reached. Bills that are advantageous to both parties (e.g., raising annual allowance or increasing the number of government-paid assistants), however, would pass promptly. Compromise and consensus are hard to obtain. Those bills over which the government and opposition parties clashed include, for example, ratification bill of the Korea-US FTA, the so-called media integration bill involving newspaper, TV, cable TV, etc.,[42] the bill on non-regular employment and others. Consequently, the National Assembly failed to perform its job of protecting important national interests and the rights and interests of the people. In many cases, it hurriedly passed bills *en masse* toward the end of the session. In some other cases, the ruling and opposition parties would reach an agreement in tough and

---

39.   For the authority (power and functions) of the national assembly as the representative and the legislative body and its failure (the failure of parliamentarianism), Dai-Kwon Choi, "Urinara bopchijuui mit uihoeju-ui-ui hoegowa jonmang."

40.   For discussions on the three-way inter-relations among the legislature, the judiciary and the people, see Koopmans, *Courts and Political Institutions*, 245–251, etc.

41.   For newspaper reports on disorders that took place at National Assembly hall, see, for example, reports of *Chosun ilbo*, December 8 and 9, 2010.

42.   See the Constitutional Court decision of October 29, 2009 (2009Hon-Ra8–9–10), cited above in n. 37).

secret negotiations, usually with a give-and-take along the partisan lines (e.g., the Capital Relocation Act, which was ruled unconstitutional in no time, etc.). In the event when bills are passed by the vote of the majority over resistance from the opposition parties to meet the government's tight legislative time schedule, a number of constitutional complaints or cases of jurisdictional dispute between departments are most likely to be filed shortly with the Constitutional Court. Recently a statutory two-third majority rule in favor of the opposition has been introduced for passage of bills in the name of facilitating the National Assembly's decision making process in 2012.[43] But the two third majority rule appears to be contrary to the constitutionally provided majority rule unless the Constitution provides otherwise (Article 49).

In any case, many of those constitutional cases filed at the Constitution Court should have been resolved in the first place at the National Assembly or otherwise politically. A good example is the impeachment against the President in 2004. When looking at the decision-making process actually practiced at the National Assembly, before accusing it of collective failure to fulfill its official duty, it can be easily imagined that even the bills passed would have a high chance of being poorly constructed so as to increase the possibility of their being ruled unconstitutional at a constitutional trial. And they would overburden the Constitutional Court with excessive loads of constitutional cases that were avoidable, resulting in an increase of opportunity cost at the national level. Despite the democratization that did put an end to the disparity phenomenon between the constitutional norms and the political reality during the past authoritarian-dictatorial era, this is perhaps another example of the remaining disparity between the constitutional norms and the political reality still remaining in the functioning of the Korean Constitution.

This is one major reason why a constitution-supporting citizen consciousness matters greatly. The problem of fundamental rights cannot be complete with the constitutionally-provided fundamental rights-guaranteeing institutions alone. Naturally, citizen consciousness in support of

---

43. See National Assembly Act Articles 71, 2 of 85 Section 1, 86 Section 3, 2 of 106 Section 6. See also a newspaper column Pyong-in Song, "Hahoetal hwanguyo-ui chamwol [Hahoe mask Hwang u-yo's *ultra vires*]," *Chosun Ilbo*, May 5, 2012.

the rights-guaranteeing institutions matters as well. From the perspective suggested above, it is obvious that in order to solve the problems and difficulties we face today it takes not a constitutional amendment that would be accompanied by controversies, divided public opinions, and waste of time and money but heightened civic virtue of the members of the Republic of Korea. This kind of civic virtue includes ability to communicate with fellow citizens having equal rights, to make concessions, compromises, or sacrifices, to love and serve the community, responsible attitudes, respect for law, the constitution-supporting consciousness, and other attitudinal-behavioral variables of the citizens that are needed for a community. Civic virtue is more strongly expected of those politicians who are the representatives of the people. Particularly, a law-abiding attitude is an indispensible part of civic virtue that should be further emphasized, without which neither constitutionalism (and the rule of law) nor the market economy can be realized. Therefore, the attitude of respect for the law on the part of the citizens and on the part of public officials comprising the state organs serves as the starting point for the guarantee of the fundamental rights institutions. Today, hotly debated political issues that involve fundamental rights matters include the National Security Act, the Assemblies and Demonstrations Act,[44] human rights in North Korea, the National Human Rights Commission of Korea, and others, but they should be resolved within the framework of constitutional democracy discussed so far.

Politician-led advocacy for constitutional amendment has been around for some years in Korea, although ordinary citizens are not necessarily enthusiastic. The major aim of the advocacy is to change the present five-year single term presidential pattern of government to a four-year, two term presidential pattern, a dual executive (president and prime minister-headed cabinet) pattern or even a parliamentary form. Some proposed amendments include those of fundamental rights and other provisions. However, there is largely no point in amending the Constitution at this time.

44. This Act was ruled inconsistent with the Constitution, requiring the National Assembly to revise the legislation by the end of June, 2010. See the Constitutional Court decision of September 24, 2009 (2008Hon-Ka25). For a critical analysis of the decision, see also Dai-Kwon Choi, "Some Thoughts on Suspended Unconstitutionality Decision-Making: with the Focus on the Constitutional Court's Assemblies and Demonstrations Act Decision," Seoul Law Journal 50/4 (2009), 141–168.

It seems instructive that "inaction" of the Korean government to initiate the dispute settlement procedure provided in the Korea-Japan agreement[45] on the former sex slaves' damage claims against the Japanese government was declared unconstitutional.[46] The Japanese government and its supreme court consistently denied responsibility for the claims on the ground that all the Korean claims against the Japanese government and/or civilian companies whatsoever incurred before World War II were met by the treaty agreement. Korean claimants, not only the former sex slaves but also male forced workers, do not and cannot agree at all in their coverage and others. They strongly claimed that they were not compensated at all with the agreement. In fact, many of them demand more the sincere apology of the Japanese government than damages as such. In any case, the agreement provides for the activation of the dispute settlement procedure when a dispute arises between the two countries concerning interpretation of its provisions. The Korean Supreme Court sided with former male forced workers in a case filed against Mitsubishi and other Japanese war industry enterprises which employed them, claiming compensation including unpaid wages.[47] After all, the popular distrust toward professional politicians, who man the political departments of the government, appears to be reflected in this kind of judicial activism. However, the force of these judicial decisions is at the most limited and more symbolic than effective (in the latter's case) unless the Japanese companies have assets in Korea.

In order to better understand development of Fundamental rights in Korea, it seems necessary to pay attention also to the semi-judicial, independent, 11-member National Human Rights Commission. Separate from the legislature, executive and judiciary, its functions range quite broadly from those of research to education, investigation, advice, opinion-making, reference, mediation and others related to human rights protection beyond the institutional confinements of judicial and other departments. Decisions made by the Commission carry only advisory power, however. The Commission was set up in 2001 to achieve the statutory goals of lev-

45. Agreement Between Japan and the Republic of Korea Concerning the Settlement of Problems in Regard to Property and Claims and Economic Cooperation (1965) Article 3.

46. Constitutional Court Decision of August 30, 2011 (2006Hon-Ma788).

47. Supreme Court Decision of May 24, 2012 (2009Da22549).

eling up individual fundamental rights protection, materializing human dignity and value, and contributing to the establishment of the democratic basic order (National Human Rights Commission Act Article 1). To some extent, the role of Commission is redundant in the sense that the very government and the judiciary constitutionally designed for protecting fundamental rights and the civic-minded citizens and their organizations are otherwise supposedly actively doing their job. However, the Commission has been contributing to the enrichment of dialogs on fundamental rights protection and hereby to the enhancement of related constitution-supporting awareness in Korean society. Occasionally it has triggered serious left-right ideological debates on human rights as well.

Lastly, let us briefly analyze whether Confucian teachings can serve as a substitute for the idea of natural law and natural rights of the West.[48] In the Choson Dynasty, Confucianism had a position of *de facto* state religion and functioned to control power and protect the minority, comparably to constitutionalism in the West, through cultivation of morality and ethics.[49] Korean society today, however, has lost much of its Confucian tradition of the past after undergoing repressive Japanese rule, its division into two Koreas following the liberation from Japan, the Korean War, industrialization and democratization. Confucianism is no longer taught in formal educational institutions. Nonetheless, Korean culture is still Confucian just as European and American societies are still Christian, although the number of churchgoers is not high today. Confucian tradition that values human dignity and worth in its own way permeates Korean society. Constitutional law, including the constitutional provisions of basic rights, as in other fields of law contains a number of such open-ended, abstract and broad clauses, in the interpretation and implementation of which public officials including judges necessarily exercise *de facto* as well as *de jure* discretionary powers. In this situation, the officials' moral/ethical senses of justice, equity, fairness, balance, etc., carry critical implications for the healthy operation of constitutional law and rights guaranteeing institutions.

48.   Dai-Kwon Choi, *Bopchiju-ui wa minjuju-ui*, 290–300.

49.   Dai-Kwon Choi, *Bopsahoehak [Sociology of Law]* (Seoul: 1983), 54–90. See also Chaihark Hahm, "Confucian Constitutionalism," (J.S.D. dissertation, Harvard Law School, 2000).

The reality we face in our daily lives is neither Western Christian nor Eastern Confucian. If we decide to take up morality and ethics as the basis of law (since law is a minimum of morality), we may conjure up Confucian or Christian morality and ethics for the job (roughly one third of the Koreans are Christian). Between the two, however, we can say that the Koreans are far more familiar with Confucian than Christian morality and ethics. Thus, particularly when we discuss the ethics of politicians or lawyers, who are involved in the operation of law, we can assert that on the behavioral level Confucian ethics is functionally more advantageous in terms of their persuasiveness than Christian ethics.[50] China, conscious that it was the leading Confucian country, particularly emphasizes Confucian "harmony" domestically and internationally, which is believed to be its national policy. Confucian harmony unaccompanied by justice, however, may well act to oppress minorities. It is insightful to notice that in his second inauguration speech President Lincoln mentioned that both the South (with its slave system) and the North (with its anti-slave policy) prayed to the same Christian God for help. We should be mindful of the fact that Confucian tradition may well be used either to justify or legitimatize certain oppressive ideas (e.g., the oppression of minorities in the name of harmony) or certain regimes (e.g., succession to power by a son) or to reinforce constitutionalism and fundamental rights. Perhaps Confucianism may well serve as an alternative to professional ethics of the lawyers including judges who are deeply involved in the operation of law if we keep the point in mind and take necessary precautions. In public officials' recruitment and training, a revival of Confucian teachings may be proposed to inculcate into them those moral and ethical principles found deficient. *Mokminsimso [Admonitions on Governing the People]*,[51] a handbook authored by Chong Yagyong, a prominent Confucian scholar (1762–1836), for public officials with which to cultivate themselves morally and ethically in the face of their official duties, could be proposed as an excellent text for the purpose.

---

50.   Dai-Kwon Choi, "Sonhan sahoeui jokon: bopchijuuirulwihan damron [The Prerequisites of Good Society: Dialogue on the Rule of Law]," *Seoul Law Journal* 40/3 (1999), 62–87.

51.   Chong Yagyong, *Admonitions on Governing the People* (Berkeley: 2010).

The Unconstitutionality of the Crime of Sodomy Under Article 92(5) of the Korean Military Penal Code

Kuk Cho[1]

INTRODUCTION

Consensual homosexual activities between civilians have never been criminalized in Korea. However, homosexual activities between military service members are criminalized under Article 92, subdivision 5 of the Korean Military Penal Code ("Article 92(5)" or "the Article"), which stipulates that "any person who commits *kyekan* [鷄姦] or any other sexual molestation with military service members shall be imprisoned not more than two years." Both consensual and non-consensual homosexual acts have been punished under Article 92(5). Under Korea's mandatory conscription system,[2] homosexual males without mental or physical deficiencies must perform military services. Thus, they are at risk of being punished during their time of service.

Although the National Human Rights Commission of Korea repeatedly recommended revising Article 92(5) for the unconstitutionality

---

1. Professor of Law, Seoul National University School of Law, Commissioner of the National Human Rights Commission of Korea 2007–2010.
2. The Military Service Act, art. 3.

of its discriminatory nature,[3] the Constitutional Court upheld its constitutionality in 2002 and 2011.[4] The goal of this article to draw international
attention to the human rights issue involving sexual minorities in Korea,
especially those in the military.

The paper begins with the review of the Korean Supreme Court's
interpretation of Article 92(5) and the two decisions rendered by the Constitutional Court of Korea. The two courts have maintained that Article
92(5) is necessary for military discipline and combat capacity and that judicial interpretation can clarify any potential ambiguities. Second, the paper
discusses legal policies and judicial decisions of major OECD countries on
homosexual acts in the military. Then, it asserts that Article 92(5) is unconstitutional because it (1) violates the right of sexual self-determination and
the privacy of military service members for the sake of national security or
military discipline; (2) is too vague in specifying the scope of punishable
conduct—for instance, it is not clear whether homosexual acts off military
bases are also punishable; and (3) is not "the less restrictive sanction" but an
overcriminalization for military discipline or combat capacity even though
administrative sanctions may be sufficient. Finally, this paper proposes (1)
an abolition of Article 92(5); (2) the use of administrative sanctions against
public homosexual activities in the military; and (3) a new provision that
punishes sexual molestation by deceit or force.

JUDICIAL INTERPRETATION OF ARTICLE 92(5)
OF THE KOREAN MILITARY PENAL CODE

Definition of the Crime

Article 92(5) of the Korean Military Penal Code criminalizes "kyekan or
any other sexual molestation between military service members." "Kyekan"
literally means "chicken copulation." It does not exactly mean sodomy. In
a social context, kyekan is interpreted as homosexual behaviors between

3.   Recommendation of the National Human Rights Commission of Korea, Dec.
8, 2010.

4.   Korean Constitutional Court [Const. Ct.], June 27, 2002 (2001Hun-Ba70);
(Mar. 31, 2011) 2008Hun-Ka21.

males. On the other hand, the Supreme Court of Korea defines it as "anal copulation,"[5] while the Ministry of Defense interprets the word to include homosexual acts between humans, as well as sexual intercourses with animals.[6] The Court defines "any other sexual molestation" as "sexual behaviors that do not fall under *kyekan* but rouse repugnance in the general public and offend the good sense of sexual morality, as well as infringe upon the sound life of the military community and its discipline."[7] "Any other sexual molestation" has been interpreted to cover oral sex and touching of another's genitals.[8]

In brief, Article 92(5) aims to punish anal sex and other non-penile/vaginal copulation-like acts, especially between male military servicemen. Henceforth, "sodomy" is used, short for "kyekan or any other sexual molestation between military service members."

Nonconsensual sodomy by force or threats between military service members warrant punishment under Articles 92(1) and 92(3) of the Military Penal Code. Thus, Article 92(5) aims to punish consensual sodomy in the military. The Supreme Court of Korea held that Article 92(5) does not apply to sodomy between a military service member and a civilian.[9] Moreover, Article 92(5) fails to prescribe specific locations of punishable sodomy. Hence, there is a possibility that it may be interpreted to apply to not only sodomy committed on a military base but also to acts committed off base. Additionally, the Article does not require sodomy to be open and notorious. Therefore, military service members' private acts of sodomy behind closed doors may also be punished.

5.   Decision of May 29, 2008 (2008Do2222) (Korean Supreme Court).

6.   Ministry of Defense Human Rights Team, "A Study of Management Policy of Homosexuals in the Military" (December 2007), 46; Legal Division of Army Headquarter, "Commentary of Military Penal Code" (2010), 383.

7.   Decision of May 29, 2008 (2008Do2222) (Korean Supreme Court).

8.   Lee Kyong-Hwan, "Punishment of Homosexual Behaviors in the Military," *Public Interests and Human Rights* 5 (2008), 67–68.

9.   Decision of September 25, 1973 (73Do1915) (Korean Supreme Court).

The Constitutional Court of Korea: Deference to the Legislative Choice or Maintaining Military Discipline

The Constitutional Court upheld the constitutionality of Article 92(5) in 2002 and 2011.

The Principle of *Lex Certa*

The majority opinion of the Constitutional Court held that Article 92(5) does not violate the principle of *lex certa*. The principle of *lex certa* requires that the criminal law define offenses and punishments in a strict and unambiguous way. It is the equivalent of the "void for vagueness" doctrine of the common law.[10] The majority concluded that the Article at issue was adequately clear, given the technicality of legislative drafting. It further stated that its judgment provided specific guidelines for interpreting prohibited behaviors and eliminated concerns about arbitrary enforcement of the statute.

Meanwhile, the dissenting opinion of the Constitutional Court in the 2002 decision argued that the Article violated the principle of *lex certa* because it failed to clarify the elements of the criminal offense. For example, the Article neither imposes any limitation on the subject or the counterpart of sexual molestation nor considers the presence of coercion in the molestation.[11]

The dissenting opinion of the Constitutional Court in its 2011 decision noted that irrational results may follow when despite the remarkable difference between non-coercive sodomy and coercive sodomy in protected legal interests, degree of illegality, and blameworthiness, they are both punished under the same provision. The court also criticized the lack of a clear standard in determining "any other sexual molestation," and ambiguity over whether the provision applied exclusively to molestation committed within the military.[12]

---

10. *Connally v. General Construction Company*, 269 U.S. 385 (1926).

11. Decision of June 27, 2002 (2001Hun-Ba70) (Korean Constitutional Court) (Song In-Joon, J., Joo Sun-Hoe, J., dissenting).

12. Decision of March 31, 2011 (2008Hun-Ka21) (Korean Constitutional Court) (Kim Jong-Dae, J., Mok Young-Dae, J., Song Doo-Hwan, J., dissenting).

The Principle of Prohibition Against Excessive Restriction

The majority of the Constitutional Court also held that Article 92(5) did not violate the principle of prohibition against excessive restriction, which requires criminal law to be *prima ratio*, not *ultima ratio*, for social control.

First, the majority reasoned that Article 92(5) did not violate the balance of legal interests because the degree of restriction imposed on the military service members' privacy cannot supersede national security, a prerequisite for national existence and freedom, as well as the protection of military discipline and a sound military community.[13] Second, the majority maintained that the Article did not violate the principle of least restrictive sanctions given the following factors: (1) simple administrative sanction alone is insufficient to effectively regulate sodomy in the military under Korea's national security situation and its conscription system; (2) the statutory punishment is not excessive compared to that of other sexual molestation crimes; and (3) probation may be imposed on a case-by-case basis because the term of the statutory punishment is less than a year.[14] Lastly, the majority held that the mere failure to specifically characterize types of indecent acts or the extent of damages, as well as proscribing all sexual molestation that infringes upon the public interest to be punishable for less than one year, did not suggest that the legislature had arbitrarily wielded its discretionary power.[15]

On the other hand, the dissenting opinion of the 2002 decision argued that in cases where sexual molestation lacks coercion and such molestation occurs in private and does not directly harms others, it is hard to determine exactly what kind of legal interest has been violated.[16] Thus, in such situations, the provision exceeded the degree of regulation necessary to achieve the legislative purpose of preserving military combat power.

Violation of the Right to Equality

The majority of the Constitutional Court held that Article 92(5) did not violate the right to equality guaranteed under Article 11(1) of the Consti-

---

13.   Decision of March 31, 2011 (2008Hun-Ka21) (Korean Constitutional Court).

14.   Ibid.

15.   Decision of June 27, 2002 (2001Hun-Ba70) (Korean Constitutional Court).

16.   Decision of June 27, 2002 (2001Hun-Ba70) (Korean Constitutional Court) (Song In-Joon, J., Joo Sun-Hoe, J., dissenting).

tution of Korea. They reasoned that allowing sodomy within the military could directly injure military combat effectiveness because the military involves a significantly higher likelihood of deviant sexual behaviors between men and a higher possibility that superiors may carry out homosexual acts against subordinates.[17] Hence, the majority decided that the provision did not infringe upon the rights of homosexuals even if it only criminalized same-sex sexual acts because there was a rational reason for such discrimination. They also concluded that Article 11(1) of the Constitution of Korea did not protect against discrimination on the basis of sexual orientation as it only protected discrimination based on "sex, religion, or social status." The dissenting opinion did not comment on this issue.

Legislative and Administrative Efforts to Revise Article 92(5)

Legislative Efforts to Revise the Article

Korea's Military Penal Code has been amended several times since it was enacted in 1962 but its punishment of consensual sodomy has not changed. Discussions to revise the Penal Code gradually developed after democratization when interest in the rights of sexual minorities grew, and with the enactment of the National Human Rights Commission Act of 2001 that regulates discrimination based on sexual orientation.[18]

An amendment to the Military Penal Code proposed by legislator Lee Kyung-Jae in 2004, stipulated that a person who uses hierarchy or force to sexually molest a military serviceperson or an equivalent in a military fortress, camp, or a ship or an aircraft or any other places, facilities, or structures built for military purposes shall be imprisoned not more than 5 years. It removed the term "sodomy," narrowed the scope of punishable behaviors to molestations using hierarchy or force, and limited places where such molestations take place. The proposal seems to reflect the suggestions of the dissenting opinion in the 2002 decision of the Constitutional Court.[19]

17.   Decision of March 31, 2011 (2008Hun-Ka21) (Korean Constitutional Court).
18.   The National Human Rights Commission Act, Art. 2 (iv).
19.   Bill No. 118, July 2, 2004 (proposed to revise the Military Penal Code).

The 2005 proposed amendment submitted by the government subdivided Article 92 into three clauses based on the manner and degree of molestation. Hence, the amended provision continued to punish sodomy or any other sexual molestation, but added monetary penalties and requirements for an aggravated punishment for molestation committed through the use of assault, threat, hierarchy, or force.[20]

In 2009, legislator Lee Joo-Young proposed an amendment that followed the framework of the proposed amendment submitted by the government in 2005 but changed the amount of the financial penalty for molestation that lack assault, threat, hierarchy, or force. This reflects the dissenting opinion of the 2002 decision of the Constitutional Court.[21] That same year, legislator Kim Ok-Ee also proposed a revision that raised the term of imprisonment for "any other sexual molestation."[22] However, all of these amendments failed to pass the National Assembly.

Response of the Ministry of National Defense— Adoption of the U.S. "Don't Ask, Don't Tell" Policy

In October 2011, the Ministry of National Defense established a "Unit Management Directive," which is a stipulated form of the 2006 "Guidelines for Supervision of Homosexual Service Members". Chapter 6 of the Directive prohibits sexual orientation surveys to include questions that help identify homosexuality, sexual experiences, details of sexual partners and other questions related to one's privacy, as well as a requirement to submit information related to one's homosexuality for the purpose of substantiating one's sexual preference. Moreover, it forbids communicating the military serviceperson's homosexuality to his or her parents, friends, and troop without his or her consent, as well as forcing homosexual soldiers to take a HIV/AIDS test or to be admitted to a hospital as a means to isolate homosexual serviceperson.[23]

---

20. Bill No. 3675, December 26, 2005 (proposed to revise the Military Penal Code).

21. Bill No. 5781, October 26, 2009 (proposed to revise the Military Penal Code).

22. Bill No. 3890, September 20, 2009 (proposed to revise the Military Penal Code).

23. Directive No. 1349 (October 11, 2011).

Although the Directive is a major step towards protecting the rights of homosexual servicepersons, it has a limitation in that it requires criminal penalties or administrative disciplinary actions under Article 92(5). The ministry's present stance is that it will not actively investigate homosexuality on base but that it will punish and impose sanctions if homosexuality is expressed through any means. This stance is a combination of the criminalization of homosexuality and the U.S. military's "Don't Ask, Don't Tell" policy, which was repealed in 2011.[24]

Consequently, as Alvin Lee points out, a homosexual Korean military serviceman is subject to an unreasonable situation: "a man who publicly announces to everyone in his unit that he is gay... evade[s] any legal recourse whereas a man who engages in a private same-sex sexual activity, which he chooses to self-report... is subject to a criminal punishment."[25]

LEGISLATION AND JUDICIAL DECISIONS OF THE MAJOR OECD COUNTRIES

European Union, Canada, and Australia— Decriminalization of Homosexuality in the Military and Allowing Homosexuals to Serve in the Military

The Treaty of Amsterdam, signed by the European Union in 1997, prohibits discrimination based on sexual orientation, and the Council of Europe agreed to prohibit discrimination on the basis of sexual orientation in Article 21 of the Charter of Fundamental Rights of the European Union.

Europe's pioneering country, The Netherlands allowed homosexuals to serve in the military as early as 1974.[26] Germany did not allow homosexuals to serve in the military as volunteers until 2000, and the Federal Administrative Court of Germany held that the decision of the Defense Minister to refuse homosexual serviceperson's request for appointment as

24.   See *infra*, text accompanying footnotes 33–38.

25.   Alvin Lee, "Assessing the Korean Military's Gay Sex Ban in the International Context," *Law and Sexuality* 19 (2010), 87–88.

26.   http://en.wikipedia.org/wiki/Sexual_orientation_and_military_service#cite_note-Bateman-31.

the sergeant was a legal exercise of personnel discretion in 1990. However, after January 2001, the Federal Ministry of Defense adopted a new standard that provided guidance on sexuality within the military and banned all types of discrimination based on sexual orientation.[27] In the United Kingdom, homosexuality within the military was decriminalized by the Criminal Justice and Public Order Act of 1994 and the policy that once prohibited military service of homosexuals was abolished in 1999[28] after a pair of decisions handed down from the European Court of Human Rights: *Lustig-Prean and Beckett v. United Kingdom*[29] and *Smith and Grady v. United Kingdom*.[30]

Canada excluded homosexuals from military service until 1988, but changed the policy to allow service but not promotions or rewards. Subsequently, the Department of National Defence abolished the discriminatory policy in 1992 after the court ruled in favor of the five servicemen who argued that the policy violated the Canadian Charter of Rights and Freedom.[31] Australia also abolished its ban on homosexual military service in 1992.[32]

The United States—
Recent Abolition of the "Don't Ask, Don't Tell" Policy

Although the Supreme Court of the United States decriminalized sodomy

27.   *Führungshilfe für Vorgesetzte*, Bd. 2, A. III. 7.

28.   Aaron Belkin and Melissa Sheridan Embser-Herbert, "The International Experience," in *The U.S. Military's "Don't Ask, Don't Tell" Policy: A Reference Handbook*, ed. Melissa Sheridan Embser-Herbert (Westport, Conn.: 2007) 72–74; Palm Center, "Gays in Foreign Militaries 2010: A Global Primer" (February 2010; http://www.palmcenter. org/files/FOREIGNMILITARIESPRIMER2010FINAL.pdf), 9–12; Lee, "Assessing the Korean Military's Gay Sex Ban," 78–80.

29.   29 Eur. H. R. 49 (1999).

30.   29 Eur. H. R. 548 (1999).

31.   Belkin and Embser-Herbert, "The International Experience," 61-62; Palm Center, "Gays in Foreign Militaries," 13–14; Lee, "Assessing the Korean Military's Gay Sex Ban," 76–77.

32.   Belkin and Embser-Herbert, "The International Experience," 68; Palm Center, "Gays in Foreign Militaries," 16–18; Lee, "Assessing the Korean Military's Gay Sex Ban," 77–78.

in the 2003 case *Lawrence v. Texas*,[33] Article 125 of the Uniform Code of Military Justice (UCMJ) adopted in 1950 continued to criminalize homosexuality between military service members. The Article, which is still effective, prohibits all "unnatural carnal copulation with another person of the same or opposite sex or with an animal." In 2004, the Court of Appeals for the Armed Forces ruled that sodomy can be constitutionally punished in *United States v. Marcum*[34] and *United States v. Stirewalt*.[35]

Against this backdrop, the Clinton administration adopted the "Don't Ask, Don't Tell" (DADT) Policy,[36] which continued in force until recently. Homosexuals were allowed to serve in the military as long as they did not publicly disclose their sexual orientation, and officials were barred from asking the sexual orientation of servicemembers. In 1998, the U.S. Court of Appeals upheld the policy, ruling that it did not violate the right to equality.[37]

However, criticism of the unconstitutionality of DADT continued. Finally in September 2010, Judge Virginia Phillips of the California District Court issued an injunction and ordered the military to suspend the DADT policy.[38] The Obama administration formally abolished the policy on September 20, 2011.[39]

33.   539 U.S. 558 (2003).

34.   60 M.J. 198 (2004).

35.   60 M.J. 297 (2004).

36.   See generally Robert I. Correales, "Don't Ask, Don't Tell: A Dying Policy on the Precipice," *California Western Law Review* 44 (2008), 413; Emily B. Hecht, "Debating the Ban: The Past, Present and Future of Don't Ask, Don't Tell," *New Jersey Law Journal* 246 (2007), 51; Lee, "Assessing the Korean Military's Gay Sex Ban," 83–84.

37.   *Able v. United States*, 155 F.3d 628 (2d Cir. 1998).

38.   *Log Cabin Republicans v. United States*, No. CV 04-08425-VAP, 2010 U.S. Dist. LEXIS 93612 (C.D. Cal. Sept. 9, 2010).

39.   See President Obama's statement: http://www.whitehouse.gov/the-press-office/2011/09/20/statement-president-repeal-dont-ask-dont-tell

The Unconstitutionality of the Crime of Sodomy

Excessive Criminalization Based on Homophobia

Article 92(5) is a product of homophobia and heterosexism. Although the provision does not explicitly limit the subject of crime to homosexuals, the legislative purpose of the Article is to punish sexual acts between homosexual military servicepersons, especially, gay servicemen. In fact, no other sexual acts have been punished under Article 92 except for consensual acts between gay military servicemen.

The Article also describes homosexual sexual activities with derogatory terms such as *kyekan*, and "molestation." The Supreme Court and the Constitutional Court also define homosexuality as an *"abnormal* act for sexual satisfaction."[40] The interpretation that the legislative intent of the Article is to protect the "sexual health of the *military family"*[41] also supports the claim that homosexuality is judged to be unhealthy. This in turn shows that the Supreme Court and the Constitutional Court distinguish between "abnormal sexual acts" and "normal sexual acts." Furthermore, the term "military family" reflects the belief that the culture of patriarchy should be manifested in the military and that patriarchy premised upon heterosexuality cannot tolerate homosexuality. In its decision reviewing the crime of adultery, two justices of the Constitutional Court wrote that "homosexuality undermines moral soundness more than adultery and is more repugnant and its moral reprehensibility is no less than that of the crime of adultery."[42]

Meanwhile, Article 92(5) purports to protect "military discipline"[43] or the military's "combat capacity"[44] but it is difficult to determine that consensual homosexual activities performed in private will hurt military

40. Decision of September 25, 1973 (73Do1975) (Korean Supreme Court); Decision of June 27, 2002 (2001Hun Ba 70) (Korean Constitutional Court) (italics inserted).

41. Decision of September 25, 1973 (73Do1975) (Korean Supreme Court) (italics inserted).

42. Decision of September 10, 1990 (89Hun-Ma82) (Korean Constitutional Court) (Han Byoung-Chae, J., Lee Si-Yoon, J., dissenting).

43. Decision of March 31, 2011 (2008Hun-Ka21) (Korean Constitutional Court).

44. Decision of June 27, 2002 (2001Hun-Ba70) (Korean Constitutional Court).

discipline or combat capacity. In fact, many defendants punished for homosexuality were recognized for integrity and fine performance in the military before their consensual homosexual acts were discovered. And there is no study that shows that major OECD countries that allow homosexuals to serve in the military have weakened military discipline or capacity.[45]

The underlying concern of Article 92(5)—the possibility of a gay serviceman sexually assaulting another serviceman within the military—is a form of homophobia. However, this cannot be the true rationale for the Article. First, such sexual assaults can be punished by other provisions. And there are no cases of sexual violence committed by a gay serviceman against another serviceman in the military according to research conducted by the National Human Rights Commission in 2003.[46] As pointed out in the 2010 decision of the National Human Rights Commission, "the essence of sexual violence between men within the military results from the exercise of hierarchy and power and less so from an uncontrollable sexual drive of the gay servicemen."[47]

Violation of the Right to Sexual Self-Determination, the Right to Equality, and Privacy

Article 92(5) imposes restrictions that are excessive and extensive. It violates the soldiers' right to sexual self-determination, which grants a person the right to choose whether or not to engage in sexual activity and with whom. The Article insists on a single method of sexual intercourse by criminalizing other means, such as oral or anal intercourse. Because it does not limit the place of conduct, there is a possibility that intercourse performed off base may also be punished.

Article 92(5) also violates the right to equality. Although the Article is not written in a manner that punishes a person based on his/her sexual orientation, it has been applied exclusively to sodomy between gay servicemen. The military law enforcement authority has never investigated and

---

45. Palm Center, "Gays in Foreign Militaries," 24–103.

46. National Human Rights Commission of Korea, "Survey of Sexual Violence in the Military" (2004), 5.

47. National Human Rights Commission of Korea, "Recommendation of December 8, 2010," 5.

prosecuted cases that involve consensual sodomy between male and female service members.

Although the freedom and privacy of personal life guaranteed under Article 17 of the Constitution may be restricted due to the nature of the military's mission and organization, such restrictions should not extend without limits in. But Article 92(5) is extremely intrusive by punishing all conduct regardless of its time, place, and operational relevance. For instance, service members' private sex life that takes place during the holidays or after work for full-time reserve officers should be constitutionally protected.

However, the majority opinion of the Constitutional Court concluded that discrimination based on sexuality is not an area that requires special constitutional protection. They supported this claim by pointing out that sexual orientation is not mentioned in Article 11(1) of the Constitution, which specifically prohibits discrimination based on "sex, religion or social status." But it is hard to accept this rationale. The provisions of Article 11(1) should be interpreted as examples of discrimination, not as an exhaustive list of the types of discrimination prohibited under the Article. Article 2 of the National Human Rights Commission Act and international human rights law prohibit discrimination based on sexual orientation, so quasi-constitutional laws are necessary to protect the equality of homosexual service members.[48] Moreover, there should be a stringent screening measures to review whether certain discrimination infringes upon the homosexuals' right to equality.

Violation of the Lex Certa Principle

As the dissenting opinion indicated in the two decisions of the Constitutional Court,[49] Article 92(5) fails to impose any limitation on punishable molestation such as the presence of coercion, the identity of the counter-

48. The National Human Rights Commission Act, Art. 2 (iv); Lee, "Assessing the Korean Military's Gay Sex Ban," 88–92.

49. Decision of June 27, 2002 (2001Hun-Ba70) (Korean Constitutional Court) (Song In-Joon, J., Joo Sun-Hoe, J., dissenting); Decision of March 31, 2011 (2008Hun-Ka21) (Korean Constitutional Court) (Kim Jong-Dae, J., Mok Young-Dae, J., Song Doo-Hwan, J., dissenting).

part, or the place of conduct. Though the Supreme Court has decided that the provision does not apply to sexual activities between a military service member and a civilian, there are still many questions to be answered to clarify the statute and its reach.

If the wording of Article 92(5) were deemed to answer all these questions, as the Supreme Court's ruling attempts to do, the Article's scope of application would still extend to a level of "blanketstrafgesetz" where supplement legal specification is needed for enforcement. This would seriously infringe fundamental rights. In conclusion, the Supreme Court's guideline for interpretation of the elements of Article 92(5) cannot resolve these ambiguities and should be held unconstitutional.

CONCLUSION

The justifiability of criminalizing consensual homosexuality between military service members is the key issue of the paper. Though Article 92(5) of the Military Penal Code does not punish a particular sexual orientation on its face, in practice it is used as a means to punish homosexual military service members.

In July 2009, the Immigration and Refugee Board of Canada (IRB) recognized a gay Korean man who objected to South Korea's mandatory military service as a refugee on the likelihood that he would be mistreated and abused in the military.[50] If homosexual military service members continue to be criminalized in Korea, such embarrassing occurrences will persist. To eliminate discrimination based on sexual orientation in the military, Article 92(5) should be abolished. Coercive sodomy and other sexual molestations can be regulated by other criminal laws and consensual homosexual acts that hurt the communal life of the military can be punished by administrative sanctions. Homosexual activities that take place outside the military base should not only be decriminalized but also exempted from administrative sanctions since there is no relationship between those activities and the weakening of military discipline or combat capacity.

50.   http://www.koreatimes.co.kr/www/news/nation/2011/12/286_100898.html

In addition to decriminalizing consensual homosexuality in the military, the requirement of a victim's complaint under Article 92(8) of the Korean Military Penal Code should be abolished.[51] According to the Article, crimes of sexual violence, such as rape and sexual molestation, can be punished only if the victim files a complaint. The rationale for such requirement is to protect the victim's privacy and dignity. However, this has been criticized for actually producing negative effects of concealing and encouraging sexual violence. Thus, abolishing such a requirement would satisfy the need to intensify the punishment of military sexual violence, as well as respect the sexual self-determination of the military service members.

The National Assembly, the Supreme Court, and the Constitutional Court should seriously consider and accept the recommendations made by the National Human Rights Commission and the policy changes adopted by OECD countries given that human rights issues of homosexuals and social minorities are now politicized. If the "Unit Management Directive" aiming to protect the rights of homosexual service members is to have any meaning, Article 92(5) must first be abolished. Otherwise, homosexual service members will leave Korea for fear of discrimination and the world will observe the backwardness of human rights protection in Korea. Homosexuality should be decriminalized in the military as a matter of principle and the elements of Article 92(5) should be amended to criminalize only sexual molestation due to hierarchy or power.

51. Regarding the requirement in the Korean Penal Code, see Kuk Cho, "The Under-Protection of Women Under Korean Criminal Law," *Columbia Journal of Asian Law* 22 (2008), 129–130.

Mergers and Acquisitions in the Corporate Reorganization Procedures of Korea

Jaewan Park[1]

INTRODUCTION

Features of M&A in Corporate Reorganization Procedures of Korea

Korea's bankruptcy regime was established as early as the 1960s, but the theory and practice of bankruptcy procedure developed in earnest only after the Asian Financial Crisis in the late 1990s. In particular, many programs were developed for a quick and efficient proceeding to tackle the rapid increase in the number of bankruptcy cases when the Company Reorganization Procedure Act, the predecessor of the current Debtor Rehabilitation and Bankruptcy Act (hereinafter "Unified Insolvency Act"), was in effect.[2] Among various options, adopting mergers and acquisitions (hereinafter "M&A") in reorganization proceedings became a conventional practice.

The objective of this article is to introduce the practice of M&A in Korean bankruptcy procedures. The terminology used in this article will mainly come from the former Company Reorganization Act since most of the practical examples and case law discussed below were formed in connection with the Act by the Bankruptcy Division of the Seoul Central Dis-

---

1. Professor of Law, Hanyang University.

2. The Company Reorganization Act, Insolvency Act, and the Composition Act are also referred to as the Three Former Insolvency Acts.

trict Court prior to the enactment of the current Unified Insolvency Act. The terminology may also be applied in the discussion of rehabilitation procedures, except in extraordinary cases.

The Bankruptcy Division of the Seoul Central District Court started adopting M&A in company reorganization proceedings in 2000. According to the Court's M&A records, there were 2 cases in 2000, 14 cases in 2001, 19 cases in 2002, 8 cases in 2003, 14 cases in 2004, and 6 cases in 2005.[3]

The first feature of M&A in company reorganization is that the contents tend to be more formal and seller-centered compared to ordinary mergers. While retaining the basic framework of ordinary mergers with regard to agreements and deal structure, M&A in company reorganization does not adopt many of the financing and funding techniques utilized in ordinary M&As. This peculiar feature results from the need to preserve the consistency of the court, which oversees multiple merging companies concurrently. However, some criticize such a feature as too rigid and unfavorable to the acquiror. The second characteristic is that most mergers accompany revisions of the reorganization program through meetings of interested parties.

The incentive of different parties to a M&A in a reorganization proceeding is as follows. The primary motivation of the court or the company undergoing reorganization is to complete the reorganization program. Though numerous companies initiated reorganization proceedings after the Asian Financial Crisis, most of them failed to meet the business goals agreed upon in the reorganization plan. Hence, most of these companies were on the brink of having their reorganization proceedings abolished if the reorganization plans were to be executed as agreed. Injection of new funds was necessary to prevent a large-scale abolition of corporate reorganization proceedings and M&A was virtually the only option.

On the other hand, there are many incentives from an acquiror's standpoint. Some use M&A to gain synergies while others seek capital gains. Others employ M&A to re-acquire companies that they had once owned. These are all common motives for both ordinary companies and companies undergoing reorganization. But the main difference between

3. The Seoul Central District Court, Bankruptcy Division, Association for Research, *Practices of Corporate Rehabilitation*, vol. 2 (Seoul: 2006), 156.

the two is that it is impossible to eliminate all possibility of residual liabilities when acquiring a distressed company in need of reorganization. There were once other factors that made companies in need of reorganization a highly appealing takeover target. But these factors have largely been mitigated or eliminated. One such example would be tax benefits from taking over distressed companies.

Overview of the Process

Time Frame
M&A for companies undergoing reorganization takes at least six months to over one year in some cases.

Process
The table below illustrates the overall flow of the M&A process.4 Because most revisions to reorganization programs in M&A happen through interested persons' meetings, the table features a process premised on such meetings.

PRE-MERGER PREPARATION PHASE

During the preparation stage, important matters include the decision to pursue an M&A, selecting the managing underwriter, and choosing the structure of the deal.

Decision on Merger

This section explores the timing and issues that decision-makers face when evaluating M&A opportunities.

Timing
The decision to pursue M&A can happen either before obtaining the reorganization approval or after obtaining one.

---

4. Hyungjoon Park, "Practice and Prospects for M&A of Companies in Receivership," *Sabop Nonjip* 44 (2004), partial modification of the Table on page 577.

Table 1	
M&A Preparation Stage	**Identify M&A opportunity** Select the managing underwriter Conduct due diligence and decide on the basic structure of the deal
Selection of an Acquiror	**Make a public announcement of M&A** Set a selection criteria for preferred bidder Accept bids Select a preferred bidder Sign MOU (Memorandum of Understanding) Preferred bidder conducts due diligence Adjust the acquisition price Sign the merger agreement
Issuance of New Shares and Payment of Debts	**Draft a proposal for revising the corporate reorganization program** Deposit the acquisition price Meetings with interested persons Attain approval of the proposed revision Implement steps: (1) paid-in capital increase (reduction of capital); (2) safeguard deposit; and (3) purchase of corporate bonds Payment of debts
Post-merger Procedure	Acquiror restructures the executive board and conducts due diligence Closing

Pursuing M&A After Obtaining Approval. The ordinary M&A transaction occurs after obtaining approval. From the late 1990s to the early 2000s, the Company Reorganization Act was revised to emphasize the expediency of reorganization proceedings. As a result, the principal problem seemed to be time pressure to pursue an M&A prior to attaining an approval for the reorganization plan. However, one of the key reasons why an M&A transaction usually occurs after approval is because companies in need of reorganization are not popular for sale in the first place and, as a result, have low success rates.

In practice, there are two main issues when pursuing an M&A after obtaining reorganization approval: (1) whether it is possible to pursue an M&A when reorganization is being executed as planned; and (2) whether it is possible to pursue an M&A when there is a substantial risk to the enterprise value of the company undergoing reorganization.

First, there are instances where existing shareholders oppose an M&A when the reorganization program is being carried out as arranged. Conventionally, reorganization programs are revised while pursuing M&As, but exigent circumstances must arise as a prerequisite for a revision. The existing shareholders can assert that the company should not pursue the M&A because there are no exigent circumstances. Ultimately, the existing shareholders are demanding control upon closing of the reorganization proceeding by pushing through the original plan.

However, such demands of the existing shareholders are rarely accepted in practice.[5] Some view such demands as infringing upon the rights of the existing shareholders.[6] The above scenario is less likely to be problematic today because the current practice is changing to promptly close the reorganization proceeding after obtaining an approval.[7]

The Unified Insolvency Act adopted a "debtor-in-possession" ("DIP") system that appoints an incumbent manager of the debtor company to continue as the manager.[8] Hence, it was possible that an M&A, which necessarily accomplishes a change in management, would conflict with the DIP system. In response, the Bankruptcy Division of the Seoul Central District

---

5. M&A and change of right are two separate issues and as long as M&A is specified in the reorganization plan, managers can pursue M&A. Since revisions to reorganization program arise from further reduction of the rights of interested persons resulting from pursuing M&A, one can say that the exigent circumstance requirement has been met. For more details, refer to Jaewan Park, "Recent Cases and Examples in the Insolvency Field," *Human Rights and Justice* 383 (2008), 43–44.

6. See Soogeun Oh, "Shareholders' Rights in Reorganization Plan," *Commercial Cases Review* (2007), 651.

7. Chung, Chuneyoung, "New Paradigm for Corporate Rehabilitation Procedure," *Jurisprudence* [Jurisdiction Development Foundation] 18 (2011), 7, 41–42.

8. This reflects the assertions that DIP system needs to be adopted.

Court revised the regulations so that an M&A may be pursued after determining the viability of the company if an incumbent manager continues in office.[9] Today, a 1–2 year grace period is granted to companies that adopt the DIP system.

For cases where there is a substantial risk to the enterprise value of the distressed company, M&A is virtually not an option because it is difficult to determine an acquisition price. This can also prevent a decision on closing. Generally, now, the indeterminacy of the enterprise value is no longer an issue upon attaining an approval for corporate reorganization.

Pursuing M&A Prior to Obtaining an Approval. There are rare cases where an M&A is pursued before attaining an approval for the reorganization program since most proposals for reorganization are not approved until they can be executed with additional funding. When additional funding is necessary for reorganization, pursuing M&A prior to obtaining approval becomes unavoidable. However, M&A may be an option if the company is unusually popular for sale.[10]

Decision-Makers

The decision-makers for an M&A include the management, the court, and a committee of directors. Since the management of the debtor company has the right to manage and control the bankrupt company, the management also decides whether to pursue an M&A or not. There is a tendency not to pursue an M&A in the initial phase of bankruptcy. The management is expected to be more apathetic to an M&A where the incumbent manager is appointed to continue as the representative under the Unified Insolvency Act.

Courts also make decisions regarding M&A's given their roles as supervisors of the management. The M&A process may be slowed down because the workload for the presiding judge in an M&A case is substantial. It is difficult for one judge to oversee three or more M&A cases at once.

The management is in charge of the details of the reorganization proceeding as well as the M&A transaction. The approach to pursuing M&A may vary across different management teams.

9. *Practices of Corporate Rehabilitation*, vol. 2, 170–71.
10. Jinro case, Dong Ah Construction case

Managing Underwriter

In this section, we will look at the selection and the role of the underwriter. Except in rare cases, most M&A deals involve a nominated underwriter. The selection of the underwriter begins when the management receives the court's approval. It does not ordinarily involve public bidding.

Usually, an underwriter is chosen from accounting firms, M&A teams in financial institutions, credit rating agencies, and companies specializing in corporate restructuring. There are some instances where an accounting firm and a law firm have become co-underwriters.

The underwriter is in charge of almost every aspect of the M&A transaction, including major responsibilities like valuation, strategic planning, drafting cover letters, drawing investing interests, and negotiating with creditors for debt adjustments. For valuation, the underwriter calculates the liquidation value and the going concern value but does not ordinarily conduct full-scale due diligence.

Provisions regarding selection criteria and compensation for underwriters are found in the M&A standards of the Bankruptcy Division of the Seoul Central District Court.

Structuring the Deal

Approach

An M&A usually takes the form of issuing new shares to third parties but it can also take the form of a business transfer or a spin-off. The greatest advantage of a third-party acquisition includes the possibility of terminating the company's operations during the reorganization proceeding or ensuring a smooth transition.

However, an M&A deal may take the form of a business transfer or a spin-off when (a) the company has multiple business lines and only some of them can be sold; or (b) it has multiple business lines that can be sold but each line is seeking different suitors; or (c) it must carry on its operations because of pending lawsuit or contingent liabilities.[11] Though choosing between a business transfer and a split-off depends on the acquiror's prefer-

---

11. *Practices of Corporate Rehabilitation*, vol. 2, 159–60.

ence or the condition of the distressed company, a spin-off is suitable when a transfer of operations is needed.[12]

When acquiring an insolvent construction company rather than one undergoing reorganization, issues such as the transfer of operation and license reinstatement become critical. There are instances where both are transferred to the acquiror as a matter of practice. Though it is theoretically difficult to explain why this is so with consistency, not all licenses are reinstated in practice. Only licenses that have been invalidated because of law are reinstated. Those that have been invalidated due to administrative penalties are not reinstated.[13]

Determining the Need for an Interested Persons' Meeting
Prior to pursuing an M&A, one must assess whether additional changes to rights in secured claims, unsecured claims, and stock are necessary. A meeting of interested persons must be held when additional changes to these rights are desired.

When the proceeds from the sale of corporate assets are not sufficient to pay off secured and unsecured claims, additional changes to rights are needed. Even when the proceeds are adequate to cover the claims, an interested persons' meeting is needed when (a) the value of shares are reduced to secure an adequate equity ratio for the acquiror, or (b) authorized capital stock needs to be increased.

When an interested persons' meeting is needed to make additional changes to rights, one must consider negotiations between creditors and shareholders. If additional changes are not necessary, one must still review the possibility of issuing new shares and transferring business through the approval of the court.

Paid-in Capital
In the case of a third-party acquisition, parts of the sale proceeds go to paid-in capital and the rest go to corporate bond takeover payments. The Bankruptcy Division of the Seoul Central District Court stipulated a 50:50 ratio for M&A transaction involving companies undergoing reorganization, which led to considerable criticism. Though the court continues to

---

12. Ibid., vol. 1, 563.
13. Dong Ah Construction, Hanyang case.

follow the principle, it takes criticism into consideration by granting extra points to instances where the paid-in capital composes more than 50% of the proceeds and deduct points when the rate falls below 50%. If the rate falls below a certain percentage, the reorganization program is eliminated. However, there have been atypical instances where the court lowered the rate to accommodate the special position of the distressed companies.[14]

Issuance at Par Value and Issuance at a Premium

Management should evaluate whether to raise capital by issuing stock at par value or at a premium. Issuance at a premium should take place when the price of shares of a listed company undergoing reorganization exceeds par value and its financial structure and business performances are good. Issuance at a premium provides preferential treatment to the acquiror. Moreover, the influx of net worth in excess of par value can be used to build up the company's financial structure and to balance out the value of the shares owned by existing shareholders. However, the management must prudently examine whether to issue stock at a premium or not and at what price because it is difficult to determine the appropriate premium. Also, there is a chance of a price decline due to the increase in uncertainty and risks post-acquisition.

Availability of LBO

Though there are requests to use LBOs ("Leveraged Buyouts"), they are not used in practice.[15] In some instances, a buyer pledges the company's assets as collateral to recover his acquisition costs at the end of the proceeding. Courts are suspicious when a buyer has committed to such collateral arrangements in advance to finance the acquisition.

BUYER SELECTION PROCESS

In this section, we will examine the selection criteria for a preferred bidder, adjustment of the acquisition price, and the formal agreement.

---

14.   *Practices of Corporate Rehabilitation*, vol. 2, 176–79.
15.   Park, "Practice and Prospects for M&A," 629–30.

Procedure

The typical buyer selection process is illustrated in the table below. This is the basic procedure for a public sale. The important components include deciding on the selection criteria for a preferred bidder, setting the acquisition price, and entering into a formal contract.

Key Stages	Note
M&A public announcement	Interested buyers conduct preliminary due diligence in data room. Going concern value and liquidation value not disclosed.
Deciding on the criteria to select a preferred bidder	
Bidding proposal received	
Selection of the preferred bidder	
Signing of MOU (Memorandum of Understanding)	Payment of 5% of the expected acquisition price
Due diligence of the preferred bidder	
Adjustment of the acquisition price	
Signing of the formal agreement	Payment of 10% of the expected acquisition price (including the above 5%)

Selection Criteria for a Preferred Bidder

General Issues in Deciding on the Criteria to Select a Preferred Bidder[16]
The criteria for selecting a preferred bidder can be divided into quantitative and qualitative indicators. The former include the acquisition price, the

16.   For details, see Park, "Practice and Prospects for M&A," 608–12; see also *Practices of Corporate Rehabilitation*, vol. 2, 179–80.

price ratio, and the financing of corporate bonds, while the latter include the ability to fund the acquisition price, the will and ability to develop the company and manage the enterprise upon acquisition, the financial soundness of the owners, and job security for employees.

In general, the scores for the price and financial composition of the acquisition comprise about 70% of the total evaluation score. In general, the scaled score is calculated by first evaluating the scores based on the price and then adjusting the score based on the proportion of paid-in capital.

When considering the conditions for financing corporate bonds, the interest rate is the most important factor. The lower the interest burden, the higher the score. The interest burden is a separate evaluation item from the size of the acquisition price. Occasionally, there are requests that repayment before maturity be made available as a condition for financing corporate bonds. But such requests are not granted in practice. On the other hand, a request to allow a conversion privilege is usually approved.

In the end, the ability to finance the acquisition becomes a matter of evidence. Submission of proof of cash and certificates of deposit, a portfolio of marketable securities, and a letter of commitment (excluding any restricted amounts) is evaluated to determine the bidder's actual ability to finance the promised amount. However, scores will be deducted for loan letters with restrictions or those that are contingent upon some other conditions or an approval from financial institutions.

The bidder's potential to run the enterprise as a responsible manager and to grow the company is another important consideration to ensure rehabilitation and sustainability of the company. Courts will consider factors such as whether the bidding company is engaged in the same or similar line of business as the target company, whether the bidding company has a long-term growth strategy, the bidder's financial soundness, debt-to-equity ratio, and interest coverage ratio[17] Though it is ideal to stress these items over the acquisition price, the latter is weighed more heavily when the funds are expected to be insufficient to repay all debts in the reorganization proceeding.

17.   When the acquiror is a consortium, the representative of the consortium is considered important in the M&A. For instance, the representative of the consortium cannot be changed though the members of the consortium may be changed within a certain range. Moreover, the representative's share may not be lower than a certain rate.

Priority Right of Existing Shareholders in the Selection Process
According to Korean commercial law, existing shareholders have priority in purchasing new shares of the reorganizing company. Likewise, some existing shareholders claim that they are entitled to priority as bidders in the selection process for bidders for an M&A with the reorganizing company. However, there is no legal basis for such a claim. There are express provisions recognizing the allocation of new shares to third parties and these provisions do not recognize the preferential status of the existing shareholders under both the Company Reorganization Act and the Unified Insolvency Act.[18] In practice, such requests are not granted.

Adjustment of the Acquisition Price

After the preferred bidder is selected and a memorandum of understanding ("MOU") is signed, the preferred bidder will conduct due diligence for two weeks to about one month. Due diligence begins at the start of the underwriter's accounting period; any changes after the start date are not taken into consideration. During due diligence, the focus is on whether the underwriter made any substantial and evident error in its evaluation.

Any adjustment of the acquisition price after the due diligence phase must follow the terms set forth in the MOU. According to the conventional MOU used for the M&As of distressed companies, the parties may request an adjustment within a 5% range of the acquisition price when the preferred bidder finds an error that is greater than 5% of the acquisition price in the underwriter's evaluation. In no case can the parties request an adjustment outside the 5% range. There are many instances where parties spend a great deal of time adjusting the acquisition price in M&A proceedings.

The Agreement

In the formal agreement, most important M&A issues—such as the acquisition price and the structure of the deal, deposit and seizure, time and method of payment, procedure for revision of reorganization program,

---

18.   Daejeon District Court [Dist. Ct.], Apr. 13, 2007 (2007Ga-Hap327),; Supreme Court, May 9, 2008, (2007Geu127); see also Park, "Recent Cases and Examples in the Insolvency Field," 43.

debt payment, delegation of task force and the closing period—are substantiated.

Regarding deposit and seizure, the buyer ordinarily pays 10% of the acquisition price as a deposit in addition to the amount already paid when selected as the preferred bidder. In general, the deposit is seized as a penalty if the buyer breaches the contract.

The time of payment is another important factor. As a principle, all payments prior to the interested persons' meeting must be paid in cash. In some cases, the delay in payment pushes back the timing of the meeting. Though rare, there are also instances where payments are made after receiving a letter of commitment based on the non-cash balance and a meeting, but before attaining a formal approval.[19]

It is common for the formal agreement to omit information on the acquiror's share of the reorganized company upon the closing of the M&A. The acquiror's share is closely related to the capital reduction rate of stock fixed during the drafting of the proposal for the reorganization plan. Demands for the share differ depending on the acquiror. Some seek 100% while others demand a special quorum resolution, and some want more than 50%. In practice, most of the acquiror's demands are granted but a retirement of 100% of the existing shares is not allowed. However, there were instances where the acquiror's share was predetermined. In theory, setting the share in the early stages of M&A seems valid because the acquiror sets the acquisition price based on the enterprise value, as well as his own share ratio.[20]

ISSUANCE OF NEW SHARES, PAYMENT OF DEBTS

In this section, we will divide the analysis into instances where an interested persons' meeting is needed and instances where it is not.

---

19.   Tongil Heavy Industries Co. and Ilsung Construction cases; *Practices of Corporate Rehabilitation*, vol. 2, 186.

20.   Park, "Practice and Prospects for M&A," 592–93.

Instances that Do and Do not Require an Interested Persons' Meeting

General

An interested persons' meeting is necessary when the revision of the reorganization plan would adversely affect the interested parties. Such a meeting is required when an additional change of right is needed. There is no adverse effect if the total sum of secured claims and unsecured claims can be paid in full and no additional change of right is needed. But when there is an adverse effect to the secured claims and unsecured claims, even more adverse changes must be made to stocks pursuant to the doctrine of equitable treatment.

In practice, a reduction of stock is presumed to cause adverse effects. On the other hand, dilution of control as a result of the issuance of new shares to third parties is not considered an adverse effect. Rather, this is seen as the intended result of the original reorganization plan.[21] But if the original arrangement did not plan for the M&A, then it is presumed to be an unfavorable effect.

When an interested persons' meeting is determined to be necessary, the management must review whether existing shareholders should also be given voting rights. It must identify whether negotiations with shareholders in addition to those with creditors are also needed. Voting rights are granted to shareholders when the company's assets exceed liabilities. In determining whether assets exceed liabilities or vice versa, the debt-to-equity swap becomes the key issue.

Claims to Be Swapped into Equity

There are some examples of reorganization proceedings where the debt-to-equity swap transaction was not effective immediately upon approval for various reasons. Some transactions also became effective only after considerable time. The bonds that are to convert into stock after the scheduled future debt-to-equity swap are known as claims to be swapped into equity (hereinafter "CSE").

---

21.   In cases where additional changes of right to shareholders are necessary, reduction must be conducted even if the control ratio of the existing shareholders is sufficiently reduced by issuing new shares to avoid the dispute on whether there was additional change of right to shareholders or not.

The critical issue turns on whether the CSE is debt or equity. Though CSE is debt in form, it is equity in substance, and this difference creates a problem.[22] In the past, CSE was treated as a claim-debt based on the emphasis on formality. Since then, M&A has been used actively in the reorganization proceeding. The distortion of voting rights due to the CSE is now highlighted to allow for review of the CSE's nature and treatment.

Current practice treats CSE as a claim security but it is not added to the amount of debt when comparing assets with the debts of a company undergoing reorganization.[23] This is because the debt-to-equity swap is not yet in effect. Theoretically, it is reasonable to consider CSE as a debt security. Moreover, the bondholders lack the authority to actually demand the payment of the sum regardless of the value of the bonds.[24]

Instances that Do Not Require an Interested Persons' Meeting

The process that omits the interested persons' meeting is quite simple. The major steps include the repayment of the full amount of secured claims and unsecured claims with the acquisition price and the issuance of new shares.

Payment of Debts

In theory, it is possible for the court to terminate the corporate reorganization proceeding without payment of debts if the existing debt is to be repaid without any obstacles. However, all liabilities must be paid before the closing of the reorganization proceeding because it is proper to have all existing liabilities paid, if possible.

In paying off debt prior to the due date, the discount rate and the advantages of paying early become key issues. In practice, there is no real problem in regard to profit because usually a provision stipulates that "reimbursement may proceed upon attaining the court's approval prior to the due date for payment." But without such a provision, the consent of the creditors must be obtained. Because the discount rate is not fixed for corporate reorganization plans, this rate must be determined through negotiations

---

22. This is commonly treated as a capital account for accounting purposes.

23. Jaejung Lee, "M&A in Corporate Reorganization Proceeding," *Human Rights and Justice* 352 (2005), 80; Il Shin Stone Co. case.

24. For details, see Park, "Practice and Prospects for M&A," 45–46.

between creditors and the companies undergoing the reorganization.[25]

Issuance of New Shares

New shares may be issued upon the court's approval. Reorganization plans drafted with an M&A option may grant authority to the management to approve increases in paid-in capital, as well as increases in authorized capital stock if necessary to execute the M&A. Moreover, the reduction of the number of existing shares and the size of the debt-to-equity swap must be set at a level that would not impede the future M&A. Thus, new shares may only be issued when the management attains the court's approval.

However, some reorganization plans drafted in the past have lacked such measures. The Supreme Court of Korea ruled that if an M&A was not considered from the very beginning of the corporate reorganization program, then subsequently including provisions on increasing the capital stock or paid-in capital would adversely affect the existing shareholders and would require an interested persons' meeting.[26]

Instances that Require an Interested Persons' Meeting

General

Any additional change of right or debt rescheduling or restructuring after the approval of the reorganization must be made through formal changes to the reorganization plan. At the interested persons' meeting, creditors and shareholders must consent to the proposed revision. This is also true for cases that involve M&A. Except for cases that have special provisions for revising the reorganization plan, the procedure for revision is the same as that of establishing the original reorganization program: through an interested persons' meeting. The computation for the amount of credit and grant of voting rights are based on the revision date. In practice, the amount of credit is computed as of the date of filing for the revised proposal and voting rights are determined as of the date of the meeting.

Though new shares may be issued solely by attaining the court's approval, they are issued at the same time as the proceeding to revise the reorganization plan for change of right is carried out.

25.　*Practices of Corporate Rehabilitation*, vol. 2, 116–17.
26.　Details in Park, "Practice and Prospects for M&A," 42–43.

Treatment of the Secured Claims

For secured claims, ensuring liquidation value is particularly problematic. In theory, we can determine whether the principles for ensuring liquidation value have been followed. But in practice, this is determined at the time of the revision of the reorganization plan. Due to depreciation, there is a disadvantage in using heavy equipment as collateral compared to using real estate.

Such imbalances among secured claims holders can be attributed to two causes. The first arises from determining liquidation value at the time of the revision of the reorganization plan. The second results from the current practice guideline that recognizes the existence of secured claims for individual objects. This guideline was formulated to reflect the demands of security holders. Changing the practice guideline can partially solve the problem of imbalance among the holders of secured claims.

In the United States, there is a device that protects the security holder from depreciation,[27] and as a result, setting liquidation value occurs almost always at the start of the proceeding. There is no such mechanism in Korea.

Based on the current practice of ensuring liquidation value at the time of the revision of the reorganization program, secured claims receive preferential treatment over unsecured claims for changes of right (when there is sufficient funds). In cases where funds are insufficient, the amount that exceeds the liquidation value can be used to change rights, just as with secured claims and unsecured claims. Or, at times, they can be given preferential treatment.[28]

Treatment of the Unsecured Claims

Rule of Fixation of a Co-debtor's Liability. The rule of fixation of a co-debtor's liability is a principle of the bankruptcy regime that modified the general principle of a co-debtor relationship under civil law. Matters that become an issue in practice are briefly discussed here.

There are conflicting viewpoints on whether the rule of fixation of a co-debtor's liability applies when the principal debtor has paid after a

---

27. The adequate protection content that safeguards the guarantor includes information where the collateral declines in value and that bonds corresponding to the decline must be treated as public interest.

28. *Practices of Corporate Rehabilitation*, vol. 2, 184, vol. 1, 525; Danon case.

bankruptcy proceeding has begun. Some persuasively argue that the rule does not apply when a principal debtor pays back his or her debt.[29] However, case law and another widely-accepted view[30] recognize the application of the rule even in such circumstances.[31] Though legal negativism has the advantage of retaining most of the general legal principles of civil law in bankruptcy proceedings, (1) there are no grounds to distinguish between when the principal debtor has paid and when he has not; and (2) presumably the fundamental purpose of the rule is to guarantee the maximum payment to the surety by preventing a decrease in the amount of credit due to the nature of surety obligations with multiple creditors.

There are times when creditors and even the companies undergoing corporate reorganization make mistakes regarding the scope of application in regards to the rule. In practice, there are also cases where the creditors submit the credit amount first and the company undergoing reorganization conducts analysis based on that amount in practice.

The confusion is aggravated because there are instances where the rule is violated within the reorganization program. In other words, there are instances where (a) a reimbursement a creditor receives from a third-party guarantor in the reorganization program initiated against the principal debtor takes the form of reimbursement bonds; (b) the reorganization program is drafted to make payments from the change of right based only on the balance left after deducting the amount received from the principal debtor using the base date set after the approval of the reorganization program; and (c) the receivables of the debtors are reduced or exempt pursuant to the reduction or exemption of receivables of the principal debtor.

Though (b) and (c) may violate the principles of equity and the guarantee of liquidation value, they are considered to be effective when an approval is confirmed.

As for (a), a lower court has held that the appropriations provision in the reorganization program cannot be declared void once the approval has been granted.[32] But if the decision on the allocation of reimbursement that

29. Yongduk Kim, "Company Reorganization Proceeding and Relationship of Multiple Parties," Seoul National University (1989), 31–34.

30. Supreme Court, Jan. 27, 2005, 2004Da27143.

31. *Practices of Corporate Rehabilitation*, vol. 1, 344.

32. Seoul High Court, July. 15, 2005, 2005Na6930. Commentary by Park, Sanggu,

a creditor receives from the guarantor is within the guarantor's right rather than that of the creditor's, there is a question of whether this issue can be addressed in the reorganization program. Thus, even if such a provision were to be included in the reorganization program and the court were to grant an approval hypothetically, there is still room for interpreting that the provision is not effective.[33]

Treatment of Claims to be Swapped into Equity. In the past, CSE was treated in the same way as a general unsecured claims but this results in excessive voting rights for convertible bondholders. To solve this problem, CSE is separated from the general secured and unsecured claims, and grouped differently in practice. Further, the voting rights of CSE are granted based on the number of shares to be issued in the future or the face value of the shares. This stems from the fact that it is difficult to assess the value of the CSE and that there are differences in requirements for attaining an approval and change of right between CSE from general security and CSE from unsecured claims.[34] Though the lowest limit for change of right of CSE can be treated like stock, it is given preference to stock in practice. Cash reimbursement is also considered possible for CSE.[35]

Treatment of Stock

As seen earlier, when creditors' rights are reduced by a revision of the reorganization program, the rights of existing shareholders must also be reduced and the rate of reduction must be greater than that of the creditors.36 In practice, the reduction of capital, ratio of reduction for control

Surety, Surety on Property and Liability of Co-debtor in Bankruptcy Law, *Commercial Cases Review* (2007), 448.

33. Supreme Court, Nov. 10, 2005, 2005Da48482. The Court held that the reorganization program that exempts the guarantor from liability is invalid even if approved; Supreme Court, Jan. 20, 2006, 2005Geu60. The Court held that the public creditor cannot appeal the approval of the revision of the reorganization program. For more details, Park, "Practice and Prospects for M&A," 39–40.

34. Lee, "M&A in Corporate Reorganization Proceeding," 79–80; Tongil Heavy Industries Co., Ilsung Construction, Il Shin Stone Co. cases.

35. Seoul District Court, Feb. 7, 2003, 98Pa10322, Tongil Heavy Industries Co case); Dist. Ct., Nov. 19, 2002, 98Pa10324, Ilsung Construction case).

36. A comparison with loan guarantee is particularly problematic.

rights, and the estimated value of stock are considered comprehensively in reducing the shareholders' rights.[37]

Forced Approval

The court may force an approval when a part of the group opposes the revision of the reorganization program at the interested persons' meetings. The Bankruptcy Division of the Seoul Central District Court often used such forced approval between 2002 and 2003. Though this resulted in an increased number of completed M&As in the context of reorganization programs, the court became more passive after concerns that buyers or managers might be at a disadvantage in negotiating with creditors when forced approval is an option.[38]

Follow-up Procedure

The follow-up stage encompasses the end of the payment of debts, issuance of new shares, and the closing of the reorganization proceeding.

Closing

The closing stage of the reorganization is one of the greatest concerns for the acquiror of a company undergoing reorganization because it is the beginning of the acquiror's exercise of independent management.

Under the Company Reorganization Act, the closing period of the reorganization is set regardless of whether an immediate appeal is available for the revision of the program or not. If an immediate appeal is not made within the period for filing an appeal, the decision on closing is made afterwards. On the other hand, if an appeal is filed on time, the decision on closing is delayed until the ruling of the appeal. The decision on the closing of the proceeding is made right away if the approval is upheld on appeal. This is because the decision of the appeals court pursuant to the Company Reorganization Act cannot be stayed and can only be challenged through a special appeal.

37.   Park, "Practice and Prospects for M&A," 45; see also Supreme Court, Dec. 10, 2004, 2002Geu121.

38.   *Practices of Corporate Rehabilitation*, vol. 2, 187.

Since the Unified Insolvency Act provides that a second appeal can be made of the the first appeal, the decision on the closing of the proceeding must technically be delayed until the Supreme Court has an opportunity to review the ruling.[39] A legislative review of this area is necessary to invigorate the use of M&A. Even if the decision on closing, in practice, must be deferred due to changes in legislation, measures such as recognizing the acquiror's exercise of control from the time of the lower court's ruling should be adopted. However, the Corporate Reorganization Act applies when the proceedings are initiated pursuant to the Act and, in such cases, the existing practices can be used.

Executive Board Restructuring

The new chief executive officer and the board members are appointed by the buyer prior to the closing of the corporate restructuring under the procedural mandates of the Bankruptcy Division of the Seoul Central District Court. This is an indispensable step for the buyer as the newly appointed executives represent the company during the process of terminating the restructuring. As for the audit, however, keeping the existing audit team is the principle.

Therefore, management exercises control before the termination of the reorganization proceeding. However, after the revision of the reorganization program is approved, the acquiror may dispatch a task force, whose scope is limited to those related to the business transition. The dispatch of the task force prior to the approval of the revision has been recognized in the past but is more of an exception.[40]

Pending Lawsuits and Closing of Reorganization Proceedings

The Supreme Court of Korea has held that pending lawsuits are abolished when reorganization proceedings close.[41] However, following the Court's holding can result in an unfair result because the defendant might receive

---

39. Ibid., 188–89.
40. Chunji Corporation case.
41. Supreme Court, Oct. 12, 2006, 2005Da59307.

an unexpected windfall.[42] One can think of a split-off to ensure that a part of the company continues for the pending lawsuit and get additional dividends as a solution.[43] Unfortunately, this procedure would be too cumbersome.

42.   For critical commentary, see Chiyong Rim, "A Practical Study on the Effect of Avoidance Power Under the Precedents," *Law Times* 623 (2008), 44.

43.   *Practices of Corporate Rehabilitation* , vol. 1, 564.

The Best Evidence Rule in a Digital Age

Sang Won Lee[1]

INTRODUCTION

The shocking world the movie *The Matrix* showed us is not just a fiction any more. Digital technology is changing human history in a way that has not been seen before. With ever-growing influence on every arena of our lives, it not only affects the criminal justice system but causes fundamental changes of criminal procedure as well.

It can be said that criminal procedure runs through evidences as they are crucial to fact finding, which constitutes the base of the whole procedure. Investigation collects evidence; trial appraises it. Evidentiary procedure seeks to get information embedded in such evidence. Traditionally, evidence has been in the form of physical objects (real evidence), documents (writings), or humans (witness testimony). With the advent of digital technology, digital evidence or electronic evidence (e-evidence: this article does not precisely distinguish the two) has found increasing significance within the criminal procedure. E-evidence is fundamentally different from traditional forms of evidence, making traditional rules of evidence less and less adequate.

In recent years, Korea has enacted laws to foster digitalization of the criminal procedure. Those are the "Act on the Use of Electronic Documents in Summary Proceedings" (hereinafter "Summary Proceedings Act") and "Act to Promote Digitalization of the Criminal Justice Proce-

---

1.   Seoul National University Law School.

dure" (hereinafter "Digitalization Act"). Both became effective on May 1, 2010. These Acts laid the institutional foundation of digital-based procedure, along with a new digital-based civil procedure created by the Act on the Use of Electronic Documents in Civil Litigation of 2010.

This paper will consider the legislation of criminal digitalization and the impact of digitalization on the existing rules, especially the best evidence rule.

Criminal Digitalization and Informal Digitalization

Recent Legislation on Criminal Digitalization

Legislative History

With the help of digital technology, Korean criminal justice agencies including the police, prosecution's office, courts and Justice Department adopted their own electronic systems for their proceedings. However, because each agency had its own separate system with no connection with each other, electronic procedure of an agency was restricted within the agency and all the information necessary for case handling had to be transformed into paper in order to be transferred to another agency. This causes various problems: (i) wastes of time and human resources, (ii) overlapping of works among agencies, and (iii) the burden on parties to submit documents separately and repeatedly.

Confronting such problems, Korea has developed the Korea Integrated Criminal Justice Information System (KICS, currently Korea Information System of Criminal Justice Services), pursuing criminal proceedings which are not only paperless but also sharing information among agencies, leading to criminal justice service for citizens. The first KICS project was implemented from 2005 to 2006, building a police investigation system and an internal portal system. The second project spanned from 2006 to 2007, building a prosecutorial investigation system and a court trial system.

Though the original intent of the KICS was to propagate a fully integrated criminal justice information system, issues over agencies' unique functions and disagreements over the range of integration made it difficult to accomplish the original goal. Thus, the suggestion on gradual constructionof criminal justice information system got more support and a legislative bill suggesting a digital-based criminal procedure for some summary proceedings was introduced to the National Assembly on November 5, 2007. The bill was discarded by expiration of the term of the then members of the National Assembly, but was again introduced in the amended form on May 18, 2009 during the next term, and passed into law, which is the Summary Proceedings Act. More fundamental efforts to digitalize the criminal justice system resulted in the Digitalization Act, which was introduced and passed on the same days as the Summary Proceedings Act. A presidential decree and Court Rules for the Acts were enacted as well.

Cyber Crime Law

Digitalization Act

The Digitalization Act is based on a long-term policy for digitalization and systematization of criminal justice information. The Act declared that its purpose is to achieve promptness, fairness and transparency in a criminal justice procedure by promoting the digitalization of the criminal justice procedure and to contribute to the extension of citizens' rights and interests by improving services to citizens in the area of criminal justice (Article 1). Instead of complete integration of systems of criminal justice agencies, it allows the independence of each system while it pursues common standards and communication among systems.

The Digitalization Act defines several categories of systems. "Criminal justice information system" (hereinafter 'system') refers to any electronic management system built by a criminal justice agency to serve to generate, acquire, store, transmit or receive criminal justice information (§2 iv). "Criminal justice information common system" (hereinafter 'common system') refers to a system shared by two or more agencies (§2 v). "Criminal justice portal" (hereinafter 'portal') refers to a system built in the common system for public services (§2 vi).

System Structure

Basically, each agency operates its own independent system (§8 i). This falls far short of the initial goals that the KICS set out to accomplish, but each system has connected channel to provide information to other agency, that is, systems are connected (§6 ii). The common system is managed by the operating institution established within the Ministry of Justice, which is KICS (§8 i). Different agencies have varying levels of integration with the system: MOJ and Prosecution's office are the most intensely connected to each other, next comes the police, and the courts are the most loosely connected with all being independent except portal.

System Operations
In the original bill, sentencing, arraignment, warrants, reports, etc. were to be written up and prepared solely through the System (Article 4 Section 1). However, this method of centralizing all processes would have concentrated undue burden and risk on one area, thus the bill was amended to simply utilize the System to store the saved data for drafts and archives of various criminal procedure documentation (§5(1)).

Thus, it is likely that the work itself is done at each agency's system, and only the completed investigative documents and lawsuit documents are uploaded to the connected system. In cases where using the system is difficult, exceptions may be provided by Presidential Decree for the systems of the MOJ, the prosecution and the police, and provided by the Supreme Court Rules for the court system (§5(1)). In this light, the system is more an independent system than a unified system.

Article 2 of the Presidential Decree contains an exception regarding (i) documents created by the suspect, victims, or others involved in the case, (ii) documents that cannot be created by the system, (iii) documents that must be drafted at a time and place where the system cannot be used, or when the system is down. This takes into consideration the possible unavailability of the system when drafting the original document. However, even in such cases, the documents can be digitized and stored in the system after drafting them. Actually, the Act asks agencies to store and keep documents in the system, but not to draft them (§5(1)).

The new system does not abolish existing systems of criminal justice agencies, which are as follows.

Name	Division	System Name	
Police	Investigation	CIMS	Crime Information Management System
		Digital map	Digital Mapping System
		Crime Statistics	Crime Statistics System
		IPAS	Investigation Performance Appraisal System
		e-Zs	Criminal Intelligence Investigation Support System
		CIAS	Criminal Intelligence Analysis System
		CRIFISS	Criminal Filing Search System
		SCAS	Scientific Crime Analysis System
		e-CRIS	Electronic Criminal Record Identification System
		IBM	Criminal record, wanted, resident checking System
		EMS	Evidence Management System
		AFIS	Automated Fingerprint Identification System
		FTIS	Footwear impression & Tire imprint Identification System
	Traffic	TAMS	Traffic Accident Management System
		Vehicle Registration	IBM mainframe
	Public Safety Bureau	Summary Disposition System	
	Public Services	National Cyber Police	
		National Anti-Cyber-Terrorism Center	
Prosecuton	Case Management	Case management/Appeal System	
	Criminal Investigation	Bureau of Inspection and Enforcement	
	Execution	Property Investigation System	
		English administration System	
		Execution of sentence System	
		Seized Property Managing System	
	Investigation Support	Audiovisual information System	
		Integrated Investigative Information System	
		Records Preservation System	
		Statistics System	
	Public Service	Homepage/Online Public Service System	

Courts	Criminal Cases	Criminal Trial/Summary Proceedings System	
		Warrant System	
		Juvenile/Family/Prostitution Case System	
		Service/Statistics System	
	Adjudication Common	Docket/Document/Preservation System	
	Information Application	Judge Support System	
		Archives Management System	
	Public Service	Public services System	
Ministry of Justice	Probation	IPIIS	Intelligent Probation Integration Information System
		PIVIS	Probation Inquiry and Viewing Information System
		PEIS	Probationary Evaluation Information System
		MOPIS	Mobile Office Probation Information System
		PGIS	Probation Geographic Information System
		CVS	Curfew Supervising Voice Verification System
	Juvenile Delinquency	Juvenile Information System	
	Custodial Medical Treatment	Custodial Information System	
	Correction	Integrated Correctional Information System	
	Immigration	Immigration Information System	
		Alien Registration Information System	

Operation of the System

Though the systems are, in the beginning, linked together with minimal integration, the Digitalization Act aims for an overall computerization and for expanded distribution and sharing of information, fostering an intimate connection among each system through standardized format of communication (Articles 3 to 6).mode based on minimal integration, the criminal procedure law aims for an overall computerization and as a result, expanded distribution and sharing of information according to the standard form for an integrated connection (Articles 3 to 6).

In principle, each criminal justice agency runs and manages the system independently and the justice department manages the common system (Article 8). Accordingly, KICS, as the managing organization established within MOJ, is in charge of the common system.

However, changes affecting the distribution standard or system-wide matters related to law enforcement are determined by unanimous agreement of the members of the Criminal Justice Information Systems Com-mittee, which is comprised of the representatives of each criminal justice agency (Articles 10 to 12). As a support, a working-level committee is established within the Committee (Article 13). The ordinance for the Digitalization Act sets out the detailed regulations.

The Protection of the Criminal Justice Information

Criminal justice agencies must take precautionary measures to ensure the safety of the criminal justice information and agents may not access, copy, or transfer criminal justice information without permission, nor use the information acquired during employment for improper purposes (Article 14). One who commits forgery, alteration, or obliteration of criminal justice information, or violates Article 14 shall be punished (Article 15).

Summary Proceedings Act

The Summary Proceedings Act implements digital procedure to such violations of the Road Traffic Act as driving under the influence or unlicensed driving first, where procedures are processed quickly and routinely. The Act regulates the use of digital documents and its effect in those cases. The Act also applies to those punishable as employer of the violators of DUI or unlicensed driving. In any case, the consent of the accused is necessary.

Target Cases

The Summary Proceedings Act only applies to cases that meet the following elements: cases eligible for summary order (Criminal Procedure Code 448); driving under the influence (Road Traffic Act 148-2(i)), unlicensed driving (Road Traffic Act 152(i), 154(ii)), and cases subject to the joint punishment provisions in connection with the two aforementioned violations; and consent of the accused. The consent of the accused means registering for the criminal justice information system and electronically submitting his or her electronic signature (Article 4 Section 1 and 5).

Procedures

In a digitalized electronic proceeding, all documents for investigation and trial get processed electronically and the procedure is operated electronically.

Creation of Documents. The Act requires certain documents to be created pursuant to a standardized electronic form that can be transferred, received, and stored. The creator of the electronic document signs an administrative electronic signature, and a person making a statement signs electronically. Documents that must be in the electronic form are as follows (Article 5):

Creator	Category	E-document
Prosecutor Judicial police officer	Investigation documents	Record of suspect's statement Record of witness's statement Arrest or release record Documents on sobriety test and result, context of driving under the influence Driver's license inquiry and Description of the violation Other investigatory documents
	Indictment documents	Request of summary order
Court	Trial documents	Summary order
	Litigation documents	Service list

In cases where non-electronic forms of documents are submitted for an electronic proceeding, the documents must be scanned and converted into an electronic file and electronically signed by the administrator. The Summary Proceedings Act refers to such documents as "digitalized documents" (Article 6). When non-electric documents are submitted to the court, court officials digitalize the documents and register these digitalized documents onto the court system.

The digitalized documents must be kept until the issuance of a summary order or final judgment (Article 6 Section 1). There is no legal requirement for their preservation thereafter but some may think it proper to require preservation for the period required for paper archives.

Courts maintain digitalized documents converted in court during the litigation, but opinions diverge regarding preservation after the issuance of a summary judgment or final judgment. There is a general view that the records should be handed over to the prosecution like ordinary records. But some believe that the court must preserve the electronic records, while others think it must discard them.

On the other hand, if the submitted documents come in the form of a book or a piece of paper that does not fit the specifications of the scanner, conversion is very difficult or unsuitable (such documents are labeled "documents difficult to convert"). Even though the Act does not expressly provide exceptions for such cases, documents deemed difficult to convert are left unconverted and kept separately. Though there were efforts to minimize abuse of such exceptions by requiring the recording of the reasons for such difficulty, there is still room for abuse since the reason for the exception is abstractly described as "technical difficulty."

Summary Order Request and Submission of Document. According to the Summary Proceedings Act Article 7, when requesting a summary order, a prosecutor shall submit electronic documents or digitalized documents. The prosecutor must submit the evidentiary document and the request for summary order electronically. However, documents that are not digitized may be submitted in paper form. When submitting electronic or digitized documents, the prosecutor must submit through the court's system and the defendant must submit through the criminal justice portal. The court and the prosecution operate under separate systems and transmit or receive necessary information by connecting them to each other. Because the Summary Proceedings Act Article 5 Section 2 requires the summary order request be made by the prosecutor through the system, the request cannot be submitted through electronic mail. The Act requires the electronic or digitalized documents to be submitted as documentary evidence to the court (Article 7), but there is no clear provision that requires those evidentiary documents to be submitted through the system. However, considering the purpose of the Summary Proceedings Act and the electronic summary proceedings system, it can be said that those evidentiary documents should also be submitted through the system.

Defendants can submit their documents to the court through the criminal justice portal, which is the common system between the criminal prosecution and the court, but since they are not required to use the criminal prosecution portal, they are allowed to submit evidence in a paper document format. In such cases, the submitted paper document must be digitalized and registered on the system. The defendant is not allowed to submit through electronic mail. This is because there is no rule that allows electronic mail submission, and also because there exists an alternative of using the criminal justice portal system. Because a submission made through electronic mail is done outside of the system, it is difficult to manage those documents, and it would place the burden on the defendants if they were required to use the criminal justice portal system.

When submitting the document through the system mentioned above, it is not clear whether the time of submission should be when the document is received or sent. More specifically, it is debatable whether the document is deemed to have been submitted when the sender clicks the send button on the prosecution or the criminal justice portal system to be sent to the court's system, or when the court confirms receipt of the document. The Rules for the Summary Proceedings Act provides that a document is deemed to be submitted when it is officially reached to the system of the court. Under this rule, the submitting party has to take the risk of non-arrival or late arrival. If we strictly stick to the rule, it will be the same even when the document does not reach the court system owing to the technical problems or heavy traffic of systems including the court system. However, this understanding is controversial. For example, it can lead to a questionable conclusion in respect to the defendant's retraction of the consent to the summary proceedings by means of electronic documents. When a defendant wants to retract her consent to the electronic proceedings, she should submit a retraction form no later than the prosecution submits the summary order request to the court. If the prosecution submit a summary order request to the court system while the defendant's retraction is not yet received because of the system delay, it is not always justifiable to regard the retraction as void.

Service. The court serves or notifies the summary order and other litigation documents electronically through the system (Article 8 Section 1). The court uploads the summary order onto the system and notifies the defendant of that fact. The document is deemed to be served when the addressee reads the uploaded summary order (Article 8 Sections 2 and 3). If the addressee does not read the uploaded order, the summary order is deemed to be served two weeks after the date when the court official informs the defendant that the summary order has been uploaded to the system. However, if the defendant irresponsibly fails to read the order and misses a deadline coming after the fictitious service, she can file a claim for relief (Article 8 Section 4). In principle, the summary order or other documents shall be served on-line, but they may be served off-line when electronic service is impossible.

Enforcement. A prosecutor shall, upon a summary order under the Act being finalized, direct the execution of the penalty imposed by the order using digital documents (Article 11 Section 1). However, if the use of electronic documents is difficult, direction of execution may be carried out through printed copy of the summary order (Section 2 of the same article).

Transition to Non-Electronic Procedure

Abbreviated electronic procedures move to non-electronic regular procedures in the following situations:

Departure from target case	When the target case gets investigated or tried together with a non-target case (§ 3② i) When electronic summary procedures are inappropriate (e.g. when applying for arrest warrants and/or confinement warrants)
Withdrawal of Agreement	When the suspect withdraws his or her agreement to an an electronic summary procedure. (§ 4③, ④)
Formal Indictment	When the prosecution doesn't request an order for an electronic summary procedure and instead files a formal indictment (§10②)
Transition to Trial	When the court remits the case to trial (§ 10①) When the defendant applies for a formal trial (§ 10①)

In the above situations, the prosecutor or the judicial police official shall convert all electronic records and documents into paper documents and file them into the case records (Article 3 Section 3, Article 4 Section 4, Article 10, paragraph 1 and paragraph 2). When the transition to trial occurs after the court procedure begins, the court electronically transmits to the prosecutor concerned all litigation documents and evidentiary documents submitted through the system, and the prosecutor prints them and then submits the printed copies to the court (Article 10 paragraph 1).

The physical copies must be printed through the system while maintaining the following: date of printing, total page numbers, an original identification number, and a cover sheet that prevents copying, falsifying, and tampering. The printed copies will be considered certified copies of the electronic documents (Article 3 section 3, article 4 section 4, article 10 section 3, article 9 section 2).

ELECTRONIC EVIDENCE AND ORIGINALITY

Original and Copy

Documents may exist not only in the form of an original but also in the form of its copies, and there have been several different concepts within the category of copies.

An "original" refers to the first document that was drafted to conclusively express certain ideas. For example, a written contract that lists the terms of agreement and was signed by contracting parties would be an original document. Another example would be a written record of examination of a suspect by a prosecutor. A "certified copy" is a document that contains the exact same information as the original, and has been certified by the original drafter. If an authorized certifying agency certifies that a copy is identical in content to the original, it is called an "exemplified copy." A certified copy is called an "authentic copy" if a public authority certifies is as such. While certified copies serve the evidentiary purpose of proving the existence and content of the original, an "authentic copy" is a document that holds the same legal significance as the original. A "reserve copy" is created for service/delivery purposes, and is generally treated as a certified copy.

An abridged copy includes part of the original contents. It serves the purpose of proving the existence of the original document and certain selective contents from the original. A "copy" refers to any document that is copied from an original document, regardless whoever makes it and regardless whether part or whole.

Handwriting being the basic method of creating documents, both the original document and its copies have typically been created by hand. When copies had to be created by hand, transcribing the entire original document was such a burden that abridged copies were favored. However, with the advent of photocopiers, it became common to copy the entire document. Of course, even with photocopying it is possible to create abridged copies by obscuring or deleting unnecessary parts of the original document. Overall, photocopying played a significant role in changing the method how document copies were created. However, the effect of such change was still limited to physical paper documents, and therefore did not present significant challenges to the existing evidentiary theories of copies.

It is different when it comes to media other than paper documents. Devices such as video and audio tapes made it possible to create records without paper documents. Computer technology goes even further through digital media. Electronic evidence followed this development. Due to the unique characteristics of electronic evidence, which is easily copyable, the conceptual boundaries between a physically distinct "original" document and its "copies" became blurred. In the case of electronic evidence, not only is there no discernible difference between the original and its copies, but in some cases there may be several "originals."

Current Law of Korea

Oral Statement and Written Statement

As an element of trial-based criminal procedure, the Supreme Court of Korea employs 'examination before the court', which includes a principle that "A trial should be based on original evidence that is closest to the fact to be proved and substitutes for original evidence should not be permitted in principle." Based on this legal principle, the Supreme Court has also found that a record of statement will not hold evidentiary significance in principle unless the person who made the statement is cross-examined in a courtroom. Also, the Supreme Court found that an appellate court should refrain from overturning the trial court's fact finding based on the court record of the testimony of the trial court's witness. This shows that original testimony is to be considered original evidence, while written record of that testimony will be perceived as a substitute for the original evidence. It also adheres to the aforementioned principle that original evidence should form the basis of a trial.

However, the Supreme Court's stance does not necessarily mean that only original evidence is admissible as evidence. The former is about a record of statement in an investigatory agency to which the defendant gave consent for the use as evidence, and the latter is about a trial court record of testimony as evidence in the appellate court. Neither denied the admissibility itself but both rather focused on the reliability of evidence. The Supreme Court seemed to think that the record of statement or testimony is a kind of substitute of original statement or testimony and to show its preference of the originals to the substitutes. Considering this, although the Supreme Court did not deny the admissibility of one over the other, but has instead created a hierarchy of reliability among different types of evidence and takes the original evidence first.

For example, a written document that lists testimony is considered to have lower credibility compared to the original testimony itself, which would be considered original evidence. Therefore, the original testimony should provide the basis for the facts over the written document.

Printed Copies of Evidentiary Documents
Nonetheless, the Supreme Court does not view the superior reliability of original evidence as being completely irrelevant to admissibility. In determining the admissibility of an abridged copy of a suspect examination record, the Supreme Court decided that the following factors were to be considered: (i) the original suspect examination record must be in existence or have been in existence, (ii) there must be circumstances that prevent or make it unduly burdensome to produce the original record, (iii) the abridged copy must accurately reflect the contents of the original record. When these three factors are satisfied, an abridged copy can be found admissible as evidence. This ruling also set out that the copied parts and hidden parts of the original record are separable from each other, but only when the hid-

den parts are unrelated to the charges at hand can the abridged copy gain admissibility based on the three aforementioned factors. This last part of the Supreme Court's ruling can be considered a fourth factor to meet the admissibility standard.

The Supreme Court's position can be summarized as follows. While it is not true that only an original document is admissible as evidence, four factors must be satisfied for a copy to be admissible as evidence: (i) the existence of the original, (ii) the impossibility or undue burden of producing the original, (iii) the accuracy of the abridged copy, and (iiii) the irrelevancy of the redacted parts. Since copies are only admissible when it has been demonstrated that the original cannot be produced, in principle only the original document has admissibility.

Audio Tapes, Video Tapes, CD Copies

Admissibility. Due to the very nature of audio tapes, video tapes, compact discs (CDs) and other audio-visual recording devices, there is no way for the writer or stater to sign or otherwise verify the authenticity of the contents. Furthermore, there is the danger of fabricating or tampering the contents intentionally or unintentionally. To address these concerns, the Supreme Court ruled that, for such media to be admissible, they must satisfy the following: (i) they must be original evidence, or (ii) in the case of copies, it must be proved that they are an exact replica of the original, and that there was no editing involved in the copying process. Since the burden of proof lies with the party that presents the evidence, this legal principle reflects the understanding that the prosecution holds the burden of proof.

Furthermore, the Supreme Court extends this principle to include tape and CD transcripts and court examination reports on such transcripts as well. Regarding the former, consider the following case: Stage 1, the defendant made certain statements in a restaurant meeting. Stage 2, one of the participants digitally recorded those statements. Stage 3, the recorded statements were transferred onto a CD. Stage 4, the contents of the CD were turned into a transcript. When the transcript from the fourth stage was presented as evidence, the Supreme Court ruled that it is not admissible because of the lack of proof that no editing occurred between the second and third stages. In regards to the latter, consider the following case: Stage 1, the defendant and victim had a conversation at the time of the alleged crime. Stage 2, the victim made a digital recording. Stage 3, the digital recording was recorded onto a cassette tape. Stage 4, the contents of the tape were turned into a transcript. Stage 5, at trial, the court examined the transcript to see whether or not the contents of the third and fourth stages were identical. However, because the court examination report at the fifth stage only shows the contents of stages 3 and 4 are identical, but not the contents between the original from stage 2 and the copy created in stage 3, it was ruled that the report of stage 5 was not admissible.

Just because the Supreme Court required the contents between stage 2 and 3 to be identical, it does not mean that later stages can be different from each other in content. To summarize, the Supreme Court requires that the contents of all copies deriving from the original evidence created in stage 2 be identical to each other in order to be admissible as evidence.

How to Prove Uniformity Between the Original and Copies. The next question is this: how to prove that the contents of the original and its copies are identical? With regards to court examination reports, the Supreme Court suggests that the court first verify the content of the original and then either take the original writer's testimony or have an expert appraise the state of recording. While vague in text, the suggestion can be interpreted as allowing any of verification, appraisal or testimony to prove the uniformity.

For example, consider the following case: Stage 1, person A and the defendant had a conversation. Stage 2, this conversation was digitally re-corded. Stage 3, the digital recording was reproduced as an audio tape. Stage 4, the audio tape was transcribed. Stage 5, the trial court issued an examination report. For the contents of the audio tape to be admissible, the contents of the original digital recording and the audio tape (which would be considered a copy) must be proven to be identical. While the court's examination and verification can be used for such a purpose, the most common method of verification used in courts (which is to play the submitted audio tape and see if the contents match the transcript) is not sufficient to establish admissibility. Case law clearly indicates that even if it is established that (i) the contents of the tape and the transcript are identical (thus, stages 3 and 4 are uniform), and that (ii) the voice in the audio tape matches the voice of the defendant, if (iii) it cannot be proven that the audio tape is an unedited, exact replica of the original evidence, the audio tape is not admissible. Furthermore, even when the stenographer who made the stage 4 transcription provided documented proof that he or she connected the digital recording and the audio tape recording when transcribing, the court found it to be insufficient to prove that stages 2 and 3 are consistent with each other.

However, it is unclear whether the person who made the original recording at the very beginning is sufficient to satisfy the idea of the "original drafter", or whether the drafters for each stage are needed individually. Consider the following case: Stage 1, defendant and persons A and B had a three-way conversation. Stage 2, the conversation was recorded. Stage 3, the recording was transcribed, and the transcript was submitted as evidence. In this case, Person A testified that he or she recorded the entire conversation and that the content of the transcript was entirely accurate. This testimony could be seen as establishing the consistency between all three stages. However, the Supreme Court ruled that for Stage 3, as a document listed under Article 313 Paragraph 1 of the Criminal Procedure Act, the drafter in Stage 3 (the stenographer) would have to testify separately for there to be admissibility. Considering that Article 313 is about hearsay, the Supreme Court can be interpreted as going toward the issue of hearsay evidence rather than consistency. Therefore, it is hard to say that this particular case set a precedent for the uniformity issue.

Computer Disks and Data Storage Media

Admissibility. The aforementioned cases in the previous section pertain to copies in the form of audio and video tapes and CDs. The legal principles established by those cases can be applied to computer disks and other forms of digital data storage as well.

The Supreme Court applied the same logic of uniformity between the original evidence and copies for cases involving computer disks and other data storage media. The following cases illustrate this line of thinking: one case where digital storage media were seized (Stage 1) and printed out to paper documents (Stage 2), and another case where out of seized digital storage media (Stage 1) hard copies or imaging files were created (Stage 1-C) were submitted as evidence, the court ruled that complete uniformity between the two stages needed to be established for admissibility to be granted. Since the evidence collected and submitted by the investigative agency would be from Stage 1, the documents from Stage 2 were created from Stage 1-a in order to prevent Stage 1 evidence from becoming altered. Thus, in this case, there was a gap in dates between the seizure of the original evidence and printing of the paper documents. The Supreme Court ruled that in such cases, it must be proved that the original evidence was not altered between the seizure date and the printing date. In short, the Supreme Court's position is that there must be complete uniformity across all stages of evidence from the original to the printed copies.

U.S. Evidence Law

Best Evidence Rule
The Best Evidence Rule governs the admission of original documents and copies. This reflects the courts' long-held preference for original writings, recordings, and photographs over secondary evidence when the contents are sought to be proved. Over time however, this preference was gradually weakened. The purpose of the Best Evidence Rule at common law was to avoid potential inaccuracies. But the development of pretrial discovery procedures that allowed close examination of whether the copies matched the original as well as the mechanical process of copying documents greatly reduced the risk of error or inaccuracies in reproduction. Some say that the Best Evidence Rule has become archaic in the Xerox era.

Origin. High illiteracy in medieval England meant emphasis on ceremony and accordingly, writings stipulating property rights and contractual rights were seen as the rights themselves instead of mere tokens of such rights. Thus, if one failed to submit the document, he or she lost the rights stipulated in the document. This approach dominated procedural law until the early 1800s. Then courts of equity began to order the obligator to fulfill obligations to the obligatee even when the written records were lost or damaged and other courts started to abandon the strict principle of requiring documents. Nevertheless, this tradition of emphasizing writing became the basis for the modern Best Evidence Rule.

Historical Development. The Best Evidence Rule has been understood to embody two concepts. The narrow concept is the rule codified in the Federal Rules of Evidence as well as state evidence law. The broader one on the other hand is a general principle of evidence law that one should submit the most accurate and persuasive piece of evidence. Most contemporary Anglo-American law scholars view that this broad principle of the Best Evidence Rule no longer exists. Simon Greenleaf, the foremost authority on evidence law in his time, expressed the Best Evidence Rule as follows: "The principle behind the Best Evidence Rule is to prevent the admission of certain evidence where better evidence is available in light of the case."

The earliest case that mentioned this broad principle was *Ford v. Hopkins* (Court of King's Bench) in 1700. In that particular case, the Chief Justice C. J. Holt said that "the best proof that the nature of the thing will afford is only required." This broad best evidence principle comes up again in 1852's *McCann v. Beach* case where the Supreme Court of California ruled that "the best evidence of which the case is susceptible must be produced."

The narrow reading of the best evidence principle is an implementation of the broader reading and this is most often applied by requiring originals. Thus, the prevailing view is that though the narrow best evidence principle originated from the broad principle, over time, the traditional broad principle faded away and only the narrow best evidence principle survived independently. However, some argue that the broad principle independent from the narrow best evidence principle as applied in evidentiary document still exists and should exist to promote both ethical and accurate trials.

Argument for the Best Evidence Rule. The Best Evidence Rule requires that the original rather than testimonies or copies be submitted to prove the content of the document. Since there is a risk of error or ambiguities when making copies of the original document by dictation and it is legally important to have the exact words contained in the document, originals are preferred over copies. In addition to these risks, testimonies and duplicates may be tainted and manipulated.

Arguments Against the Best Evidence Rule
1. Pretrial Discovery. Pretrial discovery has an effect of replacing the Best Evidence Rule. In the early days, it was rare for a party to use pretrial discovery procedure to demand originals. But as pretrial discovery expanded

in scope, litigants were permitted to review original documents to find errors and fraud. This allowed a more effective control than under the Best Evidence Rule. As a result, need for the Best Evidence Rule has significantly lessened.

2. Development of Technology. Another factor that undermined the usefulness of the Best Evidence Rule was the development of copy machines and computers. With the development of carbon paper, duplicate originals became legal (duplicate original doctrine). Many courts viewed carbon copies as primary evidence because they are duplicate originals (produced simultaneously as the originals) but rejected copies made after the production of the originals (deemed secondary evidence). However, many fiercely argued that insisting litigants to submit only the originals or duplicate originals and rejecting photographs or Xerox copies since they are secondary evidence was a needless expenditure of time and cost since they were identical to the originals in content. Copies reproduced by modern technology have significantly less room for error and so the key function of the Best Evidence Rule, which is the prevention of error, carries less meaning today.

3. Difficulty in Preventing Fraud. One of the arguments for the Best Evidence Rule is prevention of fraud. But in reality, it is hard to achieve this goal using the Best Evidence Rule since litigants can fabricate the evidence and submit it as an original. This is especially true with modern technology that allows for sophisticated forgery.

4. Unnecessary Waste of Time and Money. Strict application of the Best Evidence Rule leads to unnecessary waste of time and money compared to the likelihood of finding error or manipulation. There is also the problem of rejecting potentially credible evidence. Moreover, litigants often appeal on the propriety of the application of the Best Evidence Rule, which has nothing to do with the actual case.

5. Lack of Clarity in Scope. The Best Evidence Rule applies only to prove the content of the evidentiary document but it is not clear whether this is to prove the content itself or something other than the content. There is also an issue of ambiguity in one of its exceptions. The Best Evidence Rule does not apply where the writing is deemed to be a collateral document (i.e. of minor importance to the matter in controversy) but what constitutes collateral documents is left unclear.

California's Abrogation of the Best Evidence Rule

California abrogated the rule in 1998 and adopted the "secondary evidence rule" instead. According to the secondary evidence rule, the content of a writing may be proved by an otherwise admissible secondary evidence unless (1) there is a genuine dispute concerning material terms of the writing and justice requires the exclusion; or (2) admission of the secondary evidence would be unfair (Cal. Evid. Code §1521). However, proving evidentiary documents through testimony is still not generally permitted. It is allowed only if: (1) the proponent does not have possession or control of a copy of the writing and the original is lost or has been destroyed without fraudulent intent on the part of the proponent of the evidence; (2) the proponent does not have possession or control of the original or a copy of the writing and (a) neither the writing nor a copy of the writing was reasonably procurable by the proponent by use of the court's process or by other available means or (b) the writing is not closely related to the controlling issues and it would be inexpedient to require its production; or (3) the writing consists of numerous accounts or other writings that cannot be examined in court without great loss of time, and the evidence sought from them is only the general result of the whole (Cal. Evid. Code §1523).

Restriction of the Best Evidence Rule in Criminal Cases. On the other hand, a limited Best Evidence Rule has been maintained in criminal proceedings. In a criminal action the court excludes secondary evidence of the content of writing if the court determines that the original is in the proponent's possession, custody, or control, and the proponent has not made the original reasonably available for inspection at or before trial. But, (1) a duplicate, (2) a writing that is not closely related to the controlling issues in the action, (3) a copy of a writing in the custody of a public entity, and (4) a copy of a writing that is recorded in the public records, are allowed even if they are secondary evidence.

Presumption of Accuracy. California evidence law presumes the accuracy of computer printouts. The printed information or programs are presumed to accurately represent the actual computer information or program and the party opposing such evidence may submit evidence challenging its accuracy or reliability to rebut the presumption. In this case, the proponent of the printed representation has the burden of proving, by a preponderance of evidence, that the printed representation is an accurate representation of the existence and content of the computer information or computer program that it purports to represent. This also applies to images stored in visual or digital media. This approach is different from Korea's approach of placing the burden of proving the identity of the copies on the prosecutors.

FRE's Limited Acceptance

FRE's Adoption. Federal Rules of Evidence (hereinafter 'FRE') codified the Best Evidence Rule as the "original document rule" in Article X to cover writing, recording, or photograph. FRE 1002 clearly states that an original writing, recording, or photograph is required in order to prove its content unless FRE or a federal statute provides otherwise.

FRE seems to include electronic evidence in its writing, recording, or photograph language. FRE 1001(1) defines a "writing" and a "recording" to consist of letters, words, or numbers, or their equivalent, set down by handwriting, typewriting, printing, photostating, photographing, magnetic impulse, mechanical or electronic recording, or other form of data compilation. The definition of "photograph" even includes still photographs, X-ray films, video tapes, and motion pictures. The notes to advisory committee for FRE 1001 state that the above definitions include computers, photographic systems, and other modern developments.

This rule applies when the content of the writing is at issue. For instance, when a witness testifies that the photograph or a videotape is identical to what he or she has experienced, the original document rule does not apply because the photograph or recording was not submitted to prove the contents but as a means for testimony. On the other hand, the rule applies when photographs or recordings are submitted as evidentiary document for intellectual property rights, defamation, infringement of privacy etc. since the content is *factum probandum.*

United States v. Bennet is an illustration of the application of the above rules. There, the key issue was whether the defendant's boat crossed the U.S. border to Mexico. Though GPS records or printed representations were not submitted in the case, the Ninth Circuit Court of Appeals held that using the testimony of the police who claimed to have seen that the defendant's boat cross the border on the GPS tracking screen violated the original document rule.

Duplicate Original. As discussed earlier, the Best Evidence Rule was developed to prevent fraud and inaccuracies but litigants started to abuse the rule as a trial strategy even in cases where such risks were absent. Thus, FRE started to recognize duplicates and codified the admissibility of duplicates under sections 1001(4) and 1003.

Under common law, duplicate referred to multiple original or duplicate original. The consideration of duplicate original depended on the author's intent so the external appearance was not taken into account. The duplicates were treated as originals as long as the contents were identical and the author intended them as originals. Secondary evidence such as copies or testimonies was only admitted when it was impossible to submit the duplicate originals.

FRE codified the duplicate originals concept but chose the term multiple originals instead. FRE 1001(3) define an "original" of a writing or recording as the writing or recording itself or any counterpart intended to have the same effect by a person executing or issuing it. An "original" of a photograph includes the negative or any print therefrom. If data are stored in a computer or similar device, any printout or other output readable by sight, shown to reflect the data accurately, is an "original." Following this provision, carbon copies of contracts given to customers such as ticket sales constitute an "original." While strictly speaking, the original of a photograph might be thought to be only the negative, practicality and common usage require that any print of the negative be regarded as an original.

FRE thus recognizes duplicates that have identical content and are intended to be originals by the author. That the duplicate originals have the same legal effect as originals is comparable to Korea's copy of certification or authentication.

Duplicate. "Duplicate" in FRE refers to a particular type of copy. A "duplicate" is a counterpart produced by the same impression as the original, or from the same matrix, or by means of photography, including enlargements and miniatures, or by mechanical or electronic re-recording, or by chemical reproduction, or by other equivalent techniques, which accurately reproduces the original.

FRE 1003 provides that a duplicate is admissible to the same extent as an original unless (1) a genuine question is raised as to the authenticity of the original or (2) in the circumstances it would be unfair to admit the duplicate in lieu of the original. This is because duplicates proven to be identical to originals allow outcomes intended to result under the original document rule. For instance, admitting photostatic copies of checks instead of original microfilm in absence of suggestion to trial judge that photostats were incorrect, and admitting concededly accurate tape recording made from original wire recording were all held as proper admission.

Some assess that the original document rule is practically meaningless with this clause. In the aforementioned *Bennett* case, if the prosecution had prepared copies or printouts of the GPS information, it could have easily avoided the original document rule.

Secondary Evidence. FRE allows the admission of other secondary evidence to prove the content represented in writing, recording, or photograph in some circumstances.

First is when the originals are lost or destroyed. Secondary evidence is permitted when the originals are lost or have been destroyed without bad faith. A party that aids or instigates the loss or damage of the originals will be deemed to have lost or destroyed the originals in bad faith.

Second is when the original is not obtainable. This also includes instances where a third party possesses the original and the litigant cannot attain it by available judicial process (e.g. *subpoena duces tecum*).

Third is when the original is in possession of opponent. At a time when an original was under the control of the party against whom offered, that party was put on notice, by the pleadings or otherwise, that the contents would be a subject of proof at the hearing, and that party does not produce the original at the hearing. The notice procedure here provided means to afford the opposite party an opportunity to produce the original.

Fourth, an original is not required if the writing, recording, or photograph is not closely related to a controlling issue.

Public Records. The contents of a public record, or of a document authorized to be recorded or filed and actually recorded or filed, including data compilation in any form, may be proved by FRE section 902, or testified to be correct by a witness who has compared it with the original. If such copy cannot be obtained by the exercise of reasonable diligence, then other evidence of the contents may be submitted. This exception for public records exists because transferring of the original record is deemed inappropriate.

Summaries. The contents of voluminous writings, recordings, or photographs which cannot conveniently be examined in court may be presented in the form of a chart, summary, or calculation. The originals, or duplicates, shall be made available for examination or copying by other parties at reasonable time and place. The court may order that they be produced in court.

Admission of Opposing Party. Contents of writings, recordings, or photographs may be proved by the testimony or deposition of the party against whom offered or by that party's written admission, without accounting for the nonproduction of the original.

Best Evidence Rule on Electronic Evidence

In the US legal system, the best evidence rule only exists in a limited form. The importance of the original evidence rule becomes even more insignificant in the context of electronic evidence.

For example, even though the parties to an online transaction are looking at the same information, they are technically looking at the information that shows up on their respective screens, which means that there are as many original copies of that information as the number of images that show up on the screen. In such situation, the webserver or the computer hard drive serves as the original document. To present this evidence, the parties can bring up the images stored in the hard drive or webserver to the court's computer terminal. But because this is very inconvenient, the parties usually print out these images on paper at their home or office, and submit those printouts as the original document. Likewise, when the transaction is done over a messenger program operated by an ISP (Internet Service Provider), the parties can print out the transaction contract on paper and submit it as the original document. This is admissible under

FRE 1001 section 3, which stipulates that data printed out from a computer system, as long as they are accurate, are considered as the original.

Furthermore, because FRE 1001 section 4 considers mechanically produced copies as duplicates, and FRE 1001 section 3 treats duplicates as the original, the screen images appearing on the computer located in the parties' home or office, or photographs of those images, are considered to have the same evidentiary power as the original.

In addition, FRE 1006 allows for the contents of voluminous evidentiary documents to be submitted in the form of a summary. When applied to a situation where database stored in the server is being submitted as evidence, the original evidence rule is relaxed.

It follows that it is pointless to insist on applying the best evidence rule when electronic and internet evidence is involved. The best evidence rule was created to apply to paper evidence and has become an artifact in the age of the internet. However, it is still required that the contents of the original and duplicate copies to be identical, even if the copy possesses similar evidentiary power as the original.

Original Evidence and Copies

Law on Original Evidence

The Korean Supreme Court treats oral testimony as the original evidence and written testimony as a substitute for the original evidence, and believes that oral testimony should be the basis for trials. Duplicate copies are given the same evidentiary power as the original only when specific criteria are met. This can be seen as the Korean Supreme Court's decision to adopt the best evidence rule.

In the US, however, the broad form of the best evidence rule has mostly disappeared and instead, the narrow form of the best evidence rule is applied only in situations where documentary evidence is concerned. But because the Korean Supreme Court applies similar law to both oral and written testimony, its approach is closer to the broad form of the best evidence rule.

The reproducible characteristic of electronic evidence makes it meaningless to differentiate between the original and the duplicate. However, it is possible to treat the very first electronic file as the original's first form of existence, and when we apply the original evidence rule, the examination of the evidence should be limited to that first electronic file.

Additional information that is automatically added to the file containing the original data (i.e. user name, group name, computer name, date, etc.), or information that the creator purposely hides (i.e. hidden text, spreadsheet formula, etc.), is called metadata (the latter type of data is also referred to as "embedded data"). In many cases, these metadata are not copied or their contents change when the original file is copied. For example, there are cases in which metadata, such as date indicating when the file was created, can serve an important evidentiary function, and if metadata is changed in the process of reproduction, examining the evidence becomes meaningless. When this happens, the original evidence must be examined.

However, in the case when examining the original becomes impossible or extremely difficult, such as when the electronic evidence exists in a mega computer server or network, it would be impossible to adhere to the original evidence rule.

Examination of Copies
If it is only the content of an electronic evidence that matters, which is true in most cases, then examining its copy is enough to fulfill the purpose of examining an evidence. However, the contents of the copy must be identical to the contents of the original evidence. This requirement must include that there must be no changes made to the copy from its creation until its examination. The prosecutor who submitted this type of evidence is responsible for its accuracy.

Existence of the Original Evidence
In a case where a copy of a suspect interrogation written record is submitted as evidence, the Korean Supreme Court ask the submitting party to prove that the original document currently exists or existed in the past. Some commentators say audio/video tapes or computer files which recorded statements require the existence of the originals as well.

The above mentioned precedent case does not mention anything about copies of electronic evidence. But when we apply this precedent case about suspect interrogation to electronic evidence as well, the submitting party must prove that the original currently exists or did exist.

In the case where electronic evidence exists but the printout of that electronic evidence is being used for examination according to Article 134-7 of the Regulation on Criminal Procedure, the original electronic evidence the printout originated from is required to exist. In contrast, when the copy itself is being submitted as evidence, the submitting party does not have to prove the existence of the original version of the evidence. This is because the copy itself can be used as an independent evidence, and the original copy is treated as a mere source of the copy. Of course, if the original does not exist, then it is difficult to prove whether the contents of the copy is identical to the contents of the original, which can weaken the evidentiary power of the copy. However, if there is indirect evidence proving that the contents of the original and the copy are identical, then a mere lack of the original version alone cannot deny the evidentiary power of the copy. Furthermore, when the original document is destroyed for whatever reason, proving through evidence can only be done through the copy of the original. Therefore, it is rather when the original does not exist that the copy finds its true evidentiary value. However, there at least needs to be proof that the original document did exist.

Impossibility or Difficulty of Submission of Original Document
Requirement? As already mentioned, the Korean Supreme Court requires proof that the submission of the original documentary evidence is impossible or difficult, before accepting the copy as evidence. However, when it comes to evidence that comes in the form of database storage, such as tape recording, video recording, CD or computer disc, the Court mostly focuses on the uniformity between the original and the copy and reviews whether the copy can serve as evidence without mentioning whether the submission of the original is impossible or difficult. In this regard, it appears that the Supreme Court, at least when it comes to the copy of electronic evidence, does not require that the submission of the original documentary evidence be impossible or difficult. Electronic copies may easily be duplicates under FRE 1001 and admitted without submission of the original. With all this, however, it goes too far to say that the impossibility or difficulty is not required at all.

Exemplified Copy and Original Copy. The Regulation on Criminal Procedure of Korea allows an exemplified copy to be submitted instead of the original when the original is text information stored in computer discs or other similar information storage devices and the copy is printed out in a readable format (Article 134-7). The Regulation applies this rule to the blueprints or pictures stored in computer discs as well.

It is not clear whether printouts can serve as evidence replacing the original document. From early on, the Court accepted copies as evidence in certain circumstances, and American law takes similar approach. In light of this, it can be understood that the printout evidence mentioned above replaces electronic evidence as an independent evidence.

However, it becomes clear that information itself stored in computer discs and other storage devices serves as evidence, when we consider these points: (i) while the precedent cases were not always about certified or exemplified copies, the Regulation stipulates submission of exemplified copies, (ii) the title of the Article is "examination of evidence on textual information stored in computer disc or other storage devices," and (iii) the rule specifically suggests that information stored in computer disc and other storage devices are documentary evidence.

This is different from submitting the printout document as evidence. In such a case, because the printout itself serves as a method of proof, it undergoes examination as an evidentiary document. In contrast, if you submit an electronic document as evidence, it does not go through the examination of an evidentiary document. The court practice includes the examination of computer discs not under "evidentiary document and other categories," but under "witness and other categories." This suggests that the Court does not treat examination of digital evidence as examination of documentary evidence.

However, the submission of a certified copy, by examining the printout document instead of directly examining the electronic evidence, is considered as a way to substitute the examination of digital evidence. It follows that when you submit a certified copy, there should be no need to separately submit computer discs and other storage devices, in addition to the printout document. Even so, because the printout certified copy is not evidence but a mere supporting document, there is no need to separately examine its own admissibility. In addition to that, it is not required that the submission of the original document must be impossible or difficult, because the Regulation does not ask it as requirement for the examination of those certified copies.

Submission of Copies and Inability to Submit the Original as Evidence. In practice, parties often request that the Court accept the printout version of the electronic evidence as the original. The Court treats this not as submitting the electronic evidence to be considered as evidence, but rather submitting the printed out version of the electronic evidence to be considered as an independent evidence. This is not ruled by Article 134-7 of the Regulation on Criminal Procedure because the Article is not about printouts as independent evidence but printouts as aids for examination of electronic evidence. Those copies submitted as independent evidence have to meet the requirements of admissibility. As mentioned above, the Supreme Court focuses on the uniformity between the original and copies.

Proof of Inability to Submit or Difficulty in Submitting Original Document is Unnecessary. As long as it is proven that the contents of the duplicate are identical to the contents of the original, there is no need to insist on submission of the original. This is because the inefficiency and costliness of insisting on the submission of the original is greater than the benefit that can be gained from it.

However, even if you can perform examination on electronic evidence through examining the certified copy of that electronic evidence, the principle requires the examination to be performed on the evidentiary document itself. This principle is clearly stated in the Criminal Procedure Act Articles 292, 292-2, etc. Article 292 requires that 'the evidentiary document' is recited when being examined, and Article 292-2 requires that 'the evidence' is submitted when being examined. This can be understood as an effort to show that the purpose of doing an examination of evidence is to examine the original document. Therefore, even though the Criminal Procedure Act Article 292-3 delegated to the Supreme Court the examination method of electronic evidence, the method should not be contradictory to the principle and the Court cannot stipulate such a contradictory Regulation. Therefore, even when a court examines the certified copy as a substitute for examining the electronic evidence, the court cannot infringe or restrict the parties' interest to the examination of the original document. As a result, even though the Criminal Procedure Act does not stipulate it, the examination of the certified copy should only be allowed with the party's agreement. If the party does not agree, then the court must solely rely on the method of examining the electronic evidence itself, and the court cannot substitute the electronic evidence with the printout evidence when conducting examination, even when the uniformity of contents between the printout and the electronic original is proved. Of course, if the party objects because the printout document does not properly reflect the electronic evidence, the court should examine the printout document that properly reflects the electronic version.

A similar type of legal reasoning can also be applied to cases where the copy of the electronic evidence itself is being submitted as evidence. To sum up, whether it is possible to submit the original evidence or not should not be a factor in determining the admissibility of the electronic evidence.

The Importance of Standardized Documents
It is essential that the contents of the circulated electronic documents between different institutions within the criminal law system are identical. Section 5-2 of Korean law on the digitalization of documents stipulates that the sender of the electronic documents must confirm that the contents of the printout are the same as the contents of the electronic documents, and indicate the print out date, print out institution, page numbers, the total number of pages, and the original document number on the print out document (Rule 3-1).

ELECTRONIC CRIMINAL PROCEEDINGS AND ORIGINALITY

Examination of Evidence in Electronic Proceedings

The Digitalization Act promotes a digital criminal procedure, where litigation through digital means is possible. The Summary Proceedings Act requires electronic submission of testimonies and defendant investigation documents in electronic summary proceedings. Non-electronic documents such as evidentiary materials can be digitized using scanners and submitted in that form. Therefore, in an electronic summary proceeding, every piece of evidence exists in a digitized format.

Electronic evidence is submitted electronically from the prosecution's criminal justice information system to the Court's criminal justice information system. In addition, the Court examines digitized evidence that was transmitted to the court system.

Single Original or Multiple Originals

Single Original Standpoint

Originality of Evidence Submitted to Court. Similarly to submitting the original version when submitting paper documents to the court, when the parties are submitting electronic evidence and the court insists on the principle that there can only be one original version, then the prosecution must destroy the electronic evidence after it transfers the evidence to the Court. By doing so, the evidence that was under the prosecution's possession comes under the court's possession.

However, when the evidence is transferred from the prosecution's system to the court's system, the same electronic signal that is stored in the prosecution's system is being copied to the court's system. Whether the electronic evidence in the prosecution's system is deleted or not is not relevant to the objective format of the electronic evidence that is submitted directly to the court. Therefore, the request to delete the file has no meaning other than what it contributes to the principle that there can only be one version of the original. But it cannot be said that the court's file is the only original file, without deleting the file on the prosecution's system.

Originality of Prosecution's Evidence. When the physical document is concerned, the first drafted electronic evidence (i.e. suspect testimony statement file) is under the possession of the police or prosecution, and the documents that the court uses to conduct its examination are the copies of those electronic evidence. However, as mentioned before, the criminal procedure rules and court administration do not disapprove of examining certified copies or the original document. Therefore, it is possible to argue that the file under the police or prosecution's possession is the original and the court is conducting its examination on the copy of that original document. This argument, however, is unreasonable because it results in the total collapse of the original evidence rule.

Multiple Originals Standpoint

Multiple Original Documents. The main characteristic of electronic evidence is that you can make unlimited number of copies with identical contents. When the electronic evidence is transferred from the police system to the prosecution's system, and then from the prosecution's system to the court system, it won't be problematic to consider all of them as the original. There would be no need to delete the files that remain in the prosecution's system after submitting it to the court, if the court acknowledges that there can exist multiple copies of the original document.

From the standpoint taking the files on the prosecution's system as originals, it can be argued that the file on the prosecution's system makes the standard to decide which is correct among various files with possibly different contents. However, there is no guarantee that the investigative branch's file is more accurate. It is more likely that the contents of the electronic evidence could be damaged after the transmission is complete than during transmission. Therefore, this kind of problem cannot be solved by sticking to the singularity of original documents, but remains the problem of authenticity of evidence.

Criteria for Multiple Original Documents. In order for multiple files to be considered as the originals, those files must be identical among each other and be authenticated. It would be a good sign for being identical that the hash values of the files are same. On the other hand, a duplicate whose metadata have been changed cannot become an original when the metadata has any evidentiary meaning. In that case, only the original document can be considered as the original.

When Transited to Non-Electronic Procedure. When an electronic summary proceeding becomes a regular summary proceeding, the prosecutor must print out the electronic evidence before submitting to the court. This printed document will then serve as evidence.

It can be argued that the electronic evidence is the original evidence and that the printout version is just a copy, or that the printout version itself is the original version. It will be more reasonable to say that the evidence submitted by the prosecutor is the printout document and the electronic evidence is the source of the printout, and to think of the printout version itself as the original evidence. This is because if the prosecution is made under the original summary proceeding from the beginning, then the prosecutor most likely would have submitted the print out version of the electronic document.

However, this interpretation has one problem. Electronic summary proceeding evidence usually includes documents that were drafted electronically, as well as documents that were converted from paper format to a digitized format. When an electronic procedure moves to a regular procedure, the prosecutor is required to also submit the printed out version of the digitized document. The digitized document originally includes the paper document that is the source of the digitized version, and it is rightful to consider these as the original version. In such cases, it would be difficult to consider printout version from the digitized document as the original version.

Therefore, even though the law requires digitized document to be submitted, when the original document of the digitized document exists, the prosecutor should submit that as well.

CONCLUSION

The "original evidence rule," which states that examination should be conducted on the original evidence only, has been considered to be one of the basic principles of the traditional evidence rule. Although the Korean criminal procedural law does not so stipulate, the Supreme Court of Korea requires submission of original evidence. However, with the increasing digitalization of evidence, the Supreme Court has loosened the strictness of its requirement. With the increased use of electronic evidence, electronic criminal proceedings have become realities. It would be unrealistic to adhere to the original evidence rule under these circumstances.

As long as it can be proved that the electronic evidence is identical to the original evidence, electronic evidence should have the same evidentiary value. Moreover, evidence that is electronically exchanged between the prosecutors and the court should also serve as the original evidence, as long as it is proven to be identical.

Conclusion

John Yoo[1]

Authors of this book's chapters gathered at Berkeley Law School on April 18, 2014, to celebrate the opening of the Korea Law Center. Their presentation of the papers underscored the Center's foundations upon its strong base of Korean alumni and demonstrated its commitment to excellence in legal scholarship. Authors had the opportunity to discuss their work with other panelists, faculty moderators, and about 100 audience members drawn from the law school, the bar, and the larger university community.

Important themes emerged from the conference. First, Korean and American approaches to legal scholarship are converging on similar questions. American readers will find familiar many of the issues of interest to Korean professors. Several papers address the fundamental problem at the root of much American legal academic writing: the counter-majoritarian difficulty. That quandary, as most famously expressed by Alexander Bickel, and then further explored by John Hart Ely and Jesse Choper, among others, asks how a democratic system of government can vest the authority to interpret the Constitution—and hence control vast swaths of policymaking in the modern state—in unelected, unaccountable judges.[2] Addressing

---

1.   Emanuel S. Heller Professor of Law; Co-Director, Korea Law Center, Berkeley Law.

2.   See Alexander Bickel, *The Least Dangerous Branch: The Supreme Court at the Bar of Politics* (Indianapolis: 1962); Jesse Choper, *Judicial Review and the National Political Process: A Functional Reconsideration of the Role of the Supreme Court* (Chicago: 1980); John Hart Ely, *Democracy and Distrust: A Theory of Judicial Review* (Cambridge, Mass.: 1980).

this problem in the Korean context, former Chief Justice Kang-Kook Lee of the Korean Constitutional Court does not view judicial review as posing a severe counter-majoritarian problem, but instead sees the Court as a means for the government to reflect the wishes of the people.[3] Professor Jibong Lim, however, directly criticizes the role of the Korean Constitutional Court in invalidating decisions of the Korean President and Assembly. In "Judicial Intervention in Policy-Making by the Constitutional Court in Korea," he describes the way in which the counter-majoritarian has arisen in Korea.[4] Like Lim, Professor Hong Sik Cho registers deep concerns about the rise of judicial review in Korea. In "The Justifiability and Limits of Judicial Governance," Professor Cho extends the worries over the competence and democratic accountability of judges to the broader phenomenon of settling political questions.[5]

It is difficult to determine whether the counter-majoritarian difficulty may be even more acute in Korea than in the United States. In the United States, the President nominates all federal judges, from the trial courts to the Supreme Court, subject to the advice and consent of the Senate. In Korea, the elected branches of government do not appoint lower court judges. Lower court judges assume office after passing a judicial entrance examination and undergoing several years of education at the Judicial Research and Training Institute. On the other hand, the President of Korea appoints the Chief Justice of the Korean Supreme Court, subject to the approval of the national assembly. After recommendation by the Chief Justice, however, the other twelve justices must receive nomination by the President and consent by the Assembly. Supreme Court Justices serve fixed, non-renewable, six-year terms as well. While the lower courts may have even less connection to the democratic process, the judges at the top of the system may have more than in the United States.

Another complication is Korea's Constitutional Court. Korea's Constitution places the Constitutional Court in the role of the sole and exclusive arbiter of constitutional questions in an institutional framework simi-

---

3. Kang-Kook Lee, "The Past and Future of Constitutional Adjudication in Korea," above.

4. Jibong Lim, "Judicial Intervention in Policy-Making by the Constitutional Court in Korea," above.

5. Hong Sik Cho, "The Justifiability and Limits of Judicial Governance," above.

lar to that in Germany and Austria. Constitutional issues can arise either in a direct lawsuit brought in the first instance before the Court—analogous to the American concept of "original jurisdiction"—or in the course of a normal lawsuit before the lower courts. The Korean Constitution divides the appointment of Constitutional Court Justices between the Chief Justice of the Supreme Court, the President, and the leaders of the National Assembly. Like their Supreme Court colleagues, the Constitutional Court Justices serve fixed terms without possibility of renewal. Berkeley political scientist Hans Kelsen supported constitutional courts because he predicted that they would remove politics—which he believed was inevitable in constitutional cases—from the adjudication and enforcement of ordinary law. Concentrating the authority to decide constitutional issues in a Court whose members are chosen by the political branches and serve short terms may seriously reduce, if not ultimately eliminate, the counter-majoritarian problem.

With the reduction in the counter-majoritarian nature of the judiciary, the protection of minority rights will become more difficult. A court system that more reflects the political preferences of the people, or at least that of the political branches, may have less independence to stand up to the majority. This should lead Korean scholars to explore less judiciary and more democratic means to enforce constitutional rights. Professor Kuk Cho, for example, disagrees with the Korean judiciary's refusal to protect the rights of homosexuals in military service.[6] His contribution to this volume calls upon the executive and legislative branches of the Korean government to take concrete measures to protect gays. In a related vein, Professor Dai-Kwon Choi emphasizes that the Korean Constitution places the primary duty on the national legislature to protect human rights.[7] But by his account, the Assembly has turned in a disappointing performance in this area, which has created the space for more activism by the courts. American scholarship, where individual rights work continues to focus on judicial enforcement, may have much to learn from Korean scholarship on the political protection of individual rights.

6.   Kuk Cho, "The Unconstitutionality of the Crime of Sodomy Under Article 92(5) of the Korean Military Penal Code," above.

7.   Dai-Kwon Choi, "The State of Fundamental Rights Protection in Korea," above.

The remaining two chapters of this book identify other areas where American legal scholarship has much to gain from its Korean counterpart. In "The Best Evidence Rule in a Digital Age," Professor Sang Wong Lee discusses the recognition by all three branches of the Korean government that information is increasingly taking a digital form.[8] To enhance the handling of this data, the police, prosecutors, Ministry of Justice and courts—supported by the legislature—established an integrated digital system for handling evidence, investigatory documents, and judicial filings. He points out that the best evidence rule in U.S. law, and its counterpart in Korean law, which stresses oral over written testimony and original documents over copies, will come under stress in a world of digital information, where copies are indistinguishable. In "Mergers and Acquisitions in the Corporate Reorganization Procedures of Korea," Professor Jaewan Park tackles an interesting phenomenon in Korea's response to the sharp recession that began in 2008.[9] In the United States, the executive and legislative branches took the lead with focuses on stimulus spending, generous monetary policy, and increased regulatory intervention. In Korea, however, courts had the opportunity to contribute to the response by encouraging the merger or acquisition of companies in bankruptcy proceedings by healthier businesses.

Korean interest in these subjects can benefit from U.S. scholarship, which may identify paths for future work. Like U.S. constitutional scholars, Korean public law professors have been interested in the problems surrounding judicial review. They could gain from extension of this inquiry into the complex workings of the government in non-constitutional areas. For the last two decades, if not more, American scholars have also questioned the relationship of the courts to the administrative state. In the 1960s and 1970s, U.S. federal courts appeared uncertain about the strictness of review to afford decisions of the agencies. But by the 1980s, under the *Chevron* doctrine, the Supreme Court ordered lower courts to display a high level of deference to decisions of executive branch and independent agencies.[10] Implicitly responding to the concerns of the counter-majoritar-

8.   Sang Won Lee, "The Best Evidence Rule in a Digital Age," above.

9.   Jaewan Park, "Mergers and Acquisitions in the Corporate Reorganization Procedures of Korea," above.

10.   *Chevron v. NRDC*, 467 U.S. 837 (1984).

ian difficulty, American judges are reluctant to overturn an agency's regulations implementing its statutory mandate or its interpretations of ambiguous laws.

A great deal of American public law scholarship in the last two decades has focused with increasing sophistication on the ability of the judiciary and Congress to control the administrative state. Some support strong deference because the executive branch is better suited to developing unified, rational policies in response to changing circumstances than either the legislature or the courts. Others criticize the delegation of authority away from democratically accountable officials toward a permanent civil service, albeit one usually headed by a thin layer of officials appointed by the President. American analysis of these issues could benefit Korean scholars and lawyers as their government considers reforms in response to the tragic April 16, 2014 sinking of the *Sewol* near Jindo Island. Korean leaders attribute fault in part to the bureaucratic "mafia," which allegedly produced lax scrutiny by regulators of the ferry's safety.

In their quest to increase the accountability of regulators, Koreans might examine the different tools that American scholars have proposed to increase political control over the administrative agencies. Perhaps the most successful, and controversial, is the Office of Management and Budget's centralized review over regulations. Under a variety of executive orders dating back to President Jimmy Carter, OMB's Office of Information and Regulatory Affairs subjects agency regulations to cost-benefit analysis.[11] Regulatory review allows the President to impose a unified vision on the varied, disconnected workings of the agencies and provides a deeper link between the administrative state to the electorate. Without regulatory review, the President's primary formal control over the administrative state reduces to the ability to appoint (usually with the advice and consent of the Senate) and remove officials, which can prove too blunt a tool to oversee the day-to-day business of the agencies. Political control over the agencies can also come from greater congressional oversight over the agencies. Congressional committees have long-term relationships with the agencies under their jurisdiction because of their power over authorizing and appropriating legislation. Committees can also pressure agencies by

---

11. Exec. Order No. 13563, 76 Fed. Reg. 3821 (Jan. 18, 2011).

holding public hearings on their performance and pursuing investigations of mistakes, errors, waste, and abuse.

One drawback to increasing political controls in a presidential constitutional system—as opposed to a parliamentary democracy—may arise because of the separation of powers. If both the President and Congress seek to exercise control over the agencies, both branches might frustrate each other's efforts. Agencies might clear an even greater space for themselves by playing the executive and legislative branches against each other.

Other approaches to controlling agencies have sought to check independence with even more independence. In 1978, Congress enacted a law to create inspectors general within the major cabinet departments to investigate waste, fraud, and abuse and to improve efficiency and effectiveness.[12] Inspectors general may seek to operate independently of the political leadership of a cabinet department and report their findings directly to Congress and the public. The Ethics in Government Act—also enacted in 1978 in the aftermath of Watergate—took independence even further by creating a prosecutor appointed by the courts and removable by the President only for cause who had an unrestrained mandate to investigate allegations against the President and cabinet. Although *Morrison v. Olson* upheld the independent counsel, Justice Antonin Scalia's lone dissent identified the serious challenge to the constitutional system posed by an unaccountable independent prosecutor.[13] Korean scholars might consider, however, whether creating independent checks on the administrative state only trades one kind of bureaucratic mafia with a different another kind.

American legal scholarship and contemporary Korean interests might also intersect over unification. Koreans have suffered from an artificial division of their territory and people since the end of World War II. The Korean government has proposed a variety of unification plans, as have think tanks and academics. These range from proposals for single, nationwide democratic elections to a power-sharing system between North and South. If unification occurs through peaceful negotiation, rather than a sudden northern collapse or military conflict, American legal scholarship on federalism could provide lessons on how to bring different regions together into

---

12.   Inspector General Act of 1978, Pub. L. No. 95-452, 92 Stat. 1101.
13.   *Morrison v. Olson*, 487 U.S. 654 (1988).

a single nation. Law and economics scholarship emphasizes the benefits from decentralization that arise when jurisdictions compete for citizens by offering different packages of policies.[14] Federalism, incidentally, could inform Korean efforts to reduce over-reliance on the central government in Seoul as part of a plan to check the power of the bureaucratic mafia. But federalism also provides a means for different regions and peoples to live within a single nation by sharing power. The American Constitution, for example, helped sealed a bargain between the northern and southern states over slavery by guaranteeing equal state representation in the Senate. A constitution can provide a commitment device that allows different groups to send costly signals that they will obey a power-sharing agreement.[15]

Our discussion of federalism also suggests a final area of interaction between Korean and U.S. legal scholarship. The essays in this volume show that Korean academics do not focus solely on textual readings of the civil code or debates solely over judicial doctrine. Korean scholars bring external viewpoints to legal problems with their strong training in comparative methods and interest in the legal systems of other countries. Their comparative approach experiencing a boost because of the tension between the Korean legal system's origins in the European and Japanese civil code and the contemporary influence of American public law. As my colleague Laurent Mayali suggests in the Introduction, the rapid changes in Korea's economy and society is accelerating the mixture of these two legal traditions. Korea's rapid development from an agrarian society to a nation built on high-technology and industrial manufacturing, within the space of two generations, places heavy demands on the legal system. Examples drawn from other nations, such as the United States, which have undergone similar transformations, provides a rich proving ground for Korean efforts to update their laws to adapt to the new economic and social environment.

Korean legal scholars might expand their vision beyond other nations to include other disciplines as well. For the last three to four decades, American legal scholarship has embraced interdisciplinary approaches to legal problems. Law and economics scholars, for example, employ increas-

---

14.   See, e.g., Robert Cooter, *The Strategic Constitution* (Princeton: 2000), 101–48.

15.   John Yoo, *Point of Attack: Preventive War, International Law, and Global Welfare* (New York: 2014), 159–192.

ingly sophisticated economic tools to reveal the incentives and consequences created by legal rules. Constitutional law has become heavily influenced by historical analysis of the original understanding of the document held by its writers and ratifiers. Both the majority and minority of the Supreme Court appealed to the history of the late eighteenth century to divine the meaning of the Second Amendment's guarantee of the right "to bear arms."[16] Scholars have turned to political science to understand the effects of constitutional and public law doctrine on the political system, and to understand the way that the political process affects the law. Korean scholars should find these approaches not only consistent with their existing openness to other legal traditions, but also profoundly illuminating of difficult legal problems under conditions of rapid change.

These chapters of this volume are therefore not just interesting in their own right. They also reveal the benefits of a new attention by Korean and American scholars to each other and the paths for future work. Korea can provide a new context for the re-examination of central dilemmas in American law, as it does with the counter-majoritarian difficulty. Or Korea can show alternative solutions to common problems, such as the rise of digital evidence or responses to the recent economic crisis. American scholarship may point the way toward a deeper application of comparative and interdisciplinary approaches to Korean problems.

16.   *District of Columbia v. Heller*, 554 U.S. 570 (2008).